The Web's Awake

The Web's Awake
An Introduction to the Field of Web Science and the Concept of Web Life

Philip Tetlow

IEEE PRESS

WILEY-INTERSCIENCE
A JOHN WILEY & SONS, INC., PUBLICATION

The material in Appendix B of this book is reproduced with permission from W3C®. See footnote on page 216 for futher details.

Published by John Wiley & Sons, Inc., Hoboken, New Jersey.
Published simultaneously in Canada.

For general information on our other products and services or for technical support, please contact our Customer Care Department within the United States at (800) 762-2974, outside the United States at (317) 572-3993 or fax (317) 572-4002.

Wiley also publishes its books in a variety of electronic formats. Some content that appears in print may not be available in electronic format. For information about Wiley products, visit our web site at www.wiley.com.

Library of Congress Cataloging-in-Publication Data is available.

ISBN 978-0-470-13794-9

Printed in the United States of America.

10 9 8 7 6 5 4 3 2 1

For VeeVon, Dude, and Kidder

"You're really not going to like it," observed Deep Thought.

"Tell us!"

"All right," said Deep Thought. "The Answer to the Great Question . . . ."

"Yes . . . !"

"Of Life, the Universe and Everything . . ." said Deep Thought.

"Yes . . . !"

"Is . . ." said Deep Thought, and paused.

"Yes . . . !"

"Is . . ."

"Yes . . . !!!"

"Forty-two," said Deep Thought, with infinite majesty and calm.

—Douglas Adams, The Hitch Hiker's Guide to the Galaxy

Contents

Foreword

Like most members, when I joined the W3C's (World Wide Web Consortium) working groups, I was pleasantly surprised. Not only did I find the dedicated group of skilled professionals I was expecting, but I also found an eclectic community of genuinely warm and imaginative individuals, all passionate about their work and the Web technologies to which they contribute. For them, novel yet rigorous thinking is the norm, and strong debate is an integral part of that thinking process. It leads to that rarest of things; a body of opinion independent of the daily squabbles of academia and business life.

It was during a W3C meeting in Bristol (UK) in 2003 that I first came across Phil Tetlow, and it was his propensity for lateral thinking that attracted me. During the course of that meeting we came to discuss many topics including the application of new Semantic Web technologies, a conversation that extended well beyond the close of proceedings. I can remember us both eventually standing on a rather cold station platform, waiting to catch our respective trains back home and yet still bouncing crazy ideas off each other. It was then that I suggested starting some work on applying Semantic Web technologies to the general field of Software Engineering, a somewhat radical proposition at the time. Upon hearing my thoughts, Phil's eyes glazed over for a few seconds as he considered the implications of my suggestion, he then smiled and nodded, and a pact was struck. Not only were we going to try and do something different and challenging, but it was obvious that a friendship had been formed that would prove rewarding from that day forward.

Unlike many of those involved with Web standards, Phil's experience does not lie solely within the confines of software construction or academic research. His years of consulting have instilled in him a pragmatic understanding of many other areas such as systems' architecture and the social drivers behind modern-day technologies. Not only does he have an interest in nurturing the raw materials behind modern-day software, but he also carries considerable experience from the "coal face," actually implementing these to architect some of the largest and most complex computer systems in existence today.

Because of this it came as little surprise to me to hear that he had been working on this book for some time. He has often voiced his frustrations with contemporary thinking on software with me, and I can fully understand why his desire to seek out best practice eventually led him to the door of the W3C and his excitement for the Web. What I find stimulating is that it was while within this community that the final threads of his ideas came together and he eventually found a way through the story he wanted to tell here.

The Web's Awake hence draws from a diverse background, pulling together a number of ideas centered on the general notion complex systems, independent of whether modern technology is involved or not. This naturally brings with it more subject matter dealing with aspects such as systems' dynamics and a variety of patterns and theories undying complex phenomena. Undoubtedly where the book distinguishes itself is in its comparison between the most complex software-based system known today (in other words the World Wide Web) and the absolute pinnacle of complex systems, life itself. Through this can be found an illuminating collection of thoughts that are bound to put the reader in a reflective mood and stir up deliberation. It is a testament to Phil's tenacity, curiosity, and integrity that such a wide ranging yet cohesive argument has been formed at all.

I know that in piecing together this work he has compared notes with some of the most authoritative minds on the planet and pushed himself well beyond his comfort zone many times to fill gaps in his reasoning as they appeared. For me this makes *The Web's Awake* both novel and informative, an off-the-wall interpretation of a number of interlinked snippets for which many Computer Scientists secretly harbor a fascination. There are other books that cover similar ground, but I am not aware of any that take such a unique perspective or specifically concentrate on the Web as the core subject matter. I know of several who have been waiting for this book to surface for some time. Now that it has finally appeared, I am sure that their wait will be rewarded many times over.

It is interesting to note that I prepared the final version of this foreword, just after attending the 5th International Semantic Web Conference (Athens, Georgia, 2006). As part of the proceedings, Phil and I, together with other colleagues from the W3C Best Practice and Deployment Working Group, successfully coordinated the International Workshop on Semantic Web Enabled Software Engineering—our second organization of such an event. Given the great numbers who took time out to attend and their overwhelmingly positive response, we are all undoubtedly in for a fascinating and fun ride in the years ahead. Welcome aboard.

JEFF Z. PAN

Department of Computing Science,
The University of Aberdeen, Scotland
World Wide Web Consortium Member

Preface

From the very birth of computer science the quest to find technology that even approximates to the salient qualities of life has proved to be somewhat of a hunt for elusive treasure. If we add to this pursuit the potential to unearth some new forms of intelligence along the way, then the prize involved quickly transforms into the magnetic mother lode of all Geekdom; no wonder it has been such a popular target for fiction writers and quasi scientists over the years.

In some respects this golden chalice has been its own worst enemy, regularly poisoning its reputation through the compounded effect of published half-truths. So why should anyone in their right mind want to join such a search knowing full well that the odds of finding a fresh and serious pathway to the truth were slim? Indeed this is a question I have asked myself often, overly appreciating that many a great mind has failed along the way before me. Why should I, even with a strong technical background and a great deal of experience, want to stick my pin in the map now? The answer is simple; I have never really deliberately sought out such treasure and there is no such map of which I know. When I first set out on my personal quest for enlightenment, I had much less provocative adventures in mind. It is merely a coincidence that the path I have taken to quell my curiosity has led me across some rather unexpectedly fertile and interesting ground.

My primary interests originally lay with the construction of large and somewhat mundane data processing systems, some distance away from the swirling vortex of life studies. Nevertheless, in my search to understand the intricacies of more and more complex computer systems, I have found myself powerless to resist the philosophical attraction of such subject matter and have been slowly pulled in over the years. On my way I have become increasingly amazed, for instance, that we still commonly construct computer systems, especially complex computer systems, using methods and patterns different from those chosen by nature in the fashioning of its own solutions. Over some time this has led me to believe that we still have a number of irreconcilable disparities in our general understanding of, and the way that we go about, the very business of computing at a number of levels, even if those who pioneered the Information Technology revolution had different ideas and were more in tune with nature's own objectives.

As a case in point, few who profess to be computer experts appreciate that computation is a concept independent of any particular physical medium, and in such respects the very Universe itself can be seen to compute. Perhaps this is the reason why we have not taken more than a few leaves out of Nature's cookbook thus far.

But this is surely a no-brainer, so have we been making some fundamental mistakes? Unlikely, I've always thought, given mans' intellectual success rate over recent millennia. Such contradictions have intrigued me deeply for some time, so consequently I set off to find some answers for myself almost 20 years ago. At first, like most, I was unsuccessful, but then, little by little, I began to realize the error of my ways; I was looking in the wrong place. I was down amongst the weeds when the real answers lay all around me.

Books about computers, bits, bytes, and the raw nuts and bolts of technology are often dry and boring, and I hate most of them with a passion. Taken at face value, they offer little more than a thin veneer, unwittingly concealing a richer treasure of far greater connected truths beneath. Books about Nature, the Universe, and complexities of life, on the other hand, have an inbuilt advantage, drawing from a never-ending well of fascination and mystery. They constantly taunt the reader, reminding them of mankind's inherent inability to truly comprehend the world in which we live. But this does not necessarily mean to say that computation or the properties of modern digital technology are any less magical or any less natural. Society's quintessential notion of its modern digital existence is one in which technology plays a role of pervasively connected enablement, at the same time being divorced of any tangible connection to the real world itself. We quite happily accept that today's computers can capably juggle everyday abstract concepts such as e-mail for us, but are somewhat less comfortable with any idea of them working in ways that even approximate to our own familiar worldly understandings. Computers may be able to control the machinery needed to make a perfect cup of coffee, for instance, but we consider the idea that they might be able to actually understand our desire for caffeine with disdain and disbelief. This is a step too far, but for whom, them or us?

Ever since the days of my earliest memories, my overriding view of the world has been one of awe and wonderment. For me, appreciation of the complex natural beauty of the Universe has always come easily, even if the understanding that accompanies it has required much more effort. Even so, combining such appreciation and learning has always been a pleasure, a release, a fascination, a property of my very identity. But my enthusiasm has not always been free-flowing. Like so many aspiring scholars interested in science and technology, during the education of my youth my head was filled with classical, Newtonian views of the world that contradicted my heartfelt instinct for how things "really were." What I was being taught was obviously right, but it somehow felt so wrong, incomplete somehow. How could the inexorable complex splendor surrounding us be described in the same types of formulae used to make clear the forced regularity of a mechanical clock? This was ludicrous, but was, nevertheless, the story of mainstream science's choosing, or so the educational system that outlined my curriculum thought, and to fight against it proved a frustrating and confining task.

For some time I succumbed to the system and, even though my inborn talents demonstrated themselves to be more artistic than scientific, my tenacious interest in technology won out and I conformed to the task at hand. I learned of basic scientific practice and gained an appreciation for simplified understandings. I learned to accept the limits of natural human cognition and I watched the constant upward march of Information Technology with much excitement, because I knew that one day soon it would enable us to look at our surroundings in different ways, ways closer to nature's scales and preferences, ways greater and grander than we have ever been capable of achieving before. Even so, the timing of my studies further worked against me and it was only after many years of aimless investigation that I learned of others also interested in the same perspectives as myself. Far more talented individuals than I were already working hard in fresh fields of mathematics and science, equipped with the new tools provided by the computer age. At first they were considered as crackpots, over-ambitious academics playing with crazy ideas, but gradually their findings started to gel, and recognized disciplines such as Chaos, Complexity, and Network Theory were born. These were all branches sprouting off one central theme, a theme that would become known as connectionism to some, systems theory to others, and nonlinear dynamics to yet more and that would still hide under numerous other pseudonyms in just about every field of modern scientific endeavor.

So I suppose it was no coincidence that in the last year of my undergraduate studies my random meanderings through the literature bore fruit and I stumbled upon a book by Sir Tony Hoare. The first passage in *Communicating Sequential Processes* reads, "Forget for a while about computers and computer programming, and think instead about objects in the world around us, which act and interact with us and with each other in accordance with some characteristic pattern of behaviour" [32], and the very moment I read this original insight a light went on somewhere in my subconscious. I had found the start of the thread I was looking for, a thread I hoped would tie together a number of intuitions, instincts almost, from both the natural and digital world that I felt were connected. What really surprised me was that others were thinking the same way too. Stuart Kauffman, one of the most respected researchers in complex systems theory, sums up this feeling far more eloquently that I ever could, stating his personal search for greater truths as aspiring to a "self-consistent big picture that ties everything together, from the origin of life as a self-organised system, to the emergence of spontaneous order in genomic regulatory systems, to the emergence of systems that are able to adapt, to nonequilibrium price formation which optimizes trade amongst organizations, to this unknown analogy of the second law of thermodynamics. It is all one picture. I really feel it is."

Many books have been written on the complexities of the natural world and the interplay between modern technology and the Universe's periodic cycles. Many more have been written on our current understanding of "life" and the prerequisites needed for its emergence. Such books collate ideas from a wide range of disciplines, but few, if any, directly relate such ideas to the single most powerful and prevalent computer technology in existence today. This is the World Wide Web, the ever-growing maelstrom of information muscle structure strung over the bones of the global Internet.

There is little doubt that the Web is having a profound effect on our personal and social existence, pulling down the barriers of time and distance and placing unequalled opportunities to access information at the fingertips of everyday people. This has attracted many authors who have attempted to categorize just what is actually going on, but few have looked at the characteristics of the Web from the perspective of holistic complexity and growth. Why is the Web evolving in the way that it is? What does the Web actually look like now and what will it look like in the future? Is "evolution" even the right word to use to describe its progression? These are all questions that have been relevant for some time, but which have appeared to be taboos in all but the most open-minded of circles. In truth a new science is needed to help address such questions, a science that combines the empirical strength of the material classics while still embracing the synthetic expression granted by the abstract worlds of computing. This is a science that must account for the atomic components of the Web all the way up to the phenomena presented by its totality. This is Web Science and from its birth should rightly come a new collection of understandings, not least of which should be some clarity on the idea of Web Life.

In the spirit of true heresy, I have hence ploughed through the jungle of works related to the various types of question asked here. In doing so, I have been exceptionally fortunate: My professional life has brought me in touch with many of the best minds in the world—first, through my employment as a Technical Architect at IBM and, second, through my membership of The World Wide Web Consortium (W3C) on IBM's behalf. Both privileges have opened many an unexpected door, and I have never been shy to grasp at opportunities and question those who might possess important answers. As such, I have been honored to meet and philosophize with a number of world experts along the way, really enjoying their company and gaining much valuable experience from the vantage point of true giants' shoulders. This has enabled me to pull together a number of ideas and conclusions from a patchwork of original, consistent, and acknowledged findings that all point to a conclusion (a finding that might currently be somewhat unorthodox in parts) that the Web is emerging as a truly natural entity.

This book attempts to lay out the case for such a conclusion, hopefully coherently stringing together observations and findings from a number of diverse fields. In parts I have deliberately borrowed writings from other writers, particularly through excellent references like www.wikipedia.org and M. Mitchell Waldrop's excellent book on complexity [67]. But this has been for no other reason than the original author(s) convey the concepts concerned far better than I ever could. This is a liberty I trust you will allow me to take, for I sincerely hope that, to quote Stuart Kauffman directly, "sometimes outsiders can make serious contributions" [52]. [1] In so doing, I also respectfully acknowledge the danger that "sometimes outsiders just make damned fools of themselves [52]." Even so, I believe that this is a risk worth taking, considering that the collection of material covered paints a provocative and compelling emergent picture, a picture of the Web as a truly natural entity, an infant alone in a cradle of its own folded reality, a child dependent on mankind for its very existence, nourishment, and upbringing.

If the evidence is correct, even in part, then it obviously brings profound responsibilities for society as well as some huge consequences for the ways that we run and organize our personal and collective lives. Most outcomes of the Web's development will undoubtedly be beneficial for us in the long term, but some will inescapably be detrimental. Many might say that this is obvious, a "natural" consequence not worth raising a fuss over. My point is exactly that. That the Web's

---

[1] Whever possible, every effort has been made to reference source materials as accurately as possible.

evolution is precisely an act of nature and by recognizing this fact we can surely utilize it for our betterment. Some have called such arguments visionary, some have called them idiotic, and some, like Sir Tim Berners-Lee, the father of the Web, have even lightheartedly commented that material of this type may be part of a wider conspiracy. Personally I have always preferred to side with the idiots, but I nevertheless feel flattered that many appear to take such thinking seriously.

But just how serious is the material presented and how should one interpret it? To paraphrase the great physicist Richard Feynman, he used to say that there were two types of scientist in the world; the Babylonians and the Greeks. By this he was referring to the opposing philosophies of those ancient civilizations. The Babylonians made Western civilization's first great strides in understanding numbers and equations and in geometry. Yet it was the later Greeks—in particular, Thales, Pythagoras, and Euclid—whom we credit with inventing mathematics. This is because Babylonians cared only whether or not a method of calculation worked—that is, adequately described a real physical situation—and not whether it was exact or fitted into any greater logical system. Thales and his Greek followers, on the other hand, first grasped the idea of theorem and proof and required that for a statement to be considered wholly true, it had to be an exact logical consequence of a system of explicit stated axioms or assumptions. To put it simply, the Babylonians focused on the phenomena, whereas the Greeks focused on the underlying order [31].

I, like the illustrious Feynman, consider myself to be a Babylonian, but freely appreciate that both approaches have merit and can be powerful. The Greek approach brings with it the full force of the logical machinery of mathematics. Philosophers and scientists of this inclination are often guided by the mathematical beauty of their developing theories, and this has led to many beautiful applications of mathematics. The Babylonian approach allows a certain freedom of imagination and frees you to follow your instinct or intuition, your "gut feeling" about nature, without worrying about rigor and justification. This aesthetic has also led to great triumphs, triumphs of intuition and "physical reasoning"—that is, reasoning based principally on the observation and interpretation of phenomena, and not driven by mathematics in the first instance. In fact, those employing this kind of thinking sometimes violate the formal rules surrounding their chosen subject, or even invent strange and unproven formulae or systems of their own based on their own understanding or interpretation of the manifestation they are studying. In some cases this has left mainstream science to follow behind, either justifying such novel ideas or investigating why their unwarranted use gives pretty accurate answers anyway.

Much of the content of this book has been structured in such a way. Several old, yet well-founded, ideas have been collected and repositioned within the new context of Web Life. The outcome of such an exercise may prove to be significant over time if subject to rigorous and proper examination, or be found to be just another misguided attempt to explain the unexplainable. Either way there is sufficient evidence on which to face the jury on behalf of our new found defendant.

In reading this book I must, however, offer both an apology and some advice to the reader, because in its writing I have unfortunately had to reach a compromise. There is a warning included too. This is not a work that aspires to be a politically, morally, or religiously correct text, nor is it necessarily aligned with any particular philosophical or religious school of thought. It is merely a personal interpretation of a rather large collection of strongly interlinked facts and findings from a wide range of sources and research areas. These range from quantum mechanics, through general systems and complexity theory, and on to the social sciences, a daunting spectrum to be sure, but one that is nonetheless necessary to do justice to this fascinating subject.

I have always believed that the concept of the Web as a living thing should be intelligible and appealing to as wide an audience as possible. For this reason I have deliberately tried not to write this book as an academic work. Instead I have chosen to use common language and phrases wherever possible. Even so, there are some reasonably complex and abstract areas that need to be covered before the complete case for a living Web can be fully presented. Therefore I must advise that this book may well be both too light in parts for the serious academic and too deep for those with merely a casual interest. For those wanting a general understanding of Web Science and Web Life, I suggest that they may wish to bypass the detail contained between Chapters 3 and 7, but for those looking for a deeper appreciation, this material may prove crutial. Regardless, at the end of the day, my primary aim in producing this work has been to provide a compelling and enjoyable read, so I hope you find the story as enthralling and thought-provoking as I still do.

Anyone wanting to keep abreast of developments, or who might also care to contribute to new understandings, can visit my website (www.thewebsawake.com). There you will find a blog of my musings and a forum where you can freely partake in open debate.

PHILIP TETLOW

Stockton on Tees, England
January 2007

Acknowledgments

First I must credit the unquestionably brilliant work of the late Professor Richard Feynman, Professor Stuart Kauffman, Professor Douglas R. Hofstadter, Professor Brian Arthur, Professor John Holland, Professor Christopher Langton, Professor Richard Dawkins, Professor Roger Penrose, Professor John Kleinberg, M. Mitchell Waldrop, Kevin Kelly, Dr. Philip Ball, and Dr. Holger Knublauch; I have drawn extensively from their groundbreaking and insightful work in this book. Next I must thank my colleagues Richard Hopkins, Derek Duerden, Kevin Jenkins, Brad Jones, David Conlon and Bruce Anderson of IBM, my good friend Craig Gannon, and Dr. Jeff Pan, Evan Wallace, Dr. Daniel Oberle, Alistair Miles, and Tom Croucher, all members of the World Wide Web Consortium (W3C), for listening to my constant jabbering and crazy ideas. At times I am sure that I have been insufferable. I must also thank Grady Booch and Bob Lojek from IBM, Professors Barrie Thompson and John Tait of Sunderland University, and Professor Keith Boddy, formerly of Newcastle University, because they have certainly been my mentors in this endeavour, although they may not have realized it. Finally I must thank my father, Dr. Alan Tetlow, because I have undoubtedly led him down a long and tortuous path. That he has chosen to follow me every step of the way is truly the mark of a great man and an even greater parent.

P. T.

Prologue

Undoubtedly the World Wide Web has provided a collection of technologies that is having a profound effect on mankind. Like the wheel, the plow, and steam power before it, it is a proving a truly differentiating tool in our world, changing the very ways in which we interact with each other, our surroundings, and our socioeconomic systems. But, unlike the great technologies that have come before it, the Web is different. Why? Because its phenomenal growth and complexity are starting to outstrip our capability to control it directly, making it impossible for us to grasp its completeness in one go. It may quite literally be taking on a life of its own. A set of emergent characteristics and behaviors are now starting to appear that we have not programmed individually. These are apparently starting to increase in number and strength, leading some to believe that the Web not only has its own life, but may also now be worthy of being considered a living organism in its own right; a new posthuman species consisting of just one isolated member.

Many have worked on the concept of emergent properties within highly complex systems, concentrating heavily on the underlying mechanics concerned. Few, however, have studied the fundamentals involved from a sociotechnical perspective. In short, the virtual anatomy of the Web remains relatively uninvestigated. This book therefore attempts to seriously explore this apparent gap, citing a number of provocative, yet objective, similarities from studies relating to both real world and digital systems. By referencing material from a broad range of fields, it presents a collage of interlinked facts, assertions, and coincidences which boldly point to a Web with a powerful potential for life.

This is not a book of definitive answers or rigorous proofs. It is a book about connections, new perspectives, immutable patterns, and the bewildering properties of complex, entangled systems. When Sir Tim Berners-Lee, the inventor of the Web, discussed its first draft at the World Wide Web Consortium's (W3C) Plenary Session in 2005, he lightheartedly referred to it as a conspiracy in the spirit of Dan Brown's best selling novel *The Da Vinci Code*. Maybe he is right, maybe he is wrong, but one thing is for sure: Herein can be found an alluring story well worth personal scrutiny.

CHAPTER *1*

The Web and Life

> The story so far: In the beginning the Universe was created. This has made a lot of
> people very angry and has been widely regarded as a bad move.
>
> —*Douglas Adams, The Restaurant at the End of the Universe*

INTRODUCTION

In some corner of a bland, ambiguous office somewhere in the world today, there is a high likelihood that the following scenario will play out. A young and rather attractive clerk will wander over to the office's token computer technician and ask, "So . . . Why do they call you a geek?" most likely as a bet from some fellow worker. Our technician will be unflustered by this question, having encountered it several times before in their unremarkable career. Nevertheless, they will still raise their head from their coffee-stained keyboard, smile and reply sincerely, "Because I talk to my computer as if it's my best friend." The clerk will never speak to the technician again.

This scene may appear to be an unrealistic and cruel caricature, but for many of those involved in the Information Technology industry it holds much truth. Scores of individuals have followed a career in computing inspired entirely by the expectation that, perhaps one day, they might be able to interact with machines as if they were alive. Whole sections of the industry openly aspire to it, with Artificial Intelligence gurus rushing from their closets to freely foretell a brave new world just over the horizon. But this world has never appeared and we are still faced with the reality of computer systems as lifeless and unnatural creations. Or are we?

A few facts are beyond question. Today, one particular example of combined computational power has emerged on a scale and power far greater than any individual or organized collective could have ever hoped to ascertain or understand in the past. This is the World Wide Web, or "Web" for short, and its unparalleled power is growing steadily by the second. Its growth is almost scary. Widespread use of the Web did not really begin until around 1995, when studies accounted for around 16 million users. By 2001 this figure had grown to over 400 million, and some estimates now predict that it should have topped 1 billion by 2005 and will surpass 2 billion by 2010 [80]—around one-third of the world's population by most common accounts. Couple the fact that the Web is well on its way to absorbing significant

The Web's Awake. By Philip Tetlow
Copyright © 2007 the Institute of Electrical and Electronics Engineers, Inc.

1

portions of mankind's joint knowledge with the raw processing power that is inherent to its technical infrastructure and a social machine the likes of which we have never experienced before is plain. As Gustavo Cardoso, professor of information and communication sciences at ISCTE, Lisbon, said in 1998, "We are in the presence of a new notion of space where physical and virtual influence each other, laying the ground for the emergence of new forms of socialisation, new lifestyles and new forms of social organisation." Some have even referred to the Web as a higher level of human consciousness, a post-human [40] existence with its own independent cognitive capabilities and conscience, a "Metaman" [1] if you will, emerging from unapparent macroevolutionary processes.

A sizable and controversial claim without a doubt. Surely no form of man-made technology could, or should, ever be considered in the same vein as life itself. Perhaps not, but there are certainly a number of apparent similarities between the type of highly complex computer systems we see today and both the development and composition of many real-world systems that natural science has chosen to classify under the heading of "life." In short, and this point is key, a number of reoccurring patterns and themes appear prevalent across both real and virtual worlds. "When a pattern recurs in different systems which bear no obvious relationship to one another, we must suspect a common causative principle, one which can be understood in the most general terms without reference to the specifics of this or that case [80]." To take one brief example, binary characteristics linked to a significant number of macro and micro natural systems have been a matter of well-proven scientific fact for some time. In particular, they are recognized to play a key role in the state transitions surrounding many of the complex systems directly related to the idea of organism. Such characteristics are also fundamental to both macro and micro control in the digital systems world, but until relatively recently these have not been investigated under the same light as their evidently similar real-world twins. It is this duality of pervasion across real and digital worlds that makes binary systems both influential and enthralling. As a recurring theme that appears in the most unexpected of guises, there is much evidence in our Universe to point to the true power of two.

At this point in our understanding there is a need to be careful, however. It is important to emphasize the term *similarity* and not confuse it with the absolute understanding of proven equivalence. Even so, by indulging the creative license granted by established prior work, it should be remembered that mankind has made many great leaps by initially recognizing similarity alone. First comes imagination, inspiration, and recognition, then speculation, investigation, and ultimately proof or disproof. Some ideas are reeled into our minds wrapped up in facts, and some burst upon us naked without the slightest evidence that they could be true but with all the conviction they are. The ideas of the latter sort are the more difficult to displace [21]. Currently, we may well be somewhere between imagination and investigation when considering ideas of life through technologies like the Web, but if one accepts this position and allows a certain level of trust in the proven research of recent decades, then at the very least a highly compelling and provocative case can be presented for others to later validate properly. Many of the observations in the pages to follow have already been substantiated, whereas others are somewhat more speculative. Nevertheless, it is hoped that where propositions are unproven, they are supported by sufficient evidence to make serious consideration at least credible, and it is in this spirit that the majority of this book is presented.

It is surely a truism to state that life has many interpretations for many good reasons. Try to encapsulate just one of these and an untold number will stand by laughing at you. In such respects, it is beyond doubt an essence—that is, an untouchable and complex collection of entangled interpretations, interactions, and dependencies across an unimaginable number of facets. But some of our latest discoveries have started to challenge many of our oldest beliefs about life. For example, today we know that life can survive in conditions far beyond those we would consider to be "normal." There are places on our planet where no light and little oxygen can be found and where temperatures can soar to levels in excess of 400°C (750°F), yet unbelievably life still thrives. These are the hydrothermal vents of the deep sea floor that teem with a fascinating array of life such as tubeworms and huge clams. Furthermore, such vents provide just one example of a seemingly intolerable habitat that life has concurred. There are many more examples, so many in fact that biology has devised a term to describe the life forms that overrun them—Extremophiles.

But such habitats do not even start to push the extremes of life as we can now perceive it. For instance, as we shall see later, more abstract interpretations of life have now been conceived that do not require even the slightest morsel of material embodiment. To be blunt, in its purest guise, life is formless. Although the human race may well be a noble illustration of its many marvels, we are but one of many millions of different occurrences of nobleness in this world. For reasons like this, it is difficult to produce a condensed, coherent, and flowing description of life, or any matter seriously associated with it. Bits of the argument simply refuse to fit into the box, flopping out over the sides at the merest hint of classification.

Although every effort has been made to string together a compelling sequence of arguments in order to associate the Web we see today with the concepts of life, any number of routes could have been taken through the various discussions included, and any number of valid interpretations of life could have been given ultimate favor. Nevertheless, a primary aim of this work is to be as accurate and factual as possible in the material presented. Reading from start to finish will undoubtedly provide an erudite set of overall ideas, but the task of highlighting the most and least convincing evidence involved has been deliberately left to personal discretion. Perhaps several attempts will be needed to take in the subtle and sometimes organic associations entailed, but it is hoped that the effort involved will all be part of an enjoyable and stimulating read.

ALMOST NONE OF THIS IS NEW

Most who are even remotely familiar with the Web would concede that it is a concept inseparably linked with the modern day digital computer. Most would also acknowledge that, although such machines are becoming "cleverer" by the day, they still do not possess one ounce of the same cleverness normally associated with any living being. The two are quite different; computers just do sums while we do something else. That's the way the world goes round: Computers simply do not think! Furthermore, computer engineers are not interested in the types of "stuff" that goes on in a living mind, are they? They are off in a land of space invaders, sort algorithms and slide rules. They can't even tie their own shoelaces let alone interact and appreciate the world to a level that could tackle the subtleties of a cognitive process. After all, why should they? They are making enough progress on their own without needing to be troubled by the challenges of such problems—they have the Web to play with now.

This is a fine parody for certain, but one that is nonetheless somewhat distant from the real truth. If you look as far back in the annals of modern computing as is practical, you will soon find that most, if not all, of the great pioneers in this area were fascinated by the concepts of life and mind. John von Neumann, for instance, one of the most influential individuals in the entire history of computing, was driven by such concepts, being fascinated by the concept of self-operating machines—often referred to as automata. In 1966 he published a book entitled *The Theory of Self-Replicating Automata.* Ted Codd, the father of relational database technology, also published in this area with his book *Cellular Automata* in 1968. So the trend went on and the search for lifelike ways of computing continued. Soon a number of new ideas and a whole collection of new fields of research began to sprout. Take, for instance, the groundbreaking work by Marvin Minsky, who started the Artificial Intelligence movement, John Holland's work on classifier systems, Friedrich Hayek and Donald Hebb's inspiring research into neural networks, and last, but not least, Chris Langton's outstanding contributions that culminated in the notion of genetic algorithms and artificial life.

In fact, until the mathematician Alan Turing first conceived the very notion of a universal programmable computing machine, the word "computer" typically referred not to an inanimate object but to a live human being. It was 1936, and people with the job of computing, in modern terms, crunched numbers. Turing's design for a machine that could do such work—one capable of computing any computable problem—set the stage for the theoretical study of computation and remains a foundation for all computer science. "But he never specified what materials should be used to build it" [83].

"Turing's conceptual machine had no electronic wires, transistors, or logic gates. Indeed he continued to imagine it as a person, one with an infinitely long piece of paper, a pencil, and a simple instruction book. His tireless computer would read a symbol, change the symbol, then move on to the next symbol, according to its programmed rules, and would keep doing so until no further rules applied. Thus the electronic computing machines made of metal and vacuum tubes that emerged in the 1940s and later evolved silicon parts may be the only 'species' of nonhuman computer most people have ever encountered. But theirs is not the only form that a computer can take" [83]. Living organisms also carry out complex physical processes under the direction of digital information. Biochemical reactions and ultimately an entire organism's operation are ruled by instructions stored in its genome, encoded in sequences of nucleic acids.

"When the workings of biomolecular machines inside cells that process deoxyri-bonucleic acid (DNA) and ribonucleic acid (RNA)[1] are compared to Turing's ma-chine, striking similarities emerge: both systems process information stored in a string of symbols taken from a fixed alphabet and both operate by moving step by step along these strings, modifying or adding symbols according to a given set of rules [83]."

But Turing is not the only significant pioneer in computing. Many others have also contributed to important computational themes indirectly. Stuart Kauffman, Brian Arthur, and even the two great physicists Richard Feynman and Murray Gell-Mann, hugely influenced the advances made. Therefore, hardly any of the material presented here is either novel or speculative. Rather, it is calculatingly borrowed from some of the most well established computational works of theory of the past century. The only thing that may be new, however, is the context in which it is ap-plied, namely the Web context. All the evidence and arguments have been applied in similar contexts before, with similar problem spaces all dealing with the same core set of parameters: large-scale dynamics, complexity and adaptation, to name a few.

WHERE TO BEGIN?—WEB MISCONCEPTIONS AND FOLKLORE

Before going any further, and certainly before probing the depths of any discussion on whether the Web may be alive or not, a number of common misconceptions must be dispensed with. The Web is not, for example, the Internet, although it is closely dependent upon it. The two are sometimes perceived as synonymous, but they are not [76]. For this reason, any use of the colloquialized term "the Net" in reference to the Web can only serve to confuse and is hence frowned upon here. The Internet is a communications network, a global framework of wires, routing de-vices and computers on which the Web rests, and to think of the Web just in terms

---

[1]Structurally, RNA is indistinguishable from DNA except for the critical presence of a hydroxyl group attached to the pentose ring in the 2' position (DNA has a hydrogen atom rather than a hydroxyl group). This hydroxyl group makes RNA less stable than DNA because it makes hydrolysis of the phosphosugar backbone easier [22].

Double-stranded RNA (or dsRNA) is RNA with two complementary strands, similar to the DNA found in all "higher" cells. dsRNA forms the genetic material of some viruses. In eukaryotes, it may play a role in the process of RNA interference and in microRNAs.

The RNA world hypothesis proposes that the universal ancestor to all life relied on RNA both to car-ry genetic information like DNA and to catalyze biochemical reactions like an enzyme. In effect, RNA was, before the emergence of the first cell, the dominant, and probably the only, form of life. This hy-pothesis is inspired by the fact that retroviruses use RNA as their sole genetic material and perform in-formation-storing tasks. RNA can also act like a catalyst, a task mainly done by proteins today. There are several ribozymes, catalytic RNAs, that have been discovered, and peptide bond formation in the ribo-some is carried out by an RNA-derived ribozyme. From this perspective, retroviruses and ribozymes are remnants, or molecular fossils, left over from that RNA world. Assuming that DNA is better suited for storage of genetic information and proteins are better suited for the catalytic needs of cells, one would expect reduced use of RNA in cells, along with greater use of DNA and proteins.

of electronics and silicon would be wrong.[2] Other terms like "Information Super Highway" may also be easily misconstrued as characterising the Web but don't really quite get there. They do not convey the truly global, pervasive nature of its vast information bank,[3] instead perhaps conjuring up unnecessarily artificial images, heavily dependent upon silicon-laden machines. The Web is not like that, it is something quite different, as we shall see.

The Web is not as young as one might first think. Computing pioneer Vannevar Bush[4] outlined the Web's core idea, hyperlinked pages, in 1945, making it a veritable pensioner of a concept on the timescale of modern computing. The word "hypertext" was also first coined by Ted Nelson[5] in 1963 and can be found in print in a college newspaper article about a lecture he gave called "Computers, Creativity, and the Nature of the Written Word" in January 1965. At that time, Nelson also tried to implement a version of Bush's original vision, but had little success connecting digital bits on a useful scale. Hence his efforts were known only to an isolated group of disciples.

Few of the hackers writing the code for the emerging Web in the 1990s knew about Nelson or his hyperlinked dream machine [35], but it is nonetheless appropriate to give credit where credit is due.

The origins of the Web as we would recognize it today eventually materialized in 1980, when Tim Berners-Lee and Robert Cailliau built a system called ENQUIRE—referring to *Enquire Within Upon Everything,* a book that Berners-Lee recalled from his youth. While it was rather different from the Web we see today, it contained many of the same core ideas.

It was not until March 1989, however, that Berners-Lee wrote *Information Management: A Proposal,* while working at CERN,[6] which referenced ENQUIRE and described a more elaborate information management system. He published a more formal proposal for the actual World Wide Web on November 12, 1990, and implementation accordingly began on November 13, 1990 when Berners-Lee wrote the first Web page. During the Christmas holiday of that year, Berners-Lee built all the tools necessary for a working Web: the first Web browser, which was a Web editor as well, and the first Web server.

To move the timeline on, in August 1991 he posted a short summary of the World Wide Web project on the *alt.hypertext* newsgroup. This date also marked the

---

[2]This entails a form of "dualism," the philosophical viewpoint advocated by the highly influential seventeenth-century philosopher and mathematician René Descartes. This asserts that there are two separate kinds of substance: "mindful stuff" and ordinary matter.

[3]It has been estimated that at the end of 2002 there were around 3 billion documents available on the Web, with several million more being added every day.

[4]Vannevar Bush was an American engineer, inventor, and politician, known for his political role in the development of the atomic bomb and for his idea of the memex—seen as a pioneering concept for the World Wide Web. He was allegedly a member of the secret committee Majestic 12 investigating UFO activities [90].

[5]Theodor Holm Nelson (born circa 1939) invented the term "hypertext" in 1965 and is a pioneer of information technology. He also coined the words hypermedia, transclusion, virtuality , intertwingularity and teledildonics [91].

[6]CERN is the European Organization for Nuclear Research (Organisation Européenne pour la Recherche Nucléaire) and is the world's largest particle physics laboratory [92].

debut of the Web as a publicly available service on the Internet. In April 1993, CERN announced that the World Wide Web would be free to anyone, with no fees due.

The Web finally gained critical mass with the 1993 release of the graphical Mosaic Web browser by the National Centre for Supercomputing Applications developed by Marc Andreessen and Eric Bina. Prior to the release of Mosaic, the Web was text-based and its popularity was less than that of older protocols in use over the Internet, such as Gopher and WAIS. Mosaic's graphical user interface allowed the Web to become by far the most popular Internet protocol.

OUR UNDERSTANDINGS OF THE WEB

In one way or another, everyone is involved in systems. From the moment we are born until the time we die, our lives are governed and controlled by systems. We are born into a particular religious system, reared under some political system, and educated in a school system. We may be looked after by a health system, warmed by a heating system, and subjected to a draft system. There are systems of rivers, systems of organizations, and systems of systems. But what actually is a system?

The variety of systems can make a general definition difficult, but to be as broad as possible, a system may be defined as a set of components, connected in some fashion, directed to some purpose [33]. In such a way it is an entity in itself which maintains its existence through the mutual interaction of its parts. The key emphasis here is one of mutual interaction, in that something is occurring between the parts over time which maintains the system. A system is, therefore, different from merely a heap or collection of things.

Needless to say, the Web is one such system and categorizing it in this way provides a significant and important distinction from other more common definitions. Systems are also processes that consume, transform, and produce information. In other words, they change information in some noticeable way. This conflicts with the popular vision of the Web solely as a source of data en masse and implies that certain elements of its being are often overlooked. Certainly this is true when one remembers that systems can further incorporate other systems, like us as individuals. And here another important point is raised, for it is us, humans, who are the driving force behind the Web. Without us the Web would not have been created and would most certainly not have evolved to its current position today. We are intrinsic to its very being and are becoming increasingly dependent upon it in turn to maintain the stability of our various modern societies, cultures, and even core beliefs. We have truly become assimilated into its very fabric, thereby producing a hybrid hyperspatial system of natural flesh and blood combined with digital information tissue—a machine of sorts, a "social machine" the likes of which we have never seen before, to quote Tim Berners-Lee. So from at least that perspective the Web can currently be viewed as being partly alive in the truest sense, with society constituting its essential living element.

But there are still more elements of the equation to consider. As a case in point, it is wrong to consider the Web as being exclusively about raw information or human-based processes. Today the Web embraces both data and automated function-ality as part of its make-up. Web Services, a recently introduced Web-friendly set of technologies, allow back-end computer systems, programs, and processes to in-teract using the Web as their door to door courier of data. Furthermore, multiple layers of data now exist on the Web, and so it is not uncommon to find cases of data about data, data about that data, and so on. This is the concept behind the newest branch of the Web, known as the Semantic Web, which points to a self-reflective world of information that freely talks about itself across multiple levels and dimen-sions. These dimensions not only add volume and weight to the descriptiveness of the Web's data, but also open doors to far greater levels of computerised automa-tion. In some quarters the Web will soon be able to dispense with its human hosts altogether and start to do real work for itself, discovering its own weaknesses and strengths along the way, extending and compensating accordingly. It will become truly autonomous, changing into a place where Web service will find Web service, and those best suited will feed off each other's peer circle of information and capa-bility. And the more powerful and connected such clusters of capabilities become, the greater the likelihood that they will produce even more superior capabilities. So an upward-spiraling current of self-feeding, self-organizing, decentralized compu-tational power will have been started, if it has not been started already. The engine to a much more powerful instrument than the global entity we see today will be kick-started, controlled only by society's collective consciousness. As we shall see later, there is strong evidence to support the case for the eventual transition of this into something far greater, something far different from the Web of today. Will we recognize this transition when it happens? Has it happened already? Will we be able to harness or even comprehend the outcome of any higher Web state? Perhaps the philosophers amongst us might like to guess at the answer, but the vastness of the Web will surely work against them. Just like a single ant climbing the trunk of a great redwood, they may no more understand any future state of the Web than the ant understands the art of bonsai.

POWER OF THE PEOPLE

The great power plants of our planet might well provide the energy that invigorates the Internet, but they are not the driving force behind the Web; "that job lies entire-ly within the realms of human motivation and our dispositions toward action" [77]. Moreover, this is a force to be reckoned with, having led to both to the highest and lowest points of man's achievement. So, if one accepts that, as a global communi-ty, we are now joined with the Web into one great seamless being, it would not be too strong a conclusion to suggest that the underlying mechanisms of the Web are actually driven by the very same system of wants and needs that control us all as human beings.

Through us the Web feels its most basic survival instinct. We not only provide it with its principal motivations, but also provide its own set of aspirations and per-sonal goals. What the Web wants for itself, the public presence of global humanity usually gets, and by that token the Web is incapable of hiding even its most secret desires. Be they good, bad, pure or debase, every one of the Web's visible aspects simply represents a manifestation of mankind's averaged cravings, the need for useful information being just one of those. In such respects the Web is the best mirror we have ever had for our collective mindset. What it shows, we have asked for without question; morality holds little sway in the process of technological advancement.

But just what does this driving force look like? How can it be described? And how can it explain the many faces of the Web?

Maslow's hierarchy of needs is a theory in psychology proposed by Abraham Maslow in 1943, a theory of human motivation which he subsequently extended and which has been constantly updated by others ever since (Figure 1.1). Even so, the core content of his theory is still considered to be a key reference in modern psychological practice, contending that as we humans meet our basic necessities, we seek to satisfy successively higher needs that occupy a set hierarchy.

This model is often depicted as a pyramid consisting of five levels: The four lower levels are grouped together as *deficiency* needs, while the top level is termed as a *being* need. While our deficiency needs must be met, our being needs to continually shape our behavior. The basic concept is that the higher needs in this hierarchy only come into focus once all the needs that are lower down in the pyramid are mainly or entirely satisfied. Growth forces create upward movement in the hierarchy, whereas regressive forces push prepotent needs further down the hierarchy.

As such, Maslow's hierarchy can be categorized as follows:

- **Physiological Needs:** The first need for the body is to achieve a consistent physical and mental state capable of maintaining daily life. This is obtained through the consumption of food, drink and air, achieving adequate sleep, a comfortable temperature, and so on. When such requirements are unmet, a human's physiological needs take the highest priority by default. For instance, if someone were to simultaneously experience the desire for love and a hunger for food, they would rather eat than engage in a sexual act. As a re-

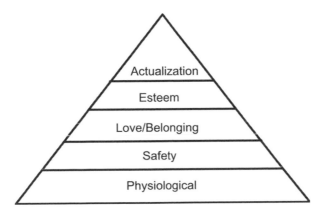

Figure 1.1. Maslow's hierarchy of needs.

sult of the potency of such physiological needs, we tend to treat all other desires and capacities with less urgency.

- **Safety Needs:** When all physiological needs are fulfilled, the need for safety becomes dominant and only in circumstances of extreme threat to physical condition will it overtake the need below it.
- **Love/Belonging Needs:** Once a person's physiological and safety needs are largely met, the third layer of human needs starts to become apparent. This involves emotionally based relationships in general, which includes the perceived need for companionship—both sexual and nonsexual—and/or having a family. There is an inherent sense of community or affiliation in our social makeup; in other words, humans want to belong to groups, whether they be clubs, work groups, religious groups, family, gangs, and so on. We need to feel wanted by others and to be accepted by them.
- **Esteem Needs:** There are two types of esteem need: (1) the need for the respect of, and recognition, by others and (2) the need for self-respect. Such needs can be seen as being motivations or drivers of behavior, as in the instinctual need of a human to make the most of their unique abilities.
- **Self-Actualization:** Self-actualization is the instinctual need of a human to make the most of their unique abilities. Maslow described it as follows: "A musician must make music, the artist must paint, a poet must write, if he is to be ultimately at peace with himself. What a man can be, he must be. This need we may call self-actualization." Although Maslow tentatively placed self-actualization at the top of his hierarchy, this element has been discounted by most modern psychologists.

What is obvious and apparent about the relationship between the Web and Maslow's famous model is that the Web can assist in satisfying needs at every level in its hierarchy. It may not provide heat, nutrition, and shelter directly, agreed, but it can make the search for such things much easier. Regardless, the Web really comes into its own in the layers above purely physiological associations, and in such respects it is much more directed toward mental, rather than physical, fulfillment. For example, it can easily hypnotize us into a sense of belonging that is falsely secure. It can easily become a surrogate companion to many of those who are somewhat less than socially adept by either character or their own making. It provides an easy option, as it were, a quick fix for large regions of our needs' landscape, and in a culture where living life in the fast lane is becoming the norm rather than the exception, such quick fixes are not only becoming socially acceptable, they also are starting to take the front seat in our wider sociological systems.

Indeed academics have proposed that Maslow's hierarchy can be used to describe the kinds of information that individuals seek at different motivational levels, whether that be via the Web or not. For example, individuals at the lowest level seek coping information in order to meet their basic needs. Information that is not directly connected to helping a person meet his or her needs in a very short time span is simply left unattended. Individuals at Maslow's safety level need helping information. They look to be assisted in finding out how they can be safe and secure.

Enlightening information is sought by those seeking to meet their belongingness needs. Quite often this can be found in materials on relationship development. Empowering information is sought by people at the esteem level. They are looking for information on how their ego can be developed. Finally, people in the growth levels of cognitive, aesthetic, and self-actualization yearn for edifying information and material on how to connect to something beyond themselves [77]. The Web perfectly fits this higher space, openly promoting an image of communal connectedness and belonging. So as the various sectors of society become more comfortable within Maslow's framework, the Web provides a natural accompaniment to their upper motivational processes.

It should also be recognized that the psychological and sociological forces behind the Web have significant power, along with the fact that the source of this power is growing at an alarming rate. In the four centuries from 1500 to 1900, the human population of this planet grew by an average of around three million people per annum. However, in the century from 1900 to 2000, the average yearly increase was close to 44 million—in truth virtually 15 times the previous rate (Figure 1.2). So by such reckoning, some estimnates conclude that more people are walking this planet today than all the humans who have ever lived—a profound conclusion if true.

THE DARK SIDE OF THE FORCE

There is, however, one notable and potent exception to the Web's preference for mental, as opposed to physical, stimulation amongst its human hosts. As intelligent beings, one of mankind's earliest discoveries was undoubtedly its capability to achieve sexual stimulation with relative ease, be that as part of the normal process of mating or through other acts of self-gratification. Over the centuries, our various

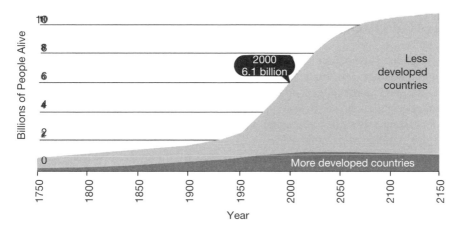

Figure 1.2. Global population growth.

cultures have controlled such activities through various rules and codes of conduct, often demoting them to a position of unacceptable public behavior. But still they are very much part of a normal human's instinctive behavior, forming an essential component of our drive to procreate the species. Sexual stimulation, after all, is nature's way of thanking us for thinking about its next generation of product, and, as such, it is a reward for which Mother Nature has deliberately created an inbuilt inclination. This is the predominant reason why pornography is so prevalent on the Web. In fact, it is so prevalent that if the Web could be visualized as a being in its own right, large parts of its skin would be colored pink through black to match our own range of exterior pigmentation.

Not wanting to be drawn into any debate about morals, from a purely technological standpoint, pornography has to be considered as a veritable plus for the Web, having forced the pace of change for many a valuable technology in the past. Throughout the history of new media, from vernacular speech to movable type, to photography, to paperback books, to videotape, to cable and pay TV, to CD-ROMs and laser discs, pornography has shown technology the way [36]. It may represent the darker side of the Web's public acceptability, but it is certainly playing a key role in its expansion and further evolution. Pornography draws curiosity seekers who stay to see what else the new media can do. And there is a convenient dovetailing in the audience for computers and pornography: Young Western males dominate both markets. Gadget-playing, girl-crazy young men will stay longer at a terminal that supplies both girls and gadgets—a sad indictment of the Web success, perhaps, but a hard reality nonetheless. Furthermore, it is from this pool of similar social demographics that most practicing technologists originate. Those who have and will make a difference in the advancement of the Web's technologies in the foreseeable future come from the predominantly caucasian economic states of the Western world. This is not a matter of racial prejudice or preference on the Web's part, but is simply an issue of macroeconomics. The Web goes where the funding is, it's as simple as that, and this in itself is causing a number of growing pains.

WHAT WOULD A WEB BE WITHOUT THE HOLES?

Although the Web certainly has the capability to be globally pervasive through the technologies and infrastructure coverage offered by the Internet, it is not truly this way yet, and significant gaps in its potential to reach a full global audience still exist. Web pages cannot be created using many character sets with regional specificity, for instance. For this reason, you will not find any native Web content including text in Ethiopic—often referred to as *Ge'ez* or *Classic Ge'ez*—one of the ancient languages of Ethiopia which is now mainly used in Ethiopian Orthodox Church as a liturgical language [37]. This is an issue predicted by the very fact that at present there is no universally recognized Ethiopic character set.[7]

---

[7]There are concerted ongoing efforts by organizations like the World Wide Web Consortium (W3C) to address such internationalization problems. For more information, please refer to http://www.w3.org/International/

This particular deficiency is not because the demand for such material is low, quite the contrary, it is purely because, up to this point, there has not been sufficient funding or knowledgeable interest to make the development to make such capability a reality—a symptom common to most, if not all, of the Web's current technological concerns.

STRUCTURE ABOUNDS

There are those who would argue that the Web is a completely unstructured place. One need only take a quick look at the NASDAQ Most Active list to support this fact, they will say, adding that Web portals and the search engines exist primarily because the Web is a tremendously disorganized space, a system where the disorder grows right alongside the overall volume. Yahoo and Google, for example, function (in a way) as man-made antidotes to the Web's natural chaos, being engineered attempts to restore structure to a system that is incapable of generating structure on its own. This is an often-noticed paradox of the Web: "The more information that flows into its reservoirs, the harder it becomes to find any single piece of information" [42].

Without a doubt, it is easy to see why the less experienced Web user might form such an opinion. The Web is certainly an impossible thing to digest in one sitting, and it isn't hard to become overwhelmed by its dominance without the help of some pretty clever tools by your side. Furthermore, it is certainly true that it is precisely for such reasons that search engine technologies have become so popular, providing a relief map of the Web based on information hewn straight from its rock face. Even so, an unstructured view of the Web's reality is still somewhat a naive interpretation of its form, being, in truth, almost as far from the actual reality as one can get.

The Web is not without structure, it simply has too much of it. It is our fault that we do not understand that vast amounts of information become a complex "intertwingularity," regardless of whatever medium it is stored in. This is due to a fundamental flaw in our mental capability. People just keep pretending that they can make complex things deeply hierarchical, categorizable, and sequential when they can't accomplish this directly; that is a task for raw complexity to achieve itself. All information becomes deeply intertwined beyond a certain point, and then such classification types begin to drift off into higher levels of framework by natural tendency. It's not that they disappear beyond recognition, it's just that there are lots of them, overlapping, merging, and generally making things difficult to comprehend from a distance. In reality, it's simply a question of not seeing the forest for the trees.

Take any two pieces of Web-friendly content, a couple of simple text-based Web pages say, and have one point to the other via a hyperlink. By this very act, structure is automatically introduced. At a finer level of detail, even the very text of each page has its own structure without the need for hyperlinks, presumably following the grammatical rules of the natural language in which it is written. In such ways the Web exudes structure to the point where it can be extremely counterproductive, often confusing its use or definition for any singular purpose. Actually that's a little unfair, because the structure we are discussing here is not just any run-of-the-mill architecture. Rather it is a composite of multiple types, layers, and hierarchies of more simplistic configurations spreading out in every direction. One could never consider the Web to be a singularly hierarchical framework, for example, although it does undoubtedly embody many thousands, if not millions, of items amassed by such configurations. In a similar manner, it is not solely a peer-to-peer, hub-and-spoke, distributed-parallel, topological, or any other type of organized system; it is all of them rolled into one complex, all encompassing whole, for many reasons and across many dimensions. But this is not just one almighty and unruly mess, because each structure carries its own purpose and identity. Furthermore, many fields of science and philosophy have a name for such arrangements. The Web's structure is in many senses a collection of "ontologies," a systematic account of existence in its own right.

In information engineering, such ontologies are the product of an attempt to formulate a conceptual description about a topic or area of interest. They are typically structures containing all the relevant entities and their relationships and rules within that area. Even so, the technological usage of the term "ontology" is derived from the much older usage of the term in philosophy, where it is also used to refer to the study of existence. The purpose of a computational ontology is therefore not to specify what does or does not 'exist', but rather to create a corpus of details containing concepts that refer to entities of interest to the examiner and that will be useful in performing certain types of computerized investigations. For this reason the rationales used by philosophical ontologists can be helpful in recognizing and avoiding potential logical ambiguities.

An ontology that is not tied to one particular area of interest, but attempts instead to generally describe things and the relationships between them, is known as a 'foundation' or 'upper' ontology, and it is from such a base that the general setup of the Web's organization is formed. This is a large open framework within which many more specialized, domain-specific ontologies are enclosed to make the artifacts presented more useful for real-world purposes. These smaller structures are hence deliberately tied to a specific subject, audience, or other kind of distribution, like the websites constituting the eBay organization for instance or the various pages on any company's intranet.

Ontologies can be referred to as being explicit specifications of particular conceptualizations, and it is across such specifications that the various search engine spiders and bots roam to collate their own interpreted indexes of the Web. In doing so, however, they only pick up nuances that suit their own particular purposes, unless, that is, they are specifically redirected. For this reason it is dangerous practice to consider the results returned by any particular search engine to be an absolute reference of the Web's true character. Google may be the Web's best ally from an approachability point of view, but it might not be considered the best candidate to act as its biographer, because it may take many more generations of new Web technologies before such a role can be fulfilled adequately. Even so, when the Web's story does eventually mature into a account worthy of accurate representation, ontological structure will almost certainly be one of the materials from which that story will be spun.

One new set of technologies that might help establish an accurate interpretation of the Web's true form in the long run are those that belong to its latest offspring, the Semantic Web. Here much more formal types of ontology are the norm, allowing far greater and more accurate levels of descriptiveness amongst the Web's content. The overall intent behind the Semantic Web is not only to make the general Web more accurate for human consumption, but to increase its capability for direct understanding by computers themselves. If successful, it will be like the Web folding back upon itself, making it capable of seeing its likeness, warts and all.

FOUR DIMENSIONS ARE NOT ENOUGH

A surreal, but nonetheless true, characteristic of the Web, as all conceptual ontologies, is the fact that it is quite literally not of this world. It is materially just a collective made up of an unimaginable number of magnetic fluctuations on the surfaces of the world's various disk drives and memory chips. In truth, in its native form it has little practical physical presence at all; you can't see it, touch it, smell it, or even taste it, and in such respects it is a truly ethereal thing. To purposefully misquote Grady Booch,[8] the famous Software Engineer, it is "invisible to most of the world. Although individuals, organizations, and nations rely on a multitude of Web-intensive systems every day, most Web content lives in the interstitial spaces of society, hidden from view except insofar as it does something tangible or useful" [57]. Furthermore, because of its physical absence the Web does not even necessarily conform in usual ways to the dimensions of space and time. For example, the fact that one Web page could theoretically link to another physically located in either the next room or the next galaxy makes no conceptual difference at all to the Web's constitution. It may take much longer for the page furthest away to render in a browser, but this is more a concern for the physical scaffolding of the Internet that underlies the Web, rather than the Web itself. This also points to that notion that the Web works on a different timescale to our own. We may see Web pages appear in front of us in the blink of an eye, but this is merely a microscopic detail, again more applicable to the Internet rather than the Web as a whole. In the Web's sphere of existence, "life" plods along at a much slower speed, synchronized to the averaged rhythm of change coming from humanity's collective stumbling en masse.

None of this means to say that the Web does not embody or aspire to comply with any of the Universe's physical laws, as we shall see from Chapter 3 onwards. It is simply a quantum leap in our joint technological capability which we do not fully understand yet. As such, it may take us some time to refocus on just what exactly is taking place inside this new technology's metabolism. The term "quantum leap" is not intended to be used as cliché here, because it perfectly describes the ideas involved. The change in mindset required to understand and harness the real power of the Web is similar to the difference in perspective needed to appreciate both Newtonian and quantum mechanics. Furthermore, this comparison has been

---

[8]Grady Booch is best known for developing the Unified Modelling Language with Ivar Jacobson and James Rumbaugh.

investigated seriously on a number of occasions already. In one example, a fascinating result was found by Jon Kleinberg, a computer scientist at Cornell University who discovered that, when the matrix of the Web is analyzed like a quantum mechanical system, stable energy states correspond to concepts under discussion [53,54].

OUR UNDERSTANDINGS OF LIFE

So what about the Web as a living thing? How can we name it so? In fact, how can we even identify and distinguish life itself, even in its most obvious of forms?

It would be foolish to pretend that we are anywhere near to understanding the true essence of life. There might be the odd fleeting moment when science unlocks another of nature's secrets, but life hides its secrets well and we soon realize that we still have an additional million locks to go. In truth we only really understand a small number of life's characteristics, a handful of its mechanics, a few of the words spoken in its native tongue as it were. But still we try, we aspire to understand, and slowly, ever so slowly, we are learning. In doing so, however, some of our most fundamental beliefs about life are being challenged.

In recent years, some have gone so far as to suggest that life may not be uniquely confined to a physical existence, for example contemplating the possibilities of consciousness and intelligence originating from purely virtual environments. The Web is most certainly one such environment, and this raises a number of profound questions. For a start, what observable properties would be required to know for certain if life existed on the Web or if the Web itself were alive? Furthermore, and perhaps more profoundly relevant, if the Web is not alive yet, but the expectation is that it might soon well be, how close to producing life are its relevant properties at the moment? For sure, these are complex and difficult questions that cannot easily be answered in one go, but there is encouraging evidence to suggest that we are not totally unequipped to tackle such conundrums. Ever since our wisest realized that they were different from the inanimate rocks that form our planet, we have tried to comprehend the very essence of our own vitality, collecting a wealth of knowledge along the way. Today we have definitive classifications for what is alive and what is not, but these mostly relate to our classical interpretations of being. Certainly they provide strong points of reference, but perhaps the real issues at hand today have now moved on. Perhaps now we should be less interested in the bipolar definitions of old and more interested in blurred edges of reality where new life forms might conceivably begin and end.

LIFE'S PLAYGROUND—A UNIVERSE OF INFINITE POSSIBILITIES

From early childhood we are urged to achieve; "eat all your greens," "be a straight 'A' student," "do the best you can" should all be familiar chants from one of society's most common mantras. Our lives are filled with goals, each one specific to a certain property of our own being. But even though we as individuals might strive to excel at anything we do, ask even the world's most successful to define "what it takes to be the best" and heads will start to scratch. "Five years training and complete dedication", an Olympic gold medalist might volunteer, "a lifetime of serenity and prayer" could easily be the answer from a devout Buddhist, while "courage, complete conviction and the willingness to go that extra mile" might well be the retort from a world leader. All are good answers, but all are nonetheless equally misdirected from nature's point of view.

If Mother Nature were privy to such testament, she would no doubt raise a wry smile, for she has indeed learned the true answer to this question through countless generations of hard-earned experience. The solution to becoming the best is no real secret and, in fact, hides a deceptively simple strategy: Just find out who or what is the best and make sure that you are better. That's all there is to it. And it doesn't make the slightest bit of difference how hard you try along the way or how long it takes you to get there. You could turn out to be a million times more superior and become so in the blink of an eye, but still, in the natural world, just being "good enough" has always been, and always will be, good enough. There are no grades handed out, no fixed pass marks to point to, and few second chances. Evolution has no long-term goal other than to make all life forms better than they were a second ago. "There is no long-distance target, no final perfection to serve as a criterion for selection, although human vanity cherishes the absurd notion that our species is the final goal of evolution" [51]. Thus there are no definite targets, just complex gray regions of competition and influence leading to black or white outcomes based on pure survival. Evolution does not care about what makes sense; it cares about what works.

But why should this be so? Why should the concept of targets be so irrelevant in the natural world? The real answer is that the Universe is an immensely large space of possibilities [67]. In fact, it is as close to being infinite in such respects as to make the very concept of boundaries practically irrelevant. Hence, in our material Universe, no matter how expansive, adaptive, or progressive any given system, it will never be constrained solely by its environment unless it attempts to transcend all but the most fundamental of its laws. Take for instance the cheetah, the fastest land animal known to exist. It could evolve and theoretically continue growing faster and faster over countless generations. On its own, it would only stop accelerating as a species when the most basic of universal laws—gravity, friction, and so on—prevented its muscle mass from propelling it any faster over its natural terrain. Moreover, without such restrictions, only the speed of light itself would stand in the way of its ever-increasing speed.

Look also at what happens with a simple species of seaweed, containing 1000 interconnected genes. To be sure of finding the highest level of adaptation to its environment, natural selection would have to examine every considerable combination of genes and appraise all conceivable mutations in order to determine the best possible variant of the species. When the total number of combinations of gene mutations is worked out, the answer isn't two multiplied by 1000, it's actually two multiplied by itself 1000 times. That's 2^{1000}, or roughly 10^{300}—a number so vast that it dwarfs even the number of potential moves in a chess game. Quite simply, the number is huge and evolution could not even begin to try out that many alternatives, not even in the time taken for the entire Universe to develop thus far. And remember that's just for seaweed. Humans and other animals roughly have 100 times as many genes, and most of these genes come in many more than two varieties [67].

In short, most adaptive systems such as life explore their way through this immense space of possibilities with no realistic hope of ever finding the single 'best' place to be [67]. They do this by a simple process of trial and error, fumbling their way to find their most appropriate evolutionary path. All that evolution can do, in essence, is look for improvements, not perfection. Hence it either builds upon the successes of previous generations or abruptly stops at the outright dead end of extinction. Through such hierarchies of successes, building blocks upon building blocks of slow progress are constructed, revealing a deep secret—namely, that hierarchy utterly transforms a system's ability to learn, evolve, and adapt [67]. But there is a price to pay for evolutionary success and higher orders of environmental fit. Through the compounded advances piled generation upon generation also comes at least one side effect; complexity. In all but the most specific of cases, this increases as a direct result of evolutionary advancement, applying its own rules and constraints from the ground up in its wake.

So, nature's systems are complex by definition and, given the meager amount of time we as a race have had to get our act together so far, it is not surprising that the man-made systems in our grasp are mostly simple by comparison. But here again there are tradeoffs. By being simple, the fabrication of our systems can be precise and efficient, whereas in comparison the complex, adaptive machinery of nature mostly cannot. A truly complicated structure has many masters, and none of them can be served exclusively. Rather than strive for optimization of any one function, a complex system can only survive by pacifying a magnitude of goals. For instance, an adaptive system must participate in a tradeoff between exploiting a known path of success, thereby optimizing a current strategy, or diverting resources to exploring new paths, thereby wasting energy to try less efficient methods.

So vast are the blended drivers in any complex natural system that it is often impossible to unravel the actual causes of its continued success or survival. Survival is a journey with many different and sometimes contradictory endpoints. Hence most living organisms are so multifaceted that they are blunt variations that happen to work, rather than precise renditions of their ultimate purposes. It is one of nature's unwritten rules; in creating something from nothing, as is nature's origin, forget elegance; if it works, it's beautiful [21]. That said, evolution's overriding cause is obviously to seek out the best possible solutions to any given problem in all possible situations; it achieves its peak fitness as it were. But in so doing, nature is always running blind. It only knows and cares about the condition of its current world and all the imperfect notions of "best" within it, infinitely stumbling in the dark to find any new options capable of stealing pole position. It is such stumbling that is evolution's defining quality. If, for example, one were theoretically able to ask it for the answer to an apparently predictable question, say "how can you cross a stream if there are three boats of different size in front of you?", completely nonsensical answers should not be unexpected. "Ignore the boats and dig a tunnel under the stream" might be one solution suggested—a ridiculous proposition maybe, but nevertheless a plausible solution. This seemingly haphazard approach to problem-solving is on of evolution's hallmarks, explaining why life continues to enlarge its own being [21]. Nature is simply an ever-expanding library of possibilities positioned in an open Universe of endless possibilities.

At first sight our modern digital world might appear to be totally different. As a species we like to think that we have progressed far beyond the point where we had to fight for our existence on the Great Plains, with our subconscious instinct for sustainability driving the search for the security and protection of certainty in our surroundings. To know our world and control it through that knowledge has been a powerful ambition of society ever since we crafted our first stone axe. Each time we have created such a new technology, we have pushed it, honed it, until it far exceeds the "just good enough" requirements of the natural world around us. We control it with ever-greater levels of precision and so involuntarily strive to push our lead in evolution's natural pecking order. In fact we have become so good at this that today we are shrouded in a world so locally precise, so digital and powerful, that we could easily account for every second of every human life on this planet and still have plenty spare computational capability left over. Nevertheless, although ours might appear to be a world destined for precise digital servitude, this is actually a somewhat naive view of our real contemporary technical context. Take a step back for a moment, in fact take 10 steps while you are at it, and you will soon see the abundance of controlled accuracy start to mount into an ever-changing, interconnected pool of swirling grayness, a swirl of interconnected system upon interconnected system not dissimilar to that from which we once fled—the imperfect and complex swirl of life itself. And the ultimate example of such interconnected technical co-evolution? Enter the Web we see today.

ENQUIRIES INTO THE DEFINITION OF LIFE

In 1872, H. C Bastian wrote: "Amongst the carbon compounds we find in our world there is an abundance of evidence to prove the existence of internal tendencies or molecular properties which may and do lead to the evolution of more and more complex chemical compounds. And it is such synthetic processes, occurring amongst the molecules of colloidal and allied substances, which seem so often to engender or give 'origin' to a kind of matter possessing that subtle combination of properties to which we are accustomed to apply the epithet 'living'" [28].

The word "life" has probably been around ever since mankind began using language. It is a word of fundamental importance to all of us, and seldom do we make it through an entire day without putting it to use. We do so, however, with only a sketchy and subjective idea of what life actually means. This is because until recently, within the last century or so, it has been easy for people to distinguish between what they call living and what they call nonliving. There has been no need to define life precisely; its meaning has typically been intuitively understood [28].

The scientific revolution of the past few centuries has brought complications into this matter, and certain new fields of science are inherently concerned with systems that would be called living by some and nonliving by others. For example, advances in medicine have brought about the discovery of microscopic 'infectious agents' such as viruses and plasmids. Are these alive? Many scientists are presently search-ing for extraterrestrial life. How will they know when they have found it, if life is not clearly defined [28]?

Scores of researchers have been, and still are, devoting their time to the study of biochemical evolution to unravel the mystery of the origin of life on Earth. Though even the ancients concerned themselves with this subject, not until recently have theories in this area depended on chemical systems whose status as living or nonliv-ing is open to debate. Linus Pauling, one of the premier chemists of the twentieth century, once said "In connection with the origin of life, I should like to say that it is sometimes easier to study a subject than to define it." Up to this point, most scien-tists have taken Pauling's 'easier' route and avoided the issue of coming to a con-sensus on definition. As the *World Book Encyclopedia* has put it: "Rather than try-ing to define life precisely, biologists concentrate on deepening their understanding of life by studying living things." So, how do they know what to study? What does the scientific community consider to be that subtle combination of properties need-ed to set all living things apart?

There are what might be considered to be classical properties of life, according to standard reference material. The 1984 *Random House College Dictionary* de-fines life as: "The condition that distinguishes animals and plants from inorganic objects and dead organisms, being manifested by growth through metabolism, re-production, and the power of adaptation to environment through changes originat-ing internally." This latter property refers to the phenomenon of homeostasis, whereby an individual organism changes itself in response to a change in its sur-roundings. In other definitions, this is referred to as "response to stimuli" or just "responsiveness." Homeostasis is not to be confused with response of the species to environmental changes through the process of natural selection. That is evolution, and it comes about through the transmission of random mutations in the organism to its offspring. This ability to transmit mutations during reproduction, and thus be subject to the processes of natural selection, is a criterion of life cited by many.

The *Encyclopaedia Britannica* concentrates on metabolism in its biochemical definition of life: "An open system of linked organic reactions catalyzed at low temperatures by specific enzymes which are themselves products of the system." Some references also include movement against a force in addition to the other cri-teria. This may include locomotion, dynamics, or, in the case of most plants, growth against the force of gravity. The transfer of matter is another standard criterion list-ed. The consumption of raw materials and the excretion of waste materials are nat-ural consequences of metabolism.

Hence, in general, life has traditionally been characterized in terms of growth, reproduction, metabolism, motion, and response through homeostasis and evolu-tion. The phrase "in terms of" is used here because each of the criteria mentioned are exhibited by different systems to varying degrees. The caveats in such defini-tions are made evident by two sets of these systems:

- Systems that we consider to be alive but that don't exhibit all of the classical properties
- Systems that we consider nonliving but that exhibit these properties

The classic example from the second set is fire. It grows, moves, metabolizes, consumes, transforms, and excretes matter, reproduces, and responds to stimuli—for example, wind. Crystals will grow in a saturated solution and reproduce more of their kind. The hydrosphere moves, as in flowing rivers, dissolves compounds and precipitates out different forms, reproduces from rain, and responds, by breaking a dam, for example. Similar analogies have even been carried as far as free radicals, a species of individual molecules that reproduce and that can grow into large polymers.

The nonreproducing mule is an often-used example from the first set. It does not take part in the process of natural selection, yet few would deny that it is alive. Various seeds, spores, and even insects can lay dormant for years without moving, growing, metabolizing, or reproducing, yet they are considered by most as part of what we call "life." This dormant life is swept under a convenient carpet commonly referred to as "cryptobiosis," meaning 'hidden life'.

There is a third category whose anomalous systems defy classification into either set. One system in this category is the virus. On one hand, it can be said that "viruses are not living organisms because they are incapable of independent existence" and must use their host's cell's metabolic machinery in order to reproduce. On the other hand, it can also be argued that it seems unreasonable to deny that viruses are living just because they need help to do so. From the latter viewpoint, the virus is considered to be a parasite, a kind of microscopic leech. In many respects too, the Web fits into this category, because in its current state it is surely incapable of surviving without our support.

Certain man-made systems are claimed to be forms of "protolife" in a classical sense, implying that they may have been the first forms of life on Earth. One category of these includes the coacervates and microspheres. These are produced through combinations of various immiscible liquids—for example: Sidney Fox's[9] thermal proteins in water. These have been shown to form "cells," also referred to as droplets, which grow and move about, bud and divide, and aggregate. Their membranes exhibit selective permeability and even catalytic activity.

Experiments have also been carried out with clay minerals. These spontaneously grow in layers. Various cations—an ion or group of ions having a positive charge and which characteristically move toward the negative electrode in electrolysis—when substituted into the silicate lattices of these clays, produce catalytically active sites. These active sites are 'reproduced' in subsequent layers that form on the clays. Thus they "are capable of replicative self-multiplication" and are subject to the process of natural selection.

[9]Arguably, Sidney Fox's best-known research was conducted in the 1950s and 1960s, when he studied the spontaneous formation of protein structures. His early work demonstrated that under certain conditions amino acids could spontaneously form small polypeptides—the first step on the road to the assembly of large proteins. The result was significant because his experimental conditions duplicated conditions that might plausibly have existed early in Earth's history.

Further work revealed that these amino acids and small peptides could be encouraged to form close spherical membranes, called microspheres. Fox has gone so far as to describe these formations as protocells, because he believed that they might be an important intermediate step in the origin of life. Microspheres might have served as a stepping stone between simple organic compounds and genuine living cells.

The systems mentioned here are just some of those that provide evidence that the classical definitions of life are not appropriate in many cases.

Some claim that there is a continuum of life complexity, with simple inorganic systems at one end and the highest life forms at the other, with the types of systems mentioned above lying somewhere in the middle of this continuum. It is therefore believed by some that there is no point along the continuum of existence from the simplest atom to the most complex animal, at which a line can be drawn separating life from nonlife. Consider the electromagnetic spectrum as an analogy: At a wavelength of 520 nm, light is green; at 470 nm, it is blue. But at what wavelength does it change from green to blue? There are an infinite number of blue-green shades in between the two extremes. The drawing of lines between green and blue, between living and nonliving, is said to be arbitrary, a matter of personal preference. Others take the stance that life is just an aspect of man's perception of matter, just as music is an aspect of his perception of sound. It is purely subjective which sequences of sounds will be perceived as music to an individual. This type of thinking has led authors such as Josephine Marquand to conclude that it is prudent to "avoid the use of the word 'life' or 'organism' in any discussion of borderline systems."

One way to draw the line between life and nonlife in such a continuum of complexity is to pick out a specific structural feature common to systems considered to be alive. The first such documented definition was that "all living systems are composed of cells." In his study on the origin of life in the 1920s, A. I. Oparin proposed that "only in discrete particles could the random chemical activity occurring in the waters of the earth be organized into harmoniously correlated chemical reactions." An effect of this definition would, obviously, be its converse: non-cellular systems are not living. But we cannot, however, deduce from this definition that all cellular systems are alive: the oil-vinegar emulsion in your salad dressing is composed of many cells, but is obviously at the nonlife end of the continuum.

Another feature of classical living systems is the ubiquity of the linear polymers of amino acids we call proteins. These make up much of the structure and catalytic machinery associated with life on Earth. Also ubiquitous are the polymers of nucleotides, the nucleic acids. DNA and RNA contain the genetic information that is passed on to the offspring of living organisms. Classical carbon-based life has been defined as that which makes use of or produces proteins and/or nucleic acids. More generally, living systems can be defined as those which exhibit optical activity and isotopic fractionation. The former refers to the rotation of polarized light by solutions of organic molecules. This is due to the chirality[10], or handedness, of these molecules. Often, when a molecule has two possible mirror images, a left one and a right one, only one of these forms is found in nature. For example, only left-handed amino acids are used in proteins and only right-handed sugars are stored for energy. Isotopic fractionation implies that life forms selectively pick out certain isotopes of the elements. This results in relative concentrations of these isotopes within them that differ from the relative concentrations in other systems—this provides the basis for carbon-14 dating. These definitions are not foolproof; some inorganic and man-

---

[10]Of or relating to the structural characteristic of a molecule that makes it impossible to superimpose it on its mirror image.

made systems also display these properties. Crystals of one handedness are produced routinely by chemists, and phase changes such as evaporation can result in isotopic fractionation.

If you grew up in Canada, you might have been led to believe that only pine trees retain their foliage during the winter. If you then defined a pine tree as 'a tree which stays green in the winter,' you would run into trouble when traveling to California, where trees that are not even part of the conifer family stay green all year. In such a way, definitions of life here on Earth may be of a similar nature. They are based on the particular, most likely random, complex mechanism by which life arose in this locale. Nevertheless, life may have arisen elsewhere or earlier on Earth under different circumstances. It may then have lacked the familiar "life signs" we recognize today, yet still be considered life by other criteria, such as reproduction or metabolism.

Many definitions of life echo the belief that "living organisms are distinguished by their specified complexity." In such definitions, the terms order, information, and complexity are frequently encountered. How are these concepts related? Complex structures and systems abound in the Universe, but most of them—the nonlife, by this definition—are random, that is, they are not specified. We could define the 'information content' of a structure as the minimum number of steps needed to specify that structure. To specify a random polypeptide—a sequence of amino acids—we need only state the proportions of the amino acids that go into making it. To specify a certain enzyme, however, we must state which acid occupies each position in the enzyme's sequence. This takes many more steps for an enzyme of the same length as the random polypeptide. Thus enzymes have higher information content. "Order" has been defined as "situations that are unlikely to occur by random processes." As the length of a specified protein goes up, the chance of producing that protein by hooking amino acids together randomly goes down exponentially. For a short protein of 10 amino acids, for instance, there is a probability of about 1 in 100 trillion that it would be formed randomly. Since proteins in organisms are usually substantially longer than this, we can hence state that they are highly ordered.

Life has also been defined not in terms of its order or information content, but in terms of its ability to transmit this information to its descendants—Its ability to replicate in other words. The human chromosome has about 10 billion bits of information in it, and the half-set of these carried by a single sperm cell contains enough information to fill 500 volumes of a large book. Certain viroids reproduce by transferring an RNA string of less than 400 nucleotides to their host cell. While this is still a substantial amount of biochemical information, it is argued that viroids should not be considered living because they require not only the nutrients of their host, but also the information contained in the host cell's reproductive machinery. Francis Crick included as a "basic requirement of life" the ability of the system to replicate both its own instructions and any machinery needed to execute them.

Erwin Schrödinger, the famous physicist, analyzed life from a statistical perspective. He noted that in all inorganic systems, it takes a statistically large number of molecules to produce a predictable result. In his "What Is Life?" lectures of 1943, he claimed that the characteristic of life is that it seems to defy the rules of statistics. Statistically speaking, in a very small number of molecules, the genotype predictably governs the structure and function of a whole organism, the phenotype. He claimed that "this situation is unknown anywhere else except in living matter."

The second law of thermodynamics states that, in any process, the total amount of entropy—apparently observed randomness—in the Universe must increase. This is a direct result of the natural tendency of the Universe toward equilibrium, a state of maximum disorder. Schrödinger wrote "It is by avoiding the rapid decay into the inert state of 'equilibrium' that an organism appears so enigmatic." How, then, do we account for the processes of life, which seem to create order out of randomness? The answer lies in the fact that living things are open systems; that is, they exchange matter and energy with their surroundings. For every bit of order created within them, a greater amount of disorder is created in their surroundings. The process of building your body produces a great deal of heat, which causes the air around you to become more disordered. Thus, such processes stay within the bounds of the Second Law.

It is through the exchange of energy that life avoids the dreaded disorderly 'equilibrium state'. Therefore, life's "exquisite regulation of energy flow" has often been included in its definition. One such definition includes the flow of energy within the organism, as opposed to between it and its surroundings: "Life is a group of chemical systems in which free energy is released as a part of the reactions of one or more of the systems and in which some of this free energy is used in the reactions of one or more of the remaining systems." The term "free energy" here refers to energy that can be put to use, as opposed to heat energy lost to the environment.

MORE CONTEMPORARY VIEWPOINTS ON LIFE

Certain groups, particularly those interested in the possible nature of extraterrestrial and artificial life, consider the preceding definitions for life to be too limiting. For example, they ask if it is relevant to differentiate between an individual organism and the entire biosphere, or between a particular website and the entire Web for that matter? A bacterium could easily mistake a person for a huge colony of one-celled organisms working in symbiosis, and, in the same way, a person could quite easily perceive the Web as a huge virtual colony of purposeful information-based technology. As such, one definition of life, from Feinberg and Shapiro's *Life Beyond Earth,* is "the activity of a biosphere" [34], and they define a biosphere as "a highly ordered system of matter and energy characterized by complex cycles that maintain or gradually increase the order of the system through an exchange of energy with its environment." The presence of the now familiar terms of order, complexity, and energy should be highlighted. Other classical notions associated with life, such as reproduction for example, are not required in this definition. So Feinberg and Shapiro propose that it might be more profitable for an organism to alter itself to adapt, rather than wait for randomly altered descendants to undergo the process of natural selection. In a perfect biosphere, with all elements in symbiosis, evolution of the parts tends to be detrimental.

Feinberg and Shapiro also allow room in their definition for the existence of physical life, as opposed to chemical life. Examples they propose include plasma life, nuclear life, and radiant life. Plasma life would exist inside stars, where inter-actions between charged particles and magnetic fields would create self-sustaining, orderly systems. One example of nuclear life would inhabit a very cold planet. It would be composed mainly of solid hydrogen and liquid helium. The spins, or mag-netic orientations of the hydrogen nuclei in the organism would be highly ordered. Magnetic fields caused by this organization of spins would induce further organiza-tion. Radiant life might inhabit interstellar nebulae, which are made of the dusty remnants of dead stars. This type of life is based on the properties of ordered radia-tion, using space dust as a tool for transforming the radiation. This can be viewed as an organized collection of self-stimulating lasers. It is interesting, however, that Feinberg and Shapiro do not include the possibility of computer-based life in their work. Perhaps this is just an accident of timing, given that they published in 1980, just before the use of computer simulations of life really took off and well before the Web materialized in its current form. Nevertheless, the 1980s and 1990s did in-deed see a great upsurge of interest in the understanding of complex systems such as life, an upsurge that led to the front door of computing for many reasons.

The goals of creating artificial intelligence and artificial life can be traced back to the very beginning of the computer age. The earliest computer scientists—Alan Turing, John von Neumann, Norbert Wiener[11], and others—were motivated in large part by visions of instilling computer programs with intelligence, with the life-like ability to self-replicate, and with the adaptive capability to learn and control their environments. These early pioneers were as much interested in biology and psy-chology as in electronics and logic, and they looked to natural real-world systems as guiding metaphors for how to achieve their visions. Thus it should be no surprise that the earliest electronic computers were applied not only to calculating missile trajectories and deciphering military codes but also to modeling the brain, mimick-ing human learning, and simulating biological evolution. These biologically moti-vated initiatives have waxed and waned over the years, but since the early 1980s they have undergone a resurgence in the computation research community. This has led to great progress in such fields as neural networks, classifier systems, artificial intelligence, genetic algorithms, evolutionary computing, and ultimately the study of artificial life, a computational concept pioneered by Chris Langton.

Artificial life, says Langton, is essentially just the inverse of conventional biolo-gy. Instead of being an effort to understand life by analysis—dissecting living com-munities into species, organisms, organs, tissues, cells, organelles, membranes, and finally molecules—artificial life is an effort to understand life by synthesis: putting simple pieces together to generate lifelike behavior in man-made systems. This can be either intentional, as in the case of Langton's experiments, or completely unin-tentional, as is the case with systems like the Web. Its belief is that life is not a prop-

[11]Norbert Wiener was a U.S. mathematician, known as the founder of cybernetics. He coined the term in his book *Cybernetics or Control and Communication in the Animal and the Machine* (MIT Press, 1948), widely recognized as one of the most important books of contemporary scientific thinking. He is also considered to be the first American-born-and-trained mathematician on an intellectual par with the tradi-tional bastions of mathematical learning in Europe. He thus represents a watershed period in American mathematics [93].

erty of matter per se, but the organization of that matter. Its operating principle is that the laws of life must be laws of dynamical form, independent of the details of any particular carbon-based chemistry that happened to arise here on Earth four billion years ago. Its promise is that by exploring other possible biologies in a new medium—computers and perhaps robots for instance—artificial life researchers can achieve what space scientists have achieved by sending probes to other planets: a new understanding of our own world through a totally different perspective gained from other worlds. "Only when we are able to view life-as-we-know-it in the context of life-as-it-could-be will we really understand the nature of the beast," Langton has declared [69].

The idea of viewing life in terms of abstract organization is perhaps the single most compelling vision to come out of early collaborative work on artificial life. And it's no accident that this vision is closely associated with computers, given that they share the same intellectual roots. Human beings have been searching for the secret of automata—machines that can generate their own behavior—at least since the time of the Pharaohs, when Egyptian craftsmen created clocks based on the steady drip of water through a small hole. In the first century A.D. Hero of Alexandria produced his *Treatise Pneumatics,* in which he described, amongst other things, how pressurized air could generate simple movements in various gadgets shaped like animals and people. In Europe, during the great age of clockworks more than a thousand years later, medieval and Renaissance craftsmen devised increasingly elaborate figures known as 'jacks', which would emerge from the interior of a clock to strike the hours; some of their public clocks eventually grew to include large numbers that acted out entire plays. And during the Industrial Revolution the technology of the clockwork automata gave rise to the still more sophisticated technology of process control, in which factory machines were guided by intricate sets of rotating cams and interlinked mechanical arms. Moreover, by incorporating such refinements as movable cams, or rotating drums with movable pegs, nineteenth-century designers soon discovered controllers that could be adjusted to generate many sequences of action from the same machine. Along with the development of calculating machines in the early twentieth century, notes Langton, "the introduction of such programmable controllers was one of the primary developments on the road to general-purpose computers" [69].

Several years prior to Langton's work, the foundation of a general theory of computing had been laid by logicians who had tried to formalize the notion of a procedure, a sequence of logical steps directed to some useful purpose. This effort peaked in the early decades of the twentieth century with the works of Alonzo Church, Kurt Gödel, and Alan Turing—of whom we shall hear much more later—along with many others, who pointed out that the essence of mechanical process, the "thing" responsible for its behavior, is not necessarily a thing at all. It is a set of rules without regard to the material of which the machine is made and in such respect is truly ethereal. Indeed, comments Langton, this abstraction is what allows us to take a piece of software from one computer and run it on another: The "machineness" of the machine is in the software, not the hardware. Furthermore, once you have accepted this, then it is a very small step to say that the "aliveness" of an organism is also in the software—in the organization of molecules, not the actual molecules themselves [69].

Admittedly, that step doesn't always look so small, especially when you consider how fluid, spontaneous, and organic life can be and how controlled computers and other machines are. At first glance it seems ludicrous even to talk about living systems in those terms [69]. But the reality behind this truth lies in a second great insight, namely that living systems are machines—that is, machines with a kind of organization and structure different from those we are used to in the "every day" sense of the word, but machines nevertheless. Instead of being designed from the top down, using a standard reductionist approach, the way a human engineer might do it, living systems almost always seem to emerge from the bottom up, from a population of much simpler systems and parts, in such a way that a computer program is the summation of all its constituent instructions and the Web is the conclusion of all its contributing resources. In biological life a cell consists of proteins, DNA, and other biomolecules, a brain consists of many millions of neurons, an embryo consists of interacting cells, an ant colony consists of a multiplicity of ants, and for that matter an entire economy consists of nothing more than firms and individuals [69]. All are simply examples of purposeful aggregates structured from the ground up.

In fact, one of the most profound and surprising lessons learned over the past few decades, as we have begun to simulate evermore complex physical systems on computers, is that complex behavior need not have complex roots. As Chris Langton has pointed out many times, "tremendously interesting and beguiling complex behavior can emerge from collections of extremely simple components" [69]. Through their work, Langton and others have managed to show that one way to achieve lifelike behavior is to simulate populations of units instead of one big complex unit. Use local control instead of global control. Let the behavior emerge from the bottom up, instead of being specified and imposed from the top down. Moreover, while you're at it, focus on the ongoing behavior instead of the final result [67]. Final results are meaningless in lifelike scenarios because living systems provide pure examples of perpetual change, only settling down into a position of closure once all life has been extinguished and death ensues. And even then change continues as the components are assimilated back into their surroundings via natural processes such as decomposition.

By taking this bottom-up idea to its logical conclusion, it is possible to see it as a new and thoroughly scientific version of vitalism—the ancient idea that life involves some kind of energy, force, or spirit that transcends matter. The plain fact is that life does transcend mere matter, and according to Langton, not because living systems are animated by some vital essence operating outside the laws of physics and chemistry, but because a population of simple things following simple rules of interaction can behave in eternally surprising ways. Life in its classical sense may involve a kind of biochemical substance, but to make such a system sentient is not to bring life to a machine; rather it is to organize a population of machines in such a way that their interacting dynamics are "alive" [67].

To accept such a premise automatically leads to a final and striking conclusion about life—that is, that there is a distinct possibility that life isn't just like a computation, in the sense of being a property of its organization rather than its physical matter. Life literally is a computation [67], independent of any physical manifestation or linkages. To see why, start with conventional biological definitions of life. As biologists and others have been pointing out for more than a century, one of the most striking characteristics of any living organism is the distinction between its genotype (the genetic blueprint encoded in its DNA) and its phenotype (the structure that is created from those instructions). In practice, of course, the actual operation of a living cell is incredibly complicated, with each gene serving as a design for a single type of protein molecule and with a myriad of proteins interacting in the body of a cell in a plethora of ways. But in effect you can think of the genotype as a collection of little computer programs all executing together, one program per gene. When activated, each of these programs enters into the complex logical maelstrom by competing and cooperating with all the other active programs in a finely tuned and self-organized overall balance. In unison, this entirety of interacting programs carries out an overall computation that is the phenotype: the structure that unfolds during the organism's development [67], thereby creating its own destiny and potentially solving a number of computational problems along the way. Indeed, Langton has managed to effectively capture a startling realism in his abstract computational framework. This is commonly referred to as artificial life, or A-Life for short, and is a model of computation that is closely analogous to higher-level computational systems such as the Web itself.

Next one can move from carbon-based biology to the more generalized biology of artificial life. The same notions apply, and to capture that fact Langton coined the term "generalized genotype," or GTYPE, to refer to any collection of low-level rules. He likewise coined the term "generalized phenotype," or PTYPE, to refer to the structure and resultant behaviour produced when those rules are activated in some specific context or environment. In a conventional computer program, for example, the GTYPE obviously represents the program code itself, and the PTYPE is the output produced by that running program as a result of the inputs by its users [67]. So, again by analogy, the Web can be viewed as being both a GTYPE and a PTYPE on the global technology scale.

Now, what is beautiful about all this is that once you have made the link between life and computation, you can bring an immense amount of theory to bear. For example, why is life quite literally full of surprises? Because, in the norm, it is impossible to start from a given set of GTYPE rules and predict what their PTYPE behavior will be—even in principle. This is the undecidability theorem, one of the most precious pearls of wisdom ever to have been discovered in the whole history of logic, and one that we will investigate in much more detail later. It states that unless a set of instructions—a computer program for want of a better term—is utterly trivial, the best way to find out what they will do is to actually execute them and see. There is no general-purpose procedure that can scan these instructions given a set of inputs and give a faster, or more accurate, answer than that. That's why traditionalists and those who do not understand the more esoteric capabilities of computing only see computers doing precisely what their programmers tell them. This is paradoxically both perfectly true and virtually irrelevant: Any piece of code that is complex enough to be interesting will always, but always, surprise its programmers, with its complexity literally stripping them of credible insight. That is why any decent software package has to be endlessly tested and reworked before it sees general release, and that's why the users always discover very quickly that the debugging involved was nearly always never perfect. Most important of all, for artificial life purposes, that is why a living system can, for instance, be materialized as a biochemical machine that is completely under the control of a program, a GTYPE, and yet still have an unexpected, apparently spontaneous behavior in its PTYPE [67].

Conversely, there are other deep theorems in computer science stating that you can't go the other way either. Given the specification for a certain type of behavior, a PTYPE, there is no general procedure for finding a set of GTYPE rules that will produce it. That's why the overall behavior of an economy can very rarely be explained by the activities of a single company and likewise why the overall character of the Web is impossible to attribute to a single website. In practice, of course, these theorems don't stop human programmers from using well-tested algorithms and design methods to solve precisely specified problems in clearly defined environments. But in poorly defined, constantly changing environments, like the Web and those faced by living systems, there seems only one way to proceed: trial and error, also known as Darwinian natural selection. This process may seem terribly crude and wasteful, but in the long run it is actually highly effective. In essence, nature does its programming by building lots of different machines with a lot of randomly differing GTYPES and then smashing the ones that don't work well. In fact this messy wasteful process may be the best that nature can do [67]. But then unlike many modern-day programs of work, it has one distinct advantage on its side: There are no deadlines in the natural world, and evolution has all the time in the Universe to get its final code right!

We have now seen scientific definitions of life spanning an unexpectedly broad range of properties and criteria, and this is undoubtedly because we still do not fully understand the medium we are dealing with. That subtle combination of properties and criteria has included structural features, complexity, growth, reproduction, metabolism, motion, response to stimuli, evolvability, information content and transfer, and control of energy flow amongst others. Obviously, the word "life" has different connotations for different individuals within many different contexts, and this often leads to confusion and disagreement. For such reasons, Leslie Orgel[12] has coined the acronym CITROENS (complex information-transforming reproducing objects that evolve by natural selection) to describe certain borderline systems that appear to ascribe to life as a definition but for whom an absolute decision is not yet available. This is a veritable mouthful of an acronym without a doubt, but one that encompasses a great deal of up to the minute thinking nonetheless. It is also is a fitting label for the Web as we move forward to examine more of its distinguishing features in depth in our search to establish its lifelike credibility.

---

[12]Leslie Eleazer Orgel is a chemist by profession. During the 1970s, Orgel suggested reconsidering the Panspermia hypothesis, according to which the earliest forms of life on Earth did not originate here, but arrived from outer space with meteorites. Together with Stanley Miller, Orgel also suggested that peptide nucleic acids, instead of ribonucleic acids, constituted the first pre-biotic systems capable of self-replication on early Earth.

CHAPTER **2**

The Spectrum of Complexity

First things first, but not necessarily in that order.
—*The Doctor, in John Flanagan and Andrew McCulloch's Meglos*

A COMPLEX WEB

To state that the Web is different from other modern technologies is an obvious and gross oversimplification. The Web is not just different, it is different in a very specific way, and its highly connected, self-organizing complexity sets it apart from all other man-made systems. But many do not understand the very basics of complexity, let alone how these might be applicable to a modern technology or its association with a concept such as life. So it is indeed appropriate to visit this supposed black art in order to give an insight into the very nature of complexity and explain just why our current understandings are so applicable to the Web at a number of levels.

The Web is not built on deterministic,[1] linear principles like so many of its digitally related forbears. Rather, it is discernibly irregular at just about every level and across every characteristic. The original language at its nucleus, the hypertext mark-up language HTML, is a "nonsequential," nonlinear technology that glues together Web resources to form a corpus of utterly unplanned global organization [4]. In short, it is complexly "messy." Unlike traditional text where the distance between the start and the end of a statement or sentence is finite and measurable, the introduction of a hypertext link renders the measurement of distance, and hence directly attained understanding, almost useless. Follow the inserted hyperlink and it could lead off on an infinitely long trail to amass the entire collective knowledge of the Universe before it eventually winds its way back to where it left. This is poles apart from the Euclidian[2] view of the world that powered the advances of the Indus-

---

[1]Determinism is the philosophical belief that every event or action is the inevitable result of preceding events and actions. Thus, in principle at least, every event or action can be completely predicted in advance, or in retrospect [94].
[2]Euclid of Alexandria was a Greek mathematician who taught at Alexandria in Egypt almost certainly during the reign (323 B.C.–283 B.C.) of Ptolemy I. Now known as "the father of geometry," his most famous work is Elements, widely considered to be history's most successful textbook. Within it, the properties of geometrical objects and integers are deduced from a small set of axioms, thereby anticipating (and partly inspiring) the axiomatic method of modern mathematics [94].

The Web's Awake. By Philip Tetlow
Copyright © 2007 the Institute of Electrical and Electronics Engineers, Inc.

trial Revolution. It is both fascinating and compelling, therefore, that the next technical revolution, the Web Revolution, has gone back to nature for its inspiration. No longer are we facing a boring world of straight lines and the predictable outcomes of cause and effect. Instead a nonlinear world of complex patterns and holistic perspectives lies ahead [6].

What is plainly interesting here is that the Web is not alone in its classification as a complex "messy" system. The Universe is full of such examples. Galaxies are messy, weather systems are messy, and coast lines are messy. In fact, nature loves messiness and the more complex a system gets, in general, the more the level of this "intertwined jumble" of messiness increases. And what is the pinnacle of intertwined jumbled systems? You guessed it—life itself!

In fairness, however, merely to state that the Web's distinguishing feature is its messy complexity and that this may be the key contributing factor in its classification as a living thing is somewhat of a throwaway comment. This is not because there is little truth in the statement; it is simply because the definition of complexity is itself complex. Complexity in its truest forms is an incomprehensible concept to most of us. When we try to capture its essence, it is like we are clutching at sand, with its very grains slipping through our fingers the harder we try and grasp. In modern culture it has many aspects and many meanings for a multiplicity of reasons.

Even so, in recent decades much progress has been made in our understandings of complexity. We now have fields of scientific endeavor specifically centered on complexity in all its guises and are able to recognize many of its distinguishing features. We know, for instance, that whenever you look at complicated systems in physics or biology, for example, you generally find that the basic components and the basic laws are quite simple; the complexity arises because you have a great many of these simple components interacting simultaneously. The complexity is actually in the organization, the structure, and the myriad of possible ways that the components of the system can interact [67].

However, there is much more to a proper understanding of complexity. Like the spectrum of colors visible to the human eye, there are an infinite number of shades of complexity. Just as when blue blurs into green and it can be hard to discern exactly where one color ends and the other begins, this is also true for complexity. It can be deceptive too. Continuing the color analogy, certain shades of light blue can appear whiter to the eye than pure white itself, and complexity also relishes in such twists of the perception. To be curt, it is simply not enough to pronounce complexity; one must be intimate with it before it will even declare its presence.

THE NATURAL MIX OF ORDER AND DISORDER

The natural world is full of ordered structure. From geology, for example, we know that most minerals are stable and regular structures organized in different lattice configurations. Ice is nothing but water molecules fixed into a regular three-dimensional pattern through chemical bonds. When we look at snow crystals closely, we see highly ordered structures. Nevertheless, if we look harder, complexity always involves both order and disorder. Ecosystems show well-defined regularities, but most populations fluctuate erratically. The brain stores vast amounts of information, however, when it is monitored using an electroencephalogram, its activity is far from regular. Our cities are large-scale structures with well-thought-out dimensions, yet their growth is more often than not organic and we know that they can eventually disappear.

In this way, complexity is neither complete order nor complete disorder. Rather, there is no fixed point on any scale that one can point to as an absolute definition. Instead, complexity relates to a broad spectrum of characteristic (Figure 2.1). At one end lies slight irregularity, while at the other end lies complete nonlinearity and randomness without meaning or purpose. Both are extremes of the same thing. When slight variation is exhibited, it is highly likely that one could accurately predict the overall pattern of the whole just by examining one tiny part, but when complete randomness is encountered, this would be pointless and impossible. In the middle lies some exciting ground—a sweet spot of complexity if you like, perched on the edge of chaos. Here, pattern is neither random nor completely ordered. Regions of differing sizes can be found all exhibiting similar features leading to the perception of some underlying theme at many different scales. This is where truly natural complexity lives. It cannot be described in terms of simple extrapolation around a few basic regularities. Instead, it displays nontrivial correlations and associations that are not necessarily reducible to smaller or more fundamental units [23].

EMERGENCE—THE COMPLEXITY SWEET SPOT

An emergent behavior or emergent property can appear when a number of simple items, entities, or agents operate in an environment, forming more complex behav-

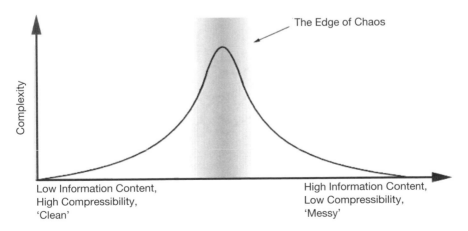

Figure 2.1. Complexity in terms of information, compressibility, and randomness.

iors as a collective, hence its obvious relevance to systems like the Web. The property itself, therefore, represents a new level of the system's evolution, signifying a step change in the overall nature of a given system.

Under certain circumstances, complex systems can demonstrate stronger types of particular correlation, some forming almost instantaneously to overwhelm their parent and transforming it into something completely and unexpectedly. This is the phenomenon we now know understand as "emergence," the process by which complex systems transition into something that they once were not (Figure 2.2). Like complexity, emergence has a spectrum of disguises, being capable of manifesting great subtlety and power. It can give rise to typhoons and take down great sections of the United States eastern seaboard power grid, and ultimately it is the driving force behind both the Universe and life itself.

The complex behaviors or properties producing emergence cannot be attributed to the aspects of any single lower-level entity, nor can they easily be predicted or deduced from behavior amongst lower-level entities. Consequently, emergence can only exist in trace amounts amongst the very lowest level constituents of a system. Emergence can be a dynamic process occurring over time, such as the evolution of the human brain over thousands of successive generations, or it can happen over disparate size scales such as the interactions between a macroscopic number of neu-

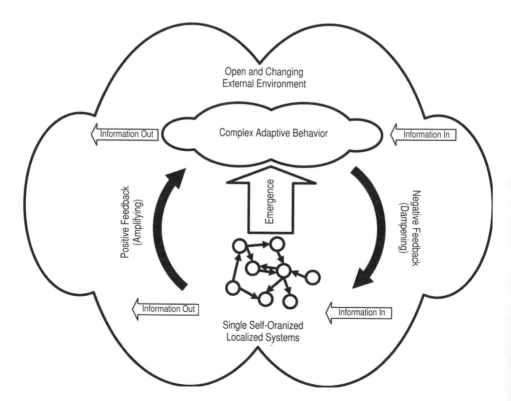

Figure 2.2. Emergence in open systems, such as the Universe or the Web.

rons producing a human brain capable of thought—even though the constituent neurons are not themselves conscious.

There is no consensus amongst scientists as to how much emergence should ever be relied upon as an explanation. It does not appear possible to unambiguously decide whether a phenomenon should be classified as emergent, and even in the cases where classification is agreed upon, it rarely helps to explain the phenomenon in any deep way. In fact, calling a phenomenon emergent is sometimes used in lieu of any better explanation.

One reason why emergent behavior occurs is that the number of interactions between components of a system increases combinatorially with the number of components, thereby potentially allowing for many new and subtle types of behavior to occur. For instance, the possible interactions between groups of molecules grows enormously with the number of molecules such that it is impossible for a computer to even count the number of arrangements for a system as small as 20 molecules.

However, merely having a large number of interactions is not enough by itself to guarantee emergent behavior. This is because many of the interactions may be negligible, may be irrelevant, or may cancel each other out. In some cases, a large number of interactions can in fact work against the emergence of interesting behavior by creating a lot of "noise" to drown out any emerging "signal" or structure. In such a way, emergent behavior may need to be temporarily isolated from other interactions before it can reach the criticality needed to become self-supporting. It is not just the sheer number of connections between components which encourages emergence, it is also how these connections are organized. A hierarchical organization is one example that can generate emergent behavior. A bureaucracy may behave in a way quite different from that of the individual humans in that bureaucracy, for example. But perhaps more interestingly, emergent behavior can also arise from more decentralized organizational structures, such as a marketplace. In such cases the system has to reach a combined threshold of diversity, organization, and connectivity before emergent behavior appears. Both of these examples also have Web equivalents; Web users will gravitate together to form hierarchical communities of interest for instance, and these loose communities will naturally couple via the osmosis of mutual interest and ideas.

Emergent structures are patterns not created by a single event or rule. There is nothing that commands systems to form such patterns, instead the interactions of each part to its immediate surroundings causes a complex process that leads to order. For such reasons, one might conclude that emergent structures are more than the sum of their parts because emergent order will not arise if the various parts simply coexist; the interaction of these parts is central.

Emergent structures can be found in many natural phenomena, from the physical through to the biological. The spatial structure and shape of galaxies is an emergent property that characterizes the large-scale distribution of energy and matter in the Universe. Weather phenomena with similar form, such as hurricanes, are emergent too. Furthermore, many speculate that consciousness and life itself are emergent properties of a network of many interacting neurons and complex molecules, as we shall see in Chapter 8. As such, many consider life as a major source of complexity and consider evolution as the major principle or driving force behind life. In this view, evolution is the main reason for the growth of complexity in the natural world. There is also a view that the beginning and development of evolution itself can be regarded as an emergent property of the laws of physics in our Universe.

But emergent structures are not just confined to the material world, being found with abundance in both virtual and conceptual domains as well. They can be found in traffic patterns, for instance, and also cities or organizational phenomena in computer simulations and cellular automata. The stock market is a well-documented example of emergence on a grand scale. As a whole, it precisely regulates the relative prices of companies across the world, yet it has no leader; there is no one entity that controls the workings of the entire market. Agents, or investors, have knowledge of only a limited number of companies within their portfolio and must follow the regulatory rules of the market. Through the interactions of individual investors, the complexity of the stock market as a whole emerges.

Popular examples for sociotechnical emergence can be found in the Linux operating system and other such open source projects like Wikipedia, the Web-based encyclopaedia. Besides the efforts of the Wikipedia founders Jim Wales and Larry Sanger, emergence is the major reason for the great success of Wikipedia. It is just one of a number of decentralized and distributed Web-based projects that would not be possible without a huge number of participants and volunteers. No participant alone knows the whole structure; instead everyone knows and edits only a small part, although all participants have the feeling of participating in something larger than themselves. This not only is a perfect description for individual parts of the Web, like the Wikipedia community, but also fits as a fine description of the Web as a whole. In such emergent systems, top-down feedback increases motivation and unity, while bottom-up contributions increase variety and diversity. This unity in diversity causes the complexity of emergent structures.

The wonderment of emergence goes on still further and there are other good examples of emergent systems that are just too compelling, not to mention all of which share underlying analogous features that should be familiar to those who are Web savvy. In physics, for example, emergence is often used to describe a property, law, or phenomenon that occurs at macroscopic scales in either space or time, but not at microscopic scales. This is despite the fact that a macroscopic system can be viewed as a large ensemble of microscopic systems. Beguiling and well understood examples of emergence in physics at both macro- and microscopic levels include the following:

Color: Elementary particles such as protons or electrons have no color; it is only when they are arranged in atoms that they absorb or emit specific wavelengths of light and thus can be said to have a color.[3]

Friction: Elementary particles are frictionless, or more precisely the forces between these particles are conservative. However, friction emerges when considering more complex structures of matter whose surfaces can absorb energy when rubbed against each other. Similar considerations apply to other emer-

---

[3]Note that while quarks have a characteristic that has been labeled color charge by physicists, this terminology is merely figurative and has no actual relation with the everyday concept of color.

gent concepts in continuum mechanics such as viscosity, elasticity, and tensile strength.

Classical Mechanics: The laws of classical mechanics can be said to emerge as a limiting case from the rules of quantum mechanics applied to large enough masses. This may be thought of as puzzling, because quantum mechanics is generally thought of as more complicated than classical mechanics, whereas lower-level rules are generally less complicated, or at least less complex, than the emergent properties.

Temperature: This well-known phenomenon is sometimes used as an example of an emergent physical macroscopic behavior. In classical dynamics, a snapshot of the instantaneous momenta of a large number of particles at equilibrium is sufficient to find the average kinetic energy per degree of freedom which is proportional to the temperature. For a small number of particles the instantaneous momenta at a given time are not statistically sufficient to determine the temperature of the system. However, using the ergodic hypothesis,[4] the temperature can still be obtained to arbitrary precision by further averaging the momenta over a long enough period of time. Also, the (constant temperature) canonical[5] distribution is perfectly well-defined even for one particle.

In some theories of particle physics, even such basic structures as mass, space, and time are viewed as emergent phenomena arising from more fundamental concepts such as the Higgs boson[6] or strings.

In some interpretations of quantum mechanics the perception of a deterministic reality, in which all objects have a definite position, momentum, and so forth, is actually an emergent phenomenon with the true state of matter being described instead by a wave function that need not have a single position or momentum. In all of this the important thing is that emergence is a fundamental property of complex systems. It is not something that can be added deliberately, nor is it something that can usually be controlled externally. In such respects it is both part of and the result of complexity.

---

[4]The ergodic hypothesis says that, over long periods of time, the time spent in some region of the phase space of microstates with the same energy is proportional to the volume of this region. That is to say that all accessible microstates are equally probable over a long period of time. Equivalently, it says that time average and average over the statistical ensemble are the same [96].

[5]In programming, canonical means "according to the rules." And noncanonical means "not according to the rules." In the early Christian church, the "canon" was the officially chosen text. In *The New Hacker's Dictionary,* Eric Raymond tells us that the word meant "reed" in its Greek and Latin origin, and a certain length of reed came to be used as a standard measure. In some knowledge areas, such as music and literature, the "canon" is the body of work that everyone studies.

The terms are sometimes used to distinguish whether a programming interface follows a particular standard or precedent or whether it departs from it.

[6]The Higgs boson is a hypothetical elementary particle predicted to exist by the Standard Model of particle physics. This boson is thought to play a fundamental role: According to the Standard Model, it is a component of the Higgs field which is thought to permeate the Universe and to give mass to other particles and to itself. As of 2005, no experiment has definitively detected the existence of the Higgs boson. The vacuum expectation of the Higgs field is perceived the same from every direction and is mostly indistinguishable from empty space [97].

It should be emphasized that each of these cases, while an emergent phenomenon at the macroscopic scale, does not directly exist at the microscopic scale. However, its existence at macroscopic scales can still be explained by the laws of physics at microscopic scales, taking into account the interactions between all the microscopic components of a macroscopic object. Thus, materially emergent phenomena can demonstrate why a reductionistic[7] physical theory, viewing all matter in terms of its component parts, and which in turn obeys a relatively small number of laws, can hope to model complex objects such as living beings. However, by the same token, emergent phenomena serve to caution against greedy reductionism, because the microscopic explanation of an emergent phenomenon may be too complicated or "low-level" to be of any practical use. For instance, if chemistry is explainable as being emergent from interactions in particle physics, cell biology as emergent from interactions in chemistry, humans as emergent from interactions in cell biology, civilizations as emergent from interactions of humans, and human history as emergent from interactions between civilizations, this does not imply that it is particularly easy or desirable to try to explain human history in terms of the laws of particle physics. Even so, this has not dissuaded some people from hypothesizing that highly complex, emergent phenomena such as human history can be described in terms of simpler laws that are more commonly associated with more fundamental systems.

MANKIND, COMPLEXITY, AND OUR ATTEMPTS TO UNDERSTAND THE UNREAL

As a race we may now be starting to gain real insight into complexity and emergent behavior for the first time, but the average human mind is still at a disadvantage when it comes to the true levels of recognition required to understand such concepts properly. In a famously ambiguous yet widely cited epigram, the seventh-century B.C. Greek poet Archilochus contrasted two disparate mammals in the metaphor: "The fox knows many things, but the hedgehog knows one great thing." This saying has caught the attention of many intellectuals in part because our brains tend to break down complexity into oversimplified categorizations. They just simply contain the "wrong wiring" to cope with many of the more complicated problems in our world. "They were designed to understand hunting and gathering, mating, and child rearing: a world of medium-sized objects in three real dimensions at moderate speeds" [51]. We are ill-equipped to understand the very large and very complex, and unfortunately the macro-characteristics of the Web fall right within such categories. We simply just cannot soak it all in, and although we may be overly familiar with it in parts, as a whole it is intangible, unrecognizable, and unreal.

---

[7]An attempt or tendency to explain a complex set of facts, entities, phenomena, or structures by another, simpler set: "For the last 400 years science has advanced by reductionism . . . . The idea is that you could understand the world, all of nature, by examining smaller and smaller pieces of it. When assembled, the small pieces would explain the whole" (John Holland).

Over the past few decades we have undoubtedly made great progress in our collective understandings of the "messiness" associated with complexity, but in doing so we have had to start by first relying on our understanding of "cleanly" ordered systems, learning some very hard lessons along the way.

The concept that all systems, no matter how complex, are merely aggregate upon aggregate of simple elemental patterns is still fundamental to the modern-day study of complex and dynamic, nonlinear systems. It is the process of combining and collecting things together that produces apparent randomness. Consequently, many interesting and complex phenomena can usefully be described as "orderly ensemble properties" and productively understood in terms of the properties and interactions of subphenomena or elements. As a race we are notoriously poor at admitting defeat, so until very recently we have invariably blamed our intellectual inadequacy for explaining such complex systems on the systems themselves, deeming them to be unfathomable or "chaotic" in a truly classical sense. Furthermore, we have been notoriously bad at admitting that even the study of complexity is difficult, thus historically proving a huge barrier to mankind's progress in this area. Given the limits of our own natural capabilities, in the past if we could not understand a complex problem in its entirety—"get our head around it" as it were—for all intents and purposes our analysis proved worthless, fueling nothing more than educated guesswork, hearsay, and myth. Thankfully, however, with the advent of modern computers our brainpower has been boosted, thereby allowing us to leap over such barriers. Previously, without such assistance, any concept involving more than a head-full of complexity would have been wasted as a byproduct of mental overflow, and it is for precisely this reason that we informally adopted the 'head-full' as complexity's yard stick many centuries ago. Ever since, we have been deliberately searching out ways to reduce complexity down into elements of lesser dimensions.

Reductionism is one such mechanism that takes us from complex phenomena to more elementary patterns and properties of components and their associations. It does this by providing consistent explanations through multiple descriptive layers. Even so, reductionism can rarely provide a coherent and consistent description from constituent parts through to an accurate picture of the whole. Understanding every single property of both hydrogen and oxygen could not, for example, provide even the slightest insight into the salient properties of water. Nor could an understanding of every single property of the water molecule provide even the slightest insight into the ultimate behavior of a tidal wave. Put a few zillion such molecules together and suddenly you have a substance that shimmers and gurgles and sloshes. Those zillions of molecules have collectively acquired a property, liquidity, that none of them possesses alone. In fact, unless you know where and how to look for it, there is nothing in even the well-understood equations of either atomic physics or chemistry to even hint at such a property [67].

For such reasons, many have been working on more a holistic method of characterising complexity, sensing that the old reductionist approaches were starting to reach a dead end. This new approach—the complex approach—is completely Taoist. In Taoism there is no inherent order. In such beliefs the world started with one, and the one became two, and the two became many, and the many led to a myriad of things in much the same way that the Web evolved. The Universe in Taoism is perceived as vast, amorphous, and ever-changing. You can never nail it down. The elements always stay the same, yet they are always rearranging themselves. So it's like a kaleidoscope; the world is a matter of patterns that change, that partly repeat, but never quite repeat, and that are always new and different [67].

More and more over the past 30 years or so, even the hard-core physicists have been getting tired with mathematical abstractions that ignore real complexity. In doing so, their half-conscious groping has started to cut across many traditional boundaries in ways that they had not done in years, maybe even centuries [67]. History tells us that where the purer sciences venture first, the more contemporary disciplines soon follow, only on this occasion it appears that convention has been broken and this new wave of scientific insight has been led from the front by the young upstarts of computer science.

But what have old-school physicists got to do with the Web as a living thing? It's simple: Scientists, like physicists, are interested in fundamentals, the very rules that underlie all systems. Furthermore, physicists are natural skeptics when it comes to modern theories on complexity and emergence, so the chances are high that they will push for truths harder than anyone else. We know that both the Web and life itself are fine examples of systems—complex systems granted, but systems nevertheless. To understand them properly it is plain that we must understand the very fundamentals on which they are built too, and who better to look to for inspiration. By investigating objective comparisons between physical systems and the Web, parallels can be found with proven real-world observables and many of the Web's characteristics. Through these a far stronger insight can be forged than through direct analysis of the Web alone.

One of the physicist's inspirations in their turn to complexity, ironically enough, appears to have been molecular biology. That's not the sort of thing that most people would expect a weapons laboratory to be interested in, but in fact, physicists have been deeply involved with molecular biology from the beginning. Many of the pioneers in the field had actually started out as physicists: One of their big motivations to switch was a slim volume entitled *What is Life?*—a series of provocative speculation about the physical and chemical basis of life published in 1944 by the Austrian physicist Erwin Schrödinger, a co-founder of quantum mechanics. One of those who was influenced by the book was Francis Crick, who deduced the molecular structure of DNA along with James Watson at Cambridge University in 1953 using data obtained from X-ray crystallography, a submicroscopic imaging technique developed by physicists decades earlier. Crick had in fact originally trained as an experimental physicist. Also George Gamow, a Ukrainian theoretical physicist who was one of the original proponents of the Big Bang theory of the origin of the Universe, became interested in the structure of the genetic code in the early 1950s and helped inspire still more physicists into the field. In particular, it was Gamow's work that inspired George Cowan, a philanthropist who conducted early research for the Manhattan Project[8] and went on to found the Santa Fe Institute to study the theory of complexity directly.

---

[8]The Manhattan Project, or, more formally, the Manhattan Engineering District, was an effort during World War II to develop the first nuclear weapon, by the United States with assistance from the United Kingdom and Canada [98].

"Almost by definition," says Cowan, "the physical sciences are fields characterised by conceptual elegance and analytical simplicity. So you make a virtue of that and avoid the other stuff." Indeed, physicists are notorious for curling their lip at "soft" sciences like sociology and psychology, which try to grapple with real-world complexity. But then came molecular biology, which described incredibly complicated living systems that were nonetheless governed by deep principles. "Once you're in partnership with biology", urges Cowan, "you give up elegance, you give up that simplicity. You're messy. And from there it's so much easier to start diffusing into economics and social issues. Once you're immersed, you might as well start swimming" [67]. In such circumstances a reductionist view of the world simply is just not good enough.

Regardless, reductionism has proved exceptionally valuable to modern science, spawning a number of philosophical approaches to shore up its weaknesses. Structuralism is one such general approach used in academic disciplines seeking to explore the interrelationships between some fundamental or reduced concepts upon which higher systemic "structures" are built and through which meaning is inherently dependent upon the relationships between participating elements.

Structuralism appeared in academic psychology for the first time in the nineteenth century and then reappeared in the second half of the twentieth century, when it grew to become one of the most popular approaches in the academic fields that are concerned with analyzing systems involving connectivity, such as language and social behavior. Structuralism in mathematics and computer science is the study of what structures define an object of interest and how the ontology of these structures should be understood. This is a growing philosophy that is not without its share of critics. Nevertheless, in many ways, structuralism can be extremely useful in dissecting the complexity of highly connected systems like the Web. For instance, it allows clusters of similar content to be accurately classified and associated at varying levels of granularity and across a number of relationship types. In short, it is well-suited to analyzing and describing multidimensional information systems.

In 1965, Paul Benacerraf[9] wrote a paper entitled "What Numbers Could Not Be" [61]. This is a seminal piece on mathematical structuralism, and it started a recognizable movement by the response it generated. In this work, Benacerraf addressed the view in mathematics which treats mathematical statements at face value, thereby committing mathematical formulae to a realm of eternally abstract objects and concepts with no direct connection to the real world. Benacerraf further posed a dilemma questioning how we could actually come to know such objects or concepts if we do not stand in causal relation to them. In other words, how could we possibly find mathematical concepts of any value if they are causally inert to the real world? Benacerraf further questioned why multiple set theories exist that allow the reduction of elementary number theory into sets—one of the most fundamental concepts in computing—thereby raising the still-to-be-solved problem of which set theory is true.

The answer to Benacerraf's concerns led to structuralism becoming a viable philosophical school of thought within mathematics through the belief that the essence of mathematical concepts or variables lies in their relationships with the

---

[9]Paul Benacerraff is an American philosopher of mathematics based at Princeton University.

wider structure of their mathematical context as a whole. This rhetoric then runs on into the area of computational theory, providing a firm basis on which to explain the same concepts in a wider "systems" context. Structures are hence exemplified in abstract systems in terms of the relations that hold true for that system. This is an essential understanding when thinking about the complexity of the Web as it provides an excellent insight into just how structure, content, and connectivity are interlinked; these being the three essential ingredients at its center.

Reductionism and Structuralism have an undeniable place in understanding complexity, but they are not the complete means to find the whole answer. Progress in understanding high complexity requires more than the study of parts in interaction. It often needs a grasp of the relevant properties of whole systems and their underlying phenomena. Only rigorous analysis can determine which phenomena are "radically emergent" and which are ultimately reducible. Therefore the void left by reductionism has spawned many new fields of modern mathematics aimed specifically at addressing the holistic nature of complexity. Today we have areas of study such as nonlinear dynamics, chaos and network theory, emergence itself, and the concept of fractals. From these our insight has started to change. Where the study of complexity begins, classical science stops, and, as we shall see in Chapter 3, all help penetrate the complex and entangled beauty of the Web, the reality of the physical Universe itself, the notion of organism, and the very idea of life itself.

COULD YOU REPEAT THAT PLEASE?

Fractals come straight from the sweet spot at the center of complexity, being "repetitions of the same general patterns, even the same details, at both ascending and descending scales" [81]. They tell us that the Universe and all that it contains is made up of folded realities within self-similar worlds, and today modern science is quickly realizing the important role that fractals have played in positioning life as the Universe's pinnacle example of such folded realities.

The term "fractal" was invented by Benoit Mandelbrot, an IBM researcher, to describe the new geometry of shapes that form in the wake of dynamic systems. Fractal patterns are all around us, above us, within us, everywhere. Trees are fractals, with their repeated pattern of large and small branches, with similar details found even in the smallest twigs. Even a single leaf shows fractal repetitions of the whole tree in both its shape and the branching in its veins. Examine a cauliflower and you find fractal geometry at its best, with florets arranged at self-similar scales. For a total fractal experience, peel the leaves from an artichoke. Photographs taken through electron microscopes and far-ranging telescopes reveal that images from vastly different scales evoke a feeling of similarity and recognition. A spiral nebula that measures hundreds of light-years across looks remarkably similar to something that measures a thousandth of a centimeter, say the eye of a firefly. One can be seen as the fractal resonance of the other, the resonance of the microcosm to the macrocosm. The patterns in the weather, the turbulence in the winds, the rhythm pounded out by an African drummer, the rituals performed by queens and shamans and celebrants of the New Year, the courtship habits of peacocks and prairie dogs, the landscapes of nature, and the inscapes of dreams all embody fractal phenomena.

These examples point to the universality of the fractal as a central organizing principle of our most complex systems, including the Web. Wherever we look in our world the complex systems of nature and time seem to preserve the look of details at finer and finer scales. Fractals show a holistic hidden order behind things, a harmony in which everything affects everything else, and, above all, an endless variety of interwoven patterns. Fractal geometry allows bounded curves of infinite length, as well as closed surfaces with infinite area. It even allows curves with positive volume and arbitrarily large groups of shapes with exactly the same boundary. This is exactly how our lungs manage to maximize their surface area. In fact, most natural objects are composed of many types of entangled fractals woven into each other, each with parts that have different fractal dimensions. For example, the bronchial tubes in the human lung have one fractal dimension for the first seven layers of branching, and then there is a divergence of geometry and a different fractal dimension appears, used in the finer grades of airway [81]. Indeed John Archibald Wheeler, a friend of Albert Einstein and a protégé of Niels Bohr, the famous quantum physicist, has been quoted as saying that "no one will be considered scientifically literate tomorrow who is not familiar with fractals" [81].

The world we live in is not naturally smooth-edged in the round; it has been fashioned with rough edges. Smooth surfaces are the exception in nature. And yet, we have thus far chosen to favor a geometry that only describes the shapes rarely, if ever, found in nature. This is commonly known as Euclidian geometry, after the Greek mathematician, and only concentrates on ideal shapes such as spheres, circles, cubes, and squares. Of course these shapes do appear in the real world, but they are mostly man-made and not born of nature [81]. Nature prefers to deal with nonuniform shapes and irregular edges. Take the human form, for example: There is certainly symmetry about it, but it is, and has always been, indescribable in terms of Euclidian geometry. It is quite simply not a uniform shape [81].

In plain English, fractal geometry is the geometry of the irregular, the geometry of nature, and, in general, fractals are characterized by infinite detail, infinite length, and the absence of smoothness or derivative.

But let us also not forget that fractals are not the sole property of the real world. They quite happily inhabit virtual realms as well. Invisible assemblies as truly intangible as traffic, a democracy, or a computer program all have the capability to embody fractal characteristics. Just as in the natural world, simple base patterns form the foundation for all the computer systems in existence today, with many such patterns sharing exactly the same characteristics as those fundamental to many naturally occurring complex phenomena.

Fractals relate to the Web in many wonderful and important ways. For instance, they provide a framework for patterned repetition on the Web, but not just any old kind of representation. Fractals allow repetition to unfold across an infinite number of dimensions and scales, thereby creating hierarchies of structure for free. Web pages within websites, websites within communities, communities with cultures and economies, and so on, all of which are complex organizations, are provided through the ubiquitous support of fractals.

There is more to fractal Web structures than just pure hierarchy support. For example, there is strong evidence to suggest that notions of knowledge and hierarchy are closely linked. Knowledge can be expressed in terms of mental hierarchies that behave very much like rules that are in competition, so that experience causes useful rules to grow stronger and causes unhelpful rules to grow weaker. Furthermore, plausible new rules are generated from a combination of old rules. In support of such thinking, psychologists like Richard Nisbett and Keith Holyoak and the philosopher Paul Thatgard[10] have produced experimental evidence to suggest that these principles could account for a wide assortment of "Aha!" type insights, ranging from Sir Isaac Newton's experience with the falling apple to such everyday abilities as understanding an analogy [67].

In particular they argue that these principles ought to cause the spontaneous emergence of default hierarchies as the basic organizational structure of human knowledge—as indeed they appear to do. We use weak general rules with stronger exceptions to make predictions about how things should be assigned into categories: "If it's streamlined and has fins and lives in the water, then it's a fish," but "if it also breaths and is big, then it's a whale." We use the same structure to make predictions about how things should be done: "It's always 'i' before 'e' except after 'c'," but "If it's a word like neighbor, weight or weird, then its 'e' before 'i'." So we use the same structure again to make predictions about causality: "If you whistle to a dog, then it may come to you," but "If the dog is growling and raising its hackles, then it probably won't."

The theory says that these default-hierarchy models ought to emerge whenever the principles are implemented and thereby promotes the notion of the Web as a mindful entity. This may not be in any conscious sense as we would traditionally recognize the concept of mind, but is a capable mechanism for storing and assimilating information nonetheless.

SELF-SIMILARITY AND RECURSION

As hinted earlier, fractals usually possess what is referred to as 'self-similarity' across scales. In such a way it is possible, for instance, to zoom in or out of the geometry of a fractal while it still maintains a similar, sometimes exactly similar, appearance.

One such example of this can be seen in the well-known Koch snowflake curve. This is created by starting with a single line segment and first replacing it, then repeatedly replacing each of its subsequent subsections, with four other lines shaped as follows: __/__ . Successively zooming in on the shape produced simply results in a shape that is exactly the same no matter what the extent of the zoom.

In such a way a Koch curve can be seen to be of itself, being defined in terms of itself [39] (Figure 2.3).

To further generalize this theme a cube, which is of course three-dimensional, can be cut into eight half-sized cubes. Hence, if the dimensions of an object are known,

[10]In 1986, all three jointly published the book *Induction* on such theory.

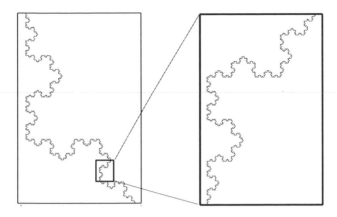

Figure 2.3. Self-similarity as displayed in the Koch cure.

be that object either real or abstract, the concepts of mathematical powers or exponents potentially afford the ability to work out how many smaller copies of itself the object can contain, of any particular size. Hence certain types of n-dimensional shape can be seen as being composed of m^n $1/m$-sized copies of themselves,[11] thereby suggesting a generalized concept of dimension which allows fractional values [81].

In 1919, Felix Hausdorff extended this notion of the similarity dimension to cover all shapes, not just those that are exactly self-similar. Hence he showed that, in general, fractal shapes that lie somewhere between dimensions have fractal Hausdorff dimension. Because Hausdorff's definition distinguishes fractal from nonfractal shapes, it is often called the fractal dimension [81].

The fractal dimension describes the fractal complexity of an object's geometry. For example, the coastline of Britain has a fractal dimension of approximately 1.26. This is about the same as a Koch curve, but slightly less than the outline of a typical cloud, which has a dimensional value of around 1.35. On this scale, a dimension of 1 means totally smooth and 2 implies increasing fractal complexity [81].

Self-similarity is normally used as a term to describe properties that are spatial in some way, such as shape or form, but the overarching concept of self-reference goes much further than that, also covering time-dependent properties like functionality and behavior as well. Under such circumstances the term 'recursion' is often used to describe particular facets of systems that operate according to rules and states that point back to their own definition and use.

In mathematics and computer science, recursion can relate to a class of instructions and data by defining a few very simple base associations that loop back on themselves. For instance, the following statements show a recursive definition of a person's ancestors:

- A person's parents are also their ancestors.
- The parents of any of their ancestors are also their ancestors.

[11]Where m is any arbitrary measure of dimension.

Thus it is convenient to think of a recursive definition as outlining something in terms of "previously defined" versions of itself. Definitions like this are often found in mathematics. For example, the following is a formal definition of natural numbers: Zero is a natural number, and each natural number has a successor, which is also a natural number. Furthermore, a function may be partly defined in terms of itself as in the Fibonacci sequence, which will be covered in much greater detail later. For such a definition to be useful, it must lead to values that are non-recursively defined.

BACK TO MEASURES OF COMPLEXITY

In the first half of the twentieth century the field of mathematics grasped the concepts of reductionism with vigor, ultimately boiling logic down into simplistic "computable" models that formed the foundation on which the modern digital revolution was built. This is an important point to remember, given that everyday users often consider computing, Information Technology, and ultimately the Web itself to be somewhat disconnected from such mundane roots. To them the Web is a much more approachable animal, magically separated from such cold worlds by many higher orders of application. But the truth is impossible to escape: Computation is just one set of models amongst many from the mathematician's tool box.

In such models, mechanisms have been established whereby any discrete piece of information or computable function can be represented as a discrete set of numbers [24], as we shall see in Chapter 3. So, systems that compute can be thought of as powerful mappings from one set of numbers onto another and hence can be treated in the same manner as other mathematical equations. This includes the Web itself, which fortunately opens it up to a great deal of mathematical analysis.

Examining both information and functionality at the extremes of mathematical reduction has proved useful in the search for valid measures of complexity, providing many quantifiable objective comparisons from differing areas of science. Well-established mathematical disciplines such as probability and statistics have established strong reference points to discern the range of measurement scales needed, providing understanding to allow the placement of endpoints of regularity and randomness in strict detail. From such coordinates a number of scientists have been working on candidate measures of "effective complexity," most of which differ but share at least one important characteristic in that strictly regular things, as well as strictly irregular things, are "simple" in a mathematically formal manner, while things that are neither simple nor irregular are "complex" [24].

At one extreme of mathematical simplicity can be found the regularity present in Euclidean geometry while at the other can be found nothing more than pure noise. Deterministic fractal patterns, while not simple, have compact algorithmic descriptions hidden beneath their elaborate structures. Fractals fail to be strictly simple because even though they are defined by short lists of instructions, these instructions must be repeated indefinitely in order to completely express the infinite self-similarity that they contain. Thus fractals are complex and lie in between the extremes of mathematical complexity. Emerging right on the edge of chaos, their iterative qualities have proved ideal for compressing the information present in nature's most complex systems. They are present in the configurations of the cosmos, as well as in the random beauty of an ever-changing coast line, and they are plentiful in the physiology of all living things.

Fractals, it appears, are nature's preferred mechanism of managing both infinite detail and the infinite expansion of that detail, bringing the ability to generate hierarchs of feature automatically. Inspect any point on such a pattern and a unique opportunity presents itself, allowing the capability to indefinitely zoom in and out of the details represented. This makes the concept of detail boundless in certain types of complex and repeatable mathematical systems. Furthermore, replace the concept of direct detail with the information used to describe it, and it should be clear that certain types of complex information systems also possess the theoretical capability to be endlessly descriptive. The Web is one such system, so it has inherited this same capability. This means that it can theoretically soak up all the knowledge we could ever throw at it, and, in common parlance, it could be seen as being infinitely "clever." This revelation is not a leap of faith, but rather a simple side effect of nothing more than pure and evolving complexity.

To be sure, the jury is still out as to how complexity should be unambiguously defined. Furthermore, it is not even clear to many people that there can exist an overall definition or measure that adequately captures any reasonable intuitive notion of what it means for something to be complex. This is especially true when one considers that there are literally dozens of conflicting measurements of the term "complexity" found in the sciences. Nevertheless, at least from more or less a philosophical point of view, there seems to be something happening between orderly things and randomness.

Is it coincidence that most of the predominant fractal types found in nature lie on the boundary between simplicity and complexity? Certainly, significant scientific thinking appears to think not. Occam's Razor is the principle that states that when one is faced with multiple but equivalent interpretations of the same phenomenon, one should always choose the simplest explanation that fits the data [24]. It is one of the guiding principles of scientific research precisely because nature almost always chooses to take the easiest way out of any given problem. Furthermore, there is strong evidence to suggest that fractals are an artifact of nature's application of this principle. Mathematically, pure randomness and perfect regularity are simpler than fractals. Even so, natural fractal structures come in such a rich variety that it may very well be that they offer the greatest amount of functionality for the least amount of underlying complexity consumed.

Certainly, fractals have been demonstrated to have huge information compression capabilities. The entire instruction set for numerous types of fractal growth, for example, can be found in DNA, which contains that information in a biochemical digital format not dissimilar to the electrical states stored in any computer's memory. By implanting a few minor deviations into extremely simplistic underlying repeating patterns, immensely complex outcomes can be produced. These can exhibit a variety and richness of form hidden by their originating equation's well-placed disguise.

THE THEORY OF COMPLEXITY

When dealing with complexity and complex phenomena such as life, an inescapable problem has to be faced—namely, that by their very nature they are multifaceted, and to reduce any description down the point of even relative simplicity would involve removing much of the very essence that we are striving to capture. In such respects it is important to remember that the theory behind complexity is still so new and wide-ranging that nobody yet knows just quite how to define it, or even where its boundaries lie. It manifests itself in everything from condensed-matter physics to society as a whole, and it is certainly present in the workings of the Web at a number of different levels. But then that's the whole point [67]. If the field seems poorly defined at the moment, it is because complexity research is trying to grapple with questions that defy all the conventional categories. As such, the theory of complexity is surfacing as a kind of "Grand Unified Holism" that can possibly run the gamut from evolutionary biology to fuzzy subjects like economics, politics, and the interactions of entire planetary consolations. It may not be quite the ultimate unified field theory sought by many physicists, but it certainly is coming tantalizingly close to unifying a number of hitherto disparate and anomalous concepts and systems independently of whether they are physical, chemical, biological, social [68], or computational. With these systems there is one thing in common, an underlying rule of systems theory if you will. At their heart they are composed of many, many agents. These might be websites, molecules, neurons, species, consumers or even corporations, but whatever their constitution, these agents constantly organize and reorganize themselves into larger structures through the clash of mutual accommodation and rivalry. Thus websites will form into communities of interest, molecules into cells, neurons into brains, species into ecosystems, and consumers and corporations into economies, and so on. At each level, new emergent structures form and engage in new emergent behaviors and organizations [67]. Complexity, in other words, is really a science of emergence [67].

But there are problems. Complexity theory is so ubiquitous that it can successfully be applied to describe both fine- and coarse-grain actualities that can be exhibited in both "cleanly" deterministic and "messy" nondeterministic ways. In short, here is a totally paradoxical situation (Figure 2.4).

Nevertheless, a lot of this so-called "mess" can now be described by the new mathematics of nonlinear dynamics. By so doing, the cleaner forms of science have had to face up to a conclusion that cuts to the very core of their understanding: that in certain circumstances the whole can indeed be greater than the sum of its parts [67].

Figure 2.4. The spectrum of complexity and its paradox in science.

For all but the most fastidious, this fact sounds pretty obvious. Its dawning was nonetheless somewhat disconcerting for the likes of physicists because they have just spent the last 300 years having a love affair with linear systems—in which the whole is precisely equal to the sum of its parts.

In fairness, physicists have plenty of reasons to feel this way. If a system is precisely equal to the sum of its parts, then each component is free to do its own thing regardless of what's happening elsewhere. That tends to make the mathematics relatively easy to analyze—the name "linear" refers to the fact that if you plot such an equation on a graph, the resultant line is straight. Besides, a great deal of nature does appear to work that way. Sound is a linear phenomenon, which is why we can hear an oboe playing over a string accompaniment and still recognize them both. The sound waves intermingle and yet retain their separate identities. Light can also be considered, in part, to be a linear observable, which is why you can see the different colors of a traffic light even on a sunny day: The light rays bouncing from the light source to the eye are not smashed to the ground by sunlight streaming down from the sky. The various light rays operate independently, passing right through each other in straight lines as if nothing were there to interfere. Furthermore, in some ways even certain aspects of the economy are linear, in the sense that small economic agents can act independently. When someone buys a newspaper at a corner shop, for instance, it has little or no effect on their decision to buy a tube of toothpaste at the supermarket the following day [67].

However, it is also true that a great deal of nature is not linear—including a lot of what is really interesting in the world. Our brains certainly aren't linear, neither in construction or function. Nor is the majority of the economy really linear. Millions of individual decisions to buy or not to buy can reinforce each other, creating a boom or recession. Moreover, that economic climate can then feed back to shape the very buying decisions that produced it. Except for the very simplest physical systems, virtually everything and everybody in the world is caught up in a vast, nonlinear "web" of incentives, constraints, and connections. That is a principal reason for why the World Wide Web is the way it is, simply modeling the nonlinear world around it. In both the Web and such real-world systems the slightest change in one place can cause currents of change elsewhere. We can't help but disturb the Universe, as T. S. Eliot[12] almost once said. The whole is almost always equal to a good deal more than the sum of its parts. And the mathematical expression for that property—to the extent that such systems can be described by mathematics at all—is a nonlinear equation: one whose graph is curvy and often extremely complex to plot.

With the advent of powerful computers to aid with simulation experiments, scientists have started to delve deep into the world of nonlinearity, finding strange and wonderful behaviors that their experience with linear systems had not prepared them for [67]. The passage of a water wave down a shallow canal, for example, turned out to have profound connections to certain subtle dynamics in

---

[12]Thomas Stearns Eliot, OM, was an American-born poet, dramatist, and literary critic, whose works, such as "The Love Song of J. Alfred Prufrock," "The Waste Land," and "Four Quartets," are considered major achievements of twentieth-century Modernist poetry [99].

quantum field theory, both being examples of isolated, self-sustaining pulses of energy called "solitons." The great red spot on Jupiter may be another soliton. A swirling hurricane bigger than Earth itself, it has sustained itself for at least 400 years. Likewise, these are just some of the abundance of nonlinear systems that infuse the natural world—high-energy physics, fluid dynamics, fusion energy research, thermonuclear blast waves, quite literally you name it. By the early 1970s, in fact, it had become clear that a good many of these fields had some sort of commonality under the covers, in the sense of having the same mathematical structure [67].

Through such realizations, mankind's understanding of raw complexity has started to reap rewards and the young science of Complexity Theory has rapidly become a recognized discipline with a well-established school of followers. Through their endeavors we now understand some of the fundamentals of complexity in its most naked forms. For example, it is well recognized that complex systems are made up from many small interacting parts, or agents, as has already been explained. Moreover, the very richness of these interactions allows the system as a whole to undergo spontaneous self-organization. Thus people trying to satisfy material needs unconsciously organize themselves through a myriad acts of buying and selling [67]. Similarly the Web satisfies our intellectual, social, and economic needs, acting as an environment in which we can connect and interconnect over and over again in a self-organizing sea of communication. This is not a conscious outcome attributable to any one individual or organization; it happens without anyone being in charge or consciously planning it. The genes in a developing embryo organize themselves in one way to make a liver cell and in another way to make a muscle cell. Collections of websites reference each other to form "rings" of self-similar content. Flying birds adapt to the actions of their neighbors, unconsciously organizing themselves into a flock. Organisms constantly adapt to each other through co-evolution, thereby organizing themselves into exquisitely tuned ecosystems. Atoms search for the minimum energy state by forming chemical bonds with each other, thereby organizing themselves into structures we have come to understand as molecules. In every case, groups of agents seeking mutual accommodation and self-consistency somehow manage to transcend themselves, acquiring collective properties such as life, thought, and purpose that they might never possess individually [67].

Furthermore, these complex, self-organizing systems are adaptive, in that they don't just passively respond to events in the way that rocks might roll around in an earthquake. They actively try to turn whatever happens to their advantage. Hence the human brain constantly organizes the reorganization of billions of neural connections so as to learn from experience. Web rings unconsciously morph to accommodate new websites and remove less popular resources. Species evolve for better survival in a changing environment, as do corporations and industries. And the marketplace responds to changing tastes and lifestyles, immigration, technological developments, shifts in the price of raw materials, and a host of other factors [67].

Finally, every one of these complex, self-organizing, adaptive systems possesses a kind of dynamism that makes them qualitatively different from static objects such as computer chips or snowflakes, which are merely complicated. Complex systems are spontaneous, more disorderly, more alive than that. At the same time, however, their peculiar dynamism is a far cry from the weirdly unpredictable gyrations at the extremes of chaos. In the past three decades, chaos theory has shaken science to its foundations with the realization that very simple dynamical rules can give rise to extraordinary intricate behavior. Yet chaos by itself doesn't explain the structure, the coherence, and the self-organizing cohesiveness of complex systems [67].

Instead all these complex systems somehow acquire the ability to bring order and chaos into a special kind of balance. This balance point—often referred to as "the edge of chaos"—is where the components of a system never quite lock into place, and yet never quite dissolve into turbulence either. The edge of chaos is where life has enough stability to sustain itself and enough creativity to deserve the name "life." The edge of chaos is where new ideas and innovative genotypes[13] are forever nibbling away at the edges of status quo and where even the most entrenched old guard will eventually be overthrown. It is a dynamic overly familiar to the Web. The edge of chaos is the constantly shifting battleground between stagnation and anarchy, the one place where a complex system can be spontaneous, adaptive, and alive [67].

The control of complex adaptive systems tends to be highly dispersed. There is no master neuron in the brain, for instance, nor is there any master cell within a developing embryo. If there is any coherent behavior in such a system, it arises from competition and cooperation amongst the agents themselves [67].

Furthermore, complex adaptive systems have many levels of organization, with agents or constituents at any one level serving as building blocks for agents at a higher level in a truly hierarchical manner. A group of proteins, lipids, and nucleic acids will form a biological cell, a group of such cells will form a tissue, a collection of tissues will form an organ, and association of organs will form a whole organism, and a group of organisms will form an ecosystem. In the brain, one group of neurons will form the speech cortex, and in precisely the same way a group of individual workers will compose a department, a group of departments will compose a division and so on through companies, corporations, economic sectors, national economies, and finally the world economy [67]. All are examples of reoccurring, self-similar patterns, one building on top of the other. They are recursive in much the same way as the fractal structures common in so many complex natural systems. In truth, for all intents and purposes, they are fractal.

Thus, when we take multiple agents, building blocks, internal models, and perpetual novelty all together, it's no wonder that complex systems are so hard to analyze with standard mathematics. Most of the conventional techniques like calculus or linear analysis are very well suited to describing unchanging objects moving in a fixed environment. But to really get a deep understanding of complex adaptive systems in general, what is needed are mathematics and computer simulation techniques that emphasize internal models, the emergence of new building blocks, and the rich network of interactions between multiple agents [67].

---

[13]A genotype is the specific genetic makeup of an organism, usually in the form of DNA in carbon-based biology. It codes for the development of that organism's physiology.

THE CROSSOVER BETWEEN ORDERLY AND CHAOTIC SYSTEMS

In many ways the Web can be compared to a specific type of computer system known as a cellular automaton. Like such systems it can be seen to generate its own behavior in a dynamic, sometimes self-organizing manner. It also exhibits structural cell-like properties at a number of levels. The pages of a website can be considered in this way, as can websites within communities, communities within economies, economies within global movements, and so on, with each cell holding the capability to be viewed as "on" or "off," or as "live" or "dead," depending upon context and circumstance.

In 1984, while still at Caltech, a physics whiz-kid named Stephen Wolfram pointed out that cellular automata not only have a rich mathematical structure, but also have deep similarities to nonlinear dynamical systems. He also highlighted that all cellular automata rules fall into one of four basic types, or universality classes. Class 1 contains what are essentially extinction rules: No matter what pattern of living or dead cells you start with, all activity in the automata just dies off—in the language of dynamic systems, such rules appear to act as a single "point attractor." Class 2 rules are a little livelier. With these rules an initial pattern that scatters "living" and "dead" cells over a computational space quickly, coalesces these cells into a set of static "blobs," with perhaps a few other blobs that exist in periodic oscillation; in the language of dynamical systems, these rules relate to a set of periodic attractors. Class 3 rules produce patterns at the opposite extreme, being too lively. They produce so much cellular activity that the system bubbles with change—again in the language of dynamical systems these rules would correspond to what are known as strange attractors or, more closely, chaotic behavior. Finally, Class 4 rules relate to those rare, impossible-to-classify circumstances that don't produce blobs of cells or result in chaos. These produce coherent structures that propagate, grow, split apart, and then recombine in wondrous and complex ways. Such structures essentially never settle down.

When the lid is lifted on these rules classes, they can essentially be related to one variable in a very simple type of equation. This relates to the probability that any given cell will be "alive" in the next iteration of the automata program and is often referred to by the Greek letter lambda (λ). At very low values of this variable, typically at around zero, nothing happens other than the formation of the dead frozen patterns characterized by Wolfram's first class of rules. Increasing this value slightly produces classical Class 2-type patterns. Jumping all the way up the scale to λ values close to 0.5 not surprisingly corresponds to Class 3 behavior. But right in between, clustered tightly around one magic value of λ—about 0.273—can be found clusters of Class 4 behaviors in all their magnificence.

This therefore indicates a sequence, a relationship between the orderly and the seemingly completely random, and also a provocative transition in dynamical systems' behavior (Table 2.1). This immediately brings to mind some kind of phase change. Suppose you think of λ as being like temperature. Then the Class 1 and Class 2 rules that are found at low values of λ would correspond to solid states of physical matter like ice, where molecules are rigidly locked into a lattice structure.

Table 2.1. The Relation Between Wolfram's Automata Rule Classes and Dynamic Systems' Behavior

Wolfram's Automata Rule Classes:	1 and 2	$\rightarrow$	4	$\rightarrow$	3
Dynamical System's Behavior:	Order	$\rightarrow$	"Complexity"	$\rightarrow$	Chaos

The Class 3 rules, found at high values of λ, would correspond to a gaseous vapor like steam, where molecules are flying around in Brownian-like[14] chaos. Class 4 rules correspond to fluid states.

This would be the instinctive answer, but upon closer inspection the analogy is not quite right. Class 4 rules typically produce effects known as "extended transients," chains of reaction that spread out like the legs of a nervous octopus. This behavior can survive and propagate for some time, and so it conflicts with the standard physical definition of a liquid. Ordinarily, liquids don't have such a property at the molecular level. In fact, in many physical respects, liquids behave in much the same way as gaseous substances, but obviously in a much denser form. In fact, by applying enough energy, under the right conditions, you can easily persuade a solid like ice to transition into steam without any noticeable latency in its fluid state. For such reasons, in general, gases and liquids can be considered to be aspects of the same materially "fluid" phase of physical matter.

Going back to the physics reveals that two forms of fundamental phase transition—first-order and second-order—are materially manifest in nature. First-order transitions are the type most commonplace in the physical world, being sharp and precise. Raise the temperature of an ice cube past 32°F, for instance, and the change from ice to water is almost instantaneous. Essentially what's happening at this point is that the ice molecules are forced into making an either–or choice between order and chaos. At temperatures below the transition, they are vibrating slowly enough that they can side with the decision for crystalline order—in other words, ice. At temperature above the transition, however, the molecules are vibrating with such ferocity that the molecular bonds start breaking faster than they can reform and the whole mass is eventually forced to take the path of chaos and become water.

Second-order phase transitions are much less common in nature—at least they are at the temperatures and pressures that humans are used to. They are much less abrupt, largely because the molecules in such systems don't have to make an either–or decision as in first-order transitions. Such systems literally combine order and chaos at the point of transition. Above a given transition temperature, for example, most of the molecules tumble over one another in a complete anarchical fluid phase. Yet amongst all this chaos are myriads of submicroscopic islands of orderly, latticework solidness, with molecules constantly dissolving and recrystallizing around the periphery. These islands are neither very large nor very long-lasting, even on a molecular scale. So the system resides mostly in a chaotic state. But as the temperature is lowered, the largest islands start to get very big indeed and begin to exist for a correspondingly long period of time. So the balance between chaos

---

[14]Brownian motion is the physical phenomenon of random motion in a gas or fluid.

and order shifts. Of course, were it taken all the way past the transition, the roles normally reverse; the material goes from being a sea of fluid dotted with small solid islands, to being a solid dotted with lakes of fluid. But right at the transition point the balance is perfect and orderly structures fill a volume precisely equal to that of the chaotic fluid. Thus, order and chaos intertwine in a complex, ever-changing duet of submicroscopic arms and fractal filaments. The largest ordered structures propagate their elongated extensions across the material for arbitrarily long distances and last for arbitrarily long durations. In this state nothing ever settles down and constant change is the norm.

Such transitions are profound because they illustrate a critical connection, being completely analogous to Wolfram's Class 4 rules for cellular automata-like computer systems. The similarities are quite astounding; the propagating tendrils of structure, the dynamics that take forever to settle down, and the intricate dance of structures that grow and split and recombine with spontaneous and surprising complexity.

So a second analogy can be shown in Table 2.2.

But the real issue at hand questions if this is anything more than an analogy. Mathematically, the answer is certainly a very strong "Yes," using the function of λ as a link between all the types of system listed. In fact, the more it is investigated, the more the similarities grow stronger and point to deep connections between phase transitions, dynamical behavior, and computation—and between computation, specific types of computer systems, and life itself [67].

The connection goes all the way back to simple computational simulations based on nature, like Conway's Game of Life,[15] first outlined in 1970. This is itself an automata variant. In such simulations, propagating structures, or tendrils, referred to as "gliders," carry "signals" across their abstract Universe from one point to another. As such, a flock of gliders going single file can be thought of as being like a stream of digital bits: "glider" present = 1; "glider" absent = 0. So, as researchers have experimented with such simulations, it has become apparent that such structures can be used to store data, or emit new signals that encode new information. Very quickly, in fact, it was realized that Game of Life-like structures can be used to build a complete computer, with data storage, information-processing capability, and all the other essential components needed to undertake computing. A Game of Life computer has nothing to do with the actual machine it's running on of course. Rather, it exists within an abstract problem space; a von Neumann universe to give it its more accurate title. In many respects such machines are a crude and inefficient computer to be sure. They are, however, a *universal* computer with all the power to compute anything computable nonetheless [67].

Such a fact is pretty amazing, especially when one considers that only comparatively few cellular automaton rules allow it to happen. Nevertheless, you can't

---

[15]The Game of Life is a cellular automaton devised by the British mathematician John Horton Conway in 1970. It is the best-known example of a cellular automaton. It made its first public appearance in the October 1970 issue of *Scientific American,* in Martin Gardner's "Mathematical Games" column. From a theoretical point of view, it is interesting because it has the power of a universal Turing machine: that is, anything that can be computed algorithmically can be computed within Conway's Game of Life. It has often been claimed that since 1970 more computer time world-wide has been devoted to the Game of Life than to any other single activity.

Table 2.2. The Relation Between Wolfram's Automata Rule Classes, Dynamic Systems' Behavior, and Material State Phases

Wolfram's Automata Rule Classes	1 and 2	→	4	→	3
Dynamical System's Behavior	Order	→	"Complexity"	→	Chaos
Physical Matter	Solid	→	Phase transition	→	Fluid

make a universal computer in a cellular automaton governed by Wolfram's Class 1 or Class 2 rules, because the structures they produce are too static; you could store data in such a universe, but you would have no way to propagate the information from place to place. Nor can you make such a computer in an unruly Class 3 automaton, given that the signals would quickly get lost in the noise, and storage structures would quickly get battered to pieces. In reality, rules that allow the construction of a universal computer are those that come from Class 4, like those in the Game of Life. These are the only rules that provide enough stability to store information and enough flexibility to send signals over arbitrary distances—two of the most essential ingredients in computation. And, of course, these are also the rules that sit right on the point of phase transition, just on the edge of chaos [67].

So, phase transition, complexity, and computation are all wrapped up together, at least in the abstract space of a universal computer. But these connections also hold true in the real world as well—in everything from social systems, to economics, to living cells, and obviously to the Web itself. In fact, once you get this close to the raw notions of complex computation, you are getting awfully close to the real essence of life itself. To an incredible degree, life is based on the ability to handle and transform information, in such respects being inseparable from the idea of computing. It gathers and stores information, as if to covert it for instance, and maps it to produce action. The famous biologist Richard Dawkins has a beautiful example of this [67]:

> If you take a rock and toss it in the air, it traces out a nice parabola. It's at the mercy of the laws of physics. It can only make a simple response to the forces that are acting upon it from outside. But now if you take a bird and throw it into the air, its behaviour is nothing like that. It flies off into the trees somewhere. The same forces are certainly acting upon this bird, but there's and awful lot of information processing going on that's responsible for its behaviour. Furthermore, that's true even if you go down to simple cells: they aren't just doing what inanimate matter does. They aren't just responding to simple forces.

Thus one of the interesting questions that can be asked about living things is, Under what conditions do systems whose dynamics are dominated by information processing arise from things that just respond to external forces? When and where does the processing of information and the storage of information become important [67]?

When the theory of computation is studied, there are an enormous number of analogies. For example, one of the first things to note about computer programs is that there is a distinction between those that "halt"—that is, take in some data and transform it to produce an answer in a finite amount of time—and those that just keep churning away forever. But that is just like the distinction between the behavior of matter at temperatures below and above a phase transition. There is a sense in which the material is constantly trying to "compute" how to arrange itself at a molecular level: If it's cold, then it reaches the answer very quickly and crystallizes completely. But if it's hot it can't reach any answer at all and remains fluid [67].

In much the same way the distinction is analogous to the one between (a) Class 1 and Class 2 cellular automata that eventually halt by freezing into a stable configuration and (b) chaotic Class 3 cellular automata that bubble indefinitely. For instance, suppose a program were written that just printed out one message on a screen, say the familiar "HELLO WORLD," and then quit. Such a program would correspond to Class 1 automata, with a λ value down around zero, which go to quiescence almost immediately. Conversely, suppose the same program were written with a serious bug in it, so that it printed out a steady stream of gibberish without ever repeating itself. Such a program would correspond to Class 3 cellular automata, with a λ value out around 0.5, where chaos is prevalent [67].

Now, let's move away from the extremes, toward transitions. In the material world, longer and longer transients would be found here: That is, as the temperature gets closer to phase transition, the molecules require more and more time to reach their decision. Likewise, as λ increases from zero in a von Neumann universe, one starts to see cellular automata that churn around a bit before calming down, with the amount of churning dependent on just the configuration of their initial state. These correspond to what are known as polynomial-time algorithms in computer science— the kind of programs that have a significant amount of work to do before they finish, but that tend to be relatively fast and efficient at that work—certain kinds of sorting algorithm, for example. As we go further and λ gets closer to phase transition, however, cellular automata that are active for a very long time indeed start to be found. These correspond to nonpolynomials, the kind of algorithms that might not halt for the lifetime of the Universe, or longer. Such algorithms are effectively useless [67].

Right at the transition point, in the material world, a given molecule might end up in either an ordered or fluid state; there are no known ways of telling in advance, because order and chaos are so intimately intertwined at the molecular level. In the computational space of a von Neumann universe, likewise, Wolfram's Class 4 rules might eventually produce a frozen configuration, or they might not. Either way the phase transition at the edge of chaos corresponds to what computer scientists call "undecidable" algorithms. These are algorithms that might halt very quickly with certain sets of inputs and run forever with others. The point is that it is impossible to tell ahead of time which outcome will be produced, even in principle. In fact, there is even a theorem to that effect, not surprisingly known as the "undecidable theorem." This was proved by Alan Turing in the 1930s. Paraphrased, it states that no matter how clever we think we are, there will always be algorithms that do things we can't predict in advance. The only way to find out what they will do is to just run them and see.

These are exactly the type of algorithms that are naturally associated with life and intelligence of course. So it is no wonder that Class 4 cellular automata appear so lifelike. They exist in the only dynamical region where complexity, computation, and life itself are truly viable, the place where the Web has also found its natural home: the edge of chaos.

Table 2.3. A Wide Range of Analogies Centered on the Edge of Chaos

	The Edge of Chaos		
Wolfram's Automata Rule Classes:	1 and 2 $\rightarrow$	4	$\rightarrow$ 3
Dynamical System's Behavior:	Order $\rightarrow$	Complexity	$\rightarrow$ Chaos
Physical Matter:	Solid $\rightarrow$	Phase transition	$\rightarrow$ Fluid
Computation:	Halting $\rightarrow$	Undecidable	$\rightarrow$ Non-Halting
Life:	Too static $\rightarrow$	Life/intelligence	$\rightarrow$ Too Noisy
Web:	Communal $\rightarrow$ regularity	Unpredictable change	$\rightarrow$ Turmoil

So now an even wider range of analogies can be formed (Table 2.3).

This all adds up to the fact that "solid" and "fluid" are just two fundamental phases of matter, as in ice versus water. They are two fundamental classes of dynamical behavior in general—including dynamical behavior in such utterly nonmaterial realms as the space of cellular automaton rules or the abstract universes of computational algorithms. Furthermore, the existence of these two fundamental classes of dynamical behavior implies the existence of a third fundamental class: "phase transition"—behavior at the edge of chaos, where complex computation and, quite possibly, life itself can be encountered [67].

ONWARDS TO CHAOS

No investigation of complexity would be complete without a brief summary of what is often considered to be its most extreme form. Beyond the mathematical upper border of complexity lies the deceptively camouflaged notion of chaos. This is not strictly analogous to the classical interpretations of its name involving shear calamity and confusion. Instead, in mathematical or computational terms, chaos relates to much simpler notions of pattern and organization. It may be random to our native observation, certainly, but it is also far more concisely describable than complexity when inspected using modern mathematical techniques. A specialized branch of mathematics has even been created to categorize such techniques and, not surprisingly, has been given the name Chaos Theory. Interestingly, like Einstein's theories of relativity, Heisenberg's[16] uncertainty principle and Kurt Gödel's incompleteness theorem, Chaos theory prescribes limits on the very foundations of knowledge itself. As a tantalizing taste of its own deep profoundness, it says that there are many things which simply cannot be known [81].

The roots of this mathematical discipline date back to about 1900 and the stud-

---

[16]Werner Karl Heisenberg was a celebrated German physicist and Nobel laureate, one of the founders of quantum mechanics and acknowledged to be one of the most important physicists of the twentieth century [100].

ies of Henri Poincaré[17] on the problem of the complex motion of three objects in mutual gravitational attraction—the so-called three-body problem. Through his work, Poincaré found that there can be orbits that are periodically irregular and yet not forever increasing nor approaching a fixed point. Later studies on similar topics were carried out by G. D. Birkhoff, A. N. Kolmogorov, M. L. Cartwright, J. E. Littlewood, and Stephen Smale. Interestingly, except for Smale, who was perhaps the first pure mathematician to investigate nonlinear dynamics, these studies were all again directly inspired by physics: the three-body problem in the case of Birkhoff, turbulence and astronomical problems in the case of Kolmogorov, and radio engineering in the case of Cartwright and Littlewood. Following such works, the term "chaos," as used in mathematics, was coined by the applied mathematician James A. Yorke [27] in 1975 in a paper entitled "Period Three Implies Chaos."

Closely entangled with the roots of later understandings of complexity, chaos theory progressed rapidly in the 1940s, 1950s, and 1960s, once more as a result of mainstream science's disillusionment with established linear theory and the advent of the electronic computer. The computer's involvement was simply because much of the mathematics of chaos theory involves the repeated iteration of simple mathematical formulae, which would be impractical to do by hand. Obviously, electronic computers made such repetition mundane, which is why, for instance, one of the earliest digital computers, the ENIAC,[18] was put to use running simple chaotic models for weather forecasting.

Edward Lorenz[19] was one early pioneer of the theory whose interest in chaos came about accidentally through exactly such work on weather prediction in 1961. Using a basic Royal McBee LPG-30 computer to run his weather simulation, he found ways to reduce the time of his work by starting his simulations in the middle of their original course. To his surprise, the weather that the machine began to predict was completely different from the weather calculated during a full run, so Lorenz went back and studied the variables that controlled his program.

It turned out that the printout he was using to provide his inputs rounded variables off to a three-digit number, whereas the computer itself worked to five digits. This

---

[17]Jules Henri Poincaré, generally known as Henri Poincaré, was one of France's greatest mathematicians, theoretical scientists, and a philosopher of science. He is often described as the last "universalist" (after Gauss) capable of understanding and contributing in virtually all parts of mathematics.
As a mathematician and physicist, he made many original fundamental contributions to mathematics, mathematical physics, and celestial mechanics. He was responsible for formulating the Poincaré conjecture, one of the most famous problems in mathematics. In his research on the three-body problem, Poincaré became the first person to discover a chaotic deterministic system and laid the foundations of modern chaos theory. Poincaré anticipated Albert Einstein's work and sketched a preliminary version of the special theory of relativity [101].
[18]ENIAC, short for Electronic Numerical Integrator and Computer, was long thought to have been the first electronic computer designed to be Turing-complete, capable of being reprogrammed by rewiring to solve a full range of computing problems.
[19]Edward Norton Lorenz is an American mathematician and meteorologist, a contributor to the chaos theory and inventor of the strange attractor notion. He coined the term "butterfly effect" [102].

difference was tiny, however, and common consensus at the time stated that it should have no practical effect on the computations involved. Nevertheless, Lorenz discovered that small changes in initial conditions produced large changes in the long-term outcome of chaos, a concept that was to become a cornerstone concept of the theory.

Through the efforts of scientists like Lorenz, chaos has come to be understood as a particular type of mathematically describable pattern, extremely sensitive to initial conditions. It most certainly does not prescribe to the linear order of Euclidian geometry or Newtonian physics, but neither does it strictly relate to the racket of complete randomness. Furthermore, it is more mathematically compressible than the most complex of complex systems, so there is no absolute fit there either. Yet systems that exhibit mathematical chaos are deterministic and thus orderly in at least some sense. Because they fundamentally enclose both order and complexity, they are therefore plentiful in the natural world too and can be viewed as more mathematically simple versions of their complex cousins. Furthermore, as with natural complexity, chaos commonly involves repetition, so chaotic systems often form using fractals patterns, also creating many of the familiar structures we see in the material world around us.

Without doubt, large parts of the Web can be seen to be chaotic. This should come as no real shock, because chaos is a natural ingredient in the volatile churnings associated with transition and life. At the edge of chaos, comparisons between the real and unreal are especially valid. Here cobwebs can be quite legitimately compared with corporate databases, and hippopotamuses can be compared with hyperlinks—most definitely some mind-bending propositions, but ones that nevertheless provide valid links between the workings of the natural world and those of computational megasystems like the Web and life itself.

MODERN-DAY APPROACHES TO COMPLEXITY

Of course complexity is a truism in all but the most mundane of large systems, be they natural or man-made. All contain significant levels of information that contribute to the whole in irreducible ways. But nature has one indisputable advantage over us when it comes to the management of such matters, quite simply having been in the business of complexity much longer. From endless years of practice it has come to understand far better how to control and optimize complexity in systems to gain the best advantage. It knows full well that too much complexity will make for the overly cumbersome or redundant, while at the same time appreciates that complex detail is the way to diversity and adaptation—the real key to survival in the microcosm of its making. We, on the other hand, are mere beginners in such matters, with complexity currently being a matter of high priority in many of our endeavors centered on construction.

But none of this signifies that we do not understand how to address many of the unwanted side effects of complexity. For example, many centuries ago we began to recognize the value of abstractions such as patterns, themes that once created can be reapplied many times over for many different purposes. Take the ubiquitous wheel,[20] one of the most important inventions in the entire history of the human race. Although it can take many forms, its primary design pattern remains essentially unchanged, being a round disk capable of rotation about a fixed point in its centre. Through this elegant and simple pattern, the wheel has been reapplied countless times for our betterment. "Architecture in general is all about such patterns and individual architectures can therefore be seen as the structuring paradigms of systems" [70]. Although we may often not appreciate it directly, we have become adept at using such techniques; and for all its apparent anarchy, even the Web itself is fundamentally dependent upon architectural thinking and pattern for its inherent strengths.

We also understand that the information involved in complexity can often be compressed. All modern number systems, for example, have been born out of a desire to compress the complexity of management and trade. When the shepherds of old wanted to account for their flocks, they needed a succinct mechanism by which to categorize the quantities of livestock they were tending. To us, in the modern world, the process we refer to as "counting" may seem a trivial and commonplace concept, but to the ancients, the mere concept of abstract numbers was an absolute revelation.

By such means we too know how to face many aspects of complexity head on, although we may infrequently practice what we preach. We are already implementing many such counter strategies in our modern-day technologies. Patterns, nonredundant data storage, and compression algorithms are all now commonplace in Information Technology, for instance, but once again nature got there long before us, implementing many strikingly similar schemes though the natural course of evolution. To see just how striking these similarities are, however, we must go back to basics and investigate much that is fundamental in the mechanics of computation and information representation, both in natural systems and in modern-day computer science.

[20]According to most authorities, the wheel was invented in ancient Mesopotamia in the fifth millennium B.C., originally in the function of potters' wheels. A possibly independent invention in China dates to around 2800 B.C. It is also thought that the invention of the wheel dated back to Ancient India. Though they did not develop the wheel proper, the Inca and certain other Western Hemisphere cultures seem to have approached the concept, because wheel-like worked stones have been found on objects identified as children's toys dating to about 1500 B.C. The wheel was apparently unknown in sub-Saharan Africa, Australia, and the Americas until relatively recent contacts with Eurasians [103].

CHAPTER 3

The Importance of Discreteness and Symmetry in Systems

Greater whorls have lesser whorls, which feed on their velocity. And lesser whorls have smaller whorls, and so on to viscosity.

—*L. F. Richardson*

LET'S BE DISCRETE

Before looking at the distinguishing complex features of the Web, there is a need to examine the basic mechanics on which later premises of Web Life will be made. In so doing, its very fundamentals must be laid bare in order to gain an insight into its workings, for such insight is plainly essential when trying to make objective comparisons between matters like the building blocks of life and the computational foundations of the Web. Besides, the comprehension entailed is also indispensable when trying to argue the case for the more philosophical ideas such as consciousness, cognition, and intelligence in technology as shall be attempted later.

Distill mainstream computational theory, and it basically boils down to the manipulation of four essential types of ingredient:

- The identifiable things and concepts that any computation is interested in.
- The associations, constraints, and/or transformations between those things and concepts.
- The methods of grouping both things and concepts together.
- The types of the things, concepts, associations, and groups used.

That's it, nothing more, nothing less. Just as long as all the ingredients involved can stand out in their own right—that they are suitably "discrete" in the vernacular of computer science—then most computation has some pretty simple roots.

Admittedly, there are forms of computation that deliberately challenge the constraints imposed by discrete outlooks on the world, and these are discussed more properly in Chapter 10, but the emphasis here must be on the simplicities of the everyday variants of computing we see around us today, in both nature and man-made technologies, not any specialized alternatives. When considering these, it can be shown for instance that, from certain perspectives and most practicable applica-

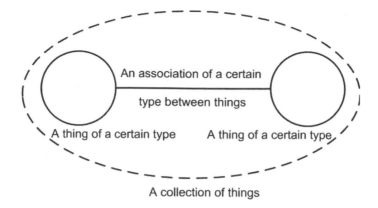

Figure 3.1. The basic mechanics of computation.

tions, all the rules, instructions, and data bound up on the Web can be treated as one particular type of information—essential distinct numeric quantities in a mathematical equation. Furthermore, it can be shown that there is only one fundamental type of logic at play on the Web—namely, Boolean logic,[1] which again rests on the notion of separation between variables. And, just as important, all the various arrangements, collections, and classifications of resources on the Web, at whatsoever level and of whatever size, can all be understood using one overriding theory, commonly known as Set Theory, of which Boolean logic is part. In fact, not only can the Web be described using Set Theory, but so too can all mathematics, with, in the broadest sense, a set being seen as a collection of things that can be thought of as a single object [81].

Thus, there is just one fundamental data type and one overall theory of aggregation, structure and logic, both being based on the discontinuity of everything they encompass and influence. In essence the basic technicalities of the Web's anatomy boil down to something really very simple. But then that's just the point. That's one of the hallmarks of a truly complex system at heart. Just as the physicists would have us do with the entire material universe and reduce it down to nothing more than a few types of subatomic particle, so too can a similarly extreme approach be taken with the complex virtual workings of the Web.

A BRIEF WORD OF WARNING

At this point it may be wise to issue a brief warning. In order to address many of the common causative features alluded to in this book, some substantial ground has to be covered in the following sections. This unfortunately journeys right to the heart

---

[1]Boolean logic is a complete system for logical operations. It was named after George Boole, an English mathematician at University College Cork who first defined an algebraic system of logic in the mid nineteenth century.

of computation and leads to some rather deep and abstract material by necessity—not something that the casual reader might care to read under normal circumstances. Furthermore, given that there is no one route through this terrain known to provide the best incremental understanding, the order in which topics are introduced may appear disjointed at times.

But there is reason behind the areas visited and the order in which they appear, although the apparent relevance of each topic covered and the interrelationships between them may not become apparent until much later. For those wanting a deep understanding of the foundations on which later arguments are based, it is recommended that you persevere, but for those who are willing just to accept the low-level detail, it is perfectly acceptable to forgo the following sections and skip straight to Chapter 6.

BOILING THE NUMBERS OUT OF COMPUTING

The notions of information and computing might, at first, seem familiar to most, but upon closer inspection it soon becomes clear that there are so many interpretations that the possibilities of unnecessary confusion are quite real. To start with, most in the modern Western World would associate such ideas with the concept of the silicon-based machines now commonplace in our everyday lives. We chose to call these "computers" by name, but it must be remembered that they are not the sole guardians of computation. For example, for many centuries, scores of men and women were gainfully employed to perform the repetitive labors now undertaken by our modern electronic friends, with many an actuary's office being filled with banks of such individuals.

Essentially, the real lesson to be learned is that computation merely refers to the act of computing and so is independent of any medium. To that extent, simply by existing, all physical systems store information. By evolving dynamically over time, they process that information. The Universe computes,[2] for instance, and information processing is written across all of nature [67]. In fact the Universe is *the* computer. It is connected, entangled so that it is hooked up into everything and is created from everything. "It does not respond to us—it is us" [87]. This implies that the ideas of computation and computers are ancient concepts rather than contemporary revolutions, having been present since the dawn of time itself. In reality, most physical entities transform information in one way or another, hiding their true behavior behind the literary camouflage of language like "functionality," "process," or "program." Systems as diverse as galaxies, giraffes, and germinating seeds are all in on the act. But this causes a problem. How can the concepts of either computation or information be debated sensibly if a huge number of definitions prevail?

---

[2]The amount of information one could process if using all the energy and matter of the universe is 10^{90} bits, and the number of elementary operations that it can have performed since the Big Bang is about 10^{120} ops. Perhaps the Universe is itself a computer, and what it's doing is performing a computation. If so, that's why the Universe is so complex and these numbers say how big that computation is [47].

What is needed is a lingua franca that can be formally tested to destruction, a vocabulary that can be pushed to the point of indisputable verification, a collection of terms where all ambiguity has been literally squeezed out—in other words, a mathematical formalism, because without such a formalism there would be no way of proving or disproving the generic capabilities common to all computing systems, no matter what their source or form.

Enter Kurt Gödel, a twentieth-century mathematician, who took the world by absolute surprise with some of his mathematical ideas on computation. Being a great believer in reductionist principles, Gödel understood the value of boiling concepts down into the simplest terms possible and recognized that any input or output to a computational process could be denoted as a sequence of letters, numbers, digits, or any other type of list—a "string" for want of a better description. Furthermore, he also understood that this principle could be applied to any computational process itself, thereby unifying the view of any computational process down to a collection of three strings—one for the inputs involved, one for the outputs, and one for the process performing the transform between the two. Where Gödel's genius became clear was when he realized that every unique value in a vocabulary of string elements could be mapped onto a similar unique natural number[3] and manipulated mathematically, thereby opening the way for reduction and making it possible to convert a computer program, input string and output string, into a set of three or less natural numbers [24].

Gödelization is therefore the term for a method for mapping many natural numbers onto a single natural number. The details of how the mapping is performed may not be very interesting, but the fact that it can be done is extremely important. Remember that the input and output of any computation can be represented as some finite-length list of values, each of which can be replaced by a natural numeric value. Also note that the computation itself can be represented in the same way. So, the relevant and interesting question is, How can multiple numbers be transposed onto just one?

The key to the whole process is the fact that every number has a unique prime factorization. If you pick any natural number, , then there is exactly one sequence of prime numbers, $Px_1, Px_2, \ldots, Px_n$, such that the product of the n prime numbers is equal to x. Now, if the computation's input is examined and there are n numbers in its sequence, then let every number in the sequence be denoted by $x_1, x_2, \ldots, x_n$. To calculate the Gödel number of the input string, use the first n prime numbers, which forms a unique natural number. Granted, Gödel numbers will tend to be huge in size, but this is not necessarily a problem.

The Gödelization Formula

$$\prod_{i=1}^{n} P_i^{x_i} = p_1^{x_1} p_2^{x_2} \ldots p_n^{x_n} \tag{3.1}$$

Given a Gödel number, it is possible to reconstruct the original string by taking the prime factorization of that number. So, if there are thirteen 2's in the prime fac-

---

[3]Natural number can mean either a positive integer (1, 2, 3, 4, . . .) or a non-negative integer (0, 1, 2, 3, 4, . . .).

torization of the Gödel number, then it follows that the first number of the original string was 13. If there are eighty-seven 3's in the prime factorization, then the second number in the original string was 87. And if there is a single 5 in the prime factorization, then the third number was 1.

Gödelization adds another simplification to studying the nature of computation. Instead of worrying about programs with multiple input and output sequences, it becomes possible to ignore most of the detail and just concentrate on transformations that take a single number as input and produce a single number as output. Even with this restriction, a computer program that operates in this manner is still doing all of the "hard" part of computing. Therefore, without loss of generalization, it is credible to speak of computation, and in such a way the Web also, as merely a manipulation of lists, the content of which is irrelevant so long as all elements are of the same type—natural numbers in this case. What really matters, however, is that the representation of a computing system's input and output can always be converted from one type of representation to another: number to string, string to image, grape to mango, it really does not matter! Gödelization powerfully clears the playing field and levels all the constituents contributing to a computational process so that all can be described, investigated, and manipulated using the same medium. This is a powerfully unifying concept beyond any question and one that removes any difference between data and functionality, at the end of the day, rendering them completely indistinct with regards to their type.

This concept may appear weird to the human mindset, but it nevertheless embodies a theme that is consistent throughout large parts of the natural world [24], being especially familiar in carbon-based life as we commonly recognize it. Early schooling teaches us that DNA carries the genetic information needed to sustain a species from generation to generation, for example. But it is less well known that as part of its normal business the same DNA contributes significantly to the process of cellular reproduction. It quite literally performs a dual role, both storing and helping to transform a cell's information. By so doing, it qualifies as a computer in its own right, yet we do not talk of DNA as having it own 'hardware' or "software," let alone its own processing unit, storage, or program. It is simply a collection of long hydrocarbons that act and interact as part of an organism's usual physiology. So, ironically we naturally view DNA's computation as if from an opposite viewpoint to our own man-made machines. Our perceptions have been established in a ground up fashion, as if the problem had been Gödelized first.

So, hydrocarbons on one hand and natural numbers on the other, what's the difference? From a material perspective, absolutely everything, which is why we don't impulsively consider armadillo's and algorithms or websites and weasels to be alike. But from a raw information content and computational standpoint they may as well be identical.

THE POWER OF TWO

Even the technophobes amongst us will be aware that all digital systems are based on the concept of binary notation—that is, the capability to represent and manipulate information using combinations of elements comprising only two types. This, by its very nature, is one of the most rudimentary patterns anywhere, and, not surprisingly, it reappears consistently at a number of levels in the digital world. Not only is it used in the zeros and ones present in binary codification, but it is also ultimately the underlying pattern for Boolean Logic, necessitated by the presence or not of the electrical charges that drive the workings of all common digital machines. It is this simple flip-flopping that is at the heart of even the most powerful of today's super mainframes, making them essentially no different from a huge collection of connected switches. So the obvious and colossal advances of the computer age are based on nothing more than the principle that, no matter how large and complex a problem, and regardless of its origins, there are very few cases where it cannot be meaningfully refined into a series of assertions and representations. These can further be distilled into a series of states being either true or false, or on or off, so long as the underlying problem is understood well enough: "But beware if you don't know anything about computers, just remember that they are machines that do exactly what you tell them but often surprise you in the result!" [51]

LET'S SPLIT THE DIFFERENCE

Despite this straightforward two-state model, many still consider the binary constraints of digital systems to be somewhat detached and different from the rules that govern the real world. Nevertheless, this viewpoint is in fact grossly misleading. Binary-based systems are also prevalent in the natural world, with their underlying characteristics often being concealed by many layers of complex diversity. At elevated levels of abstraction, such binary schemes can appear in more subtle ways. Consider a system, any system, which exists in an arbitrary steady state. This could be a galaxy, a chemical compound, a moving object, or a procedure for processing tax returns—the choice is yours. In such circumstances the known laws of the Universe dictate that it will continue to behave in exactly the same way forever, unless something eventually causes it to change. Not surprisingly, there are only two possible types of source for this impetus: Either instability inside the system increases to such a point where its condition changes spontaneously, or some external influence has a direct impact and so induces involuntary change. Combinations of both merely mask the fact that ultimately a two-type mechanism is responsible for tipping the system into the change process.

Even in such potentially unpredictable circumstances, there are further binary patterns at work. If one were to study the condition of a system sufficiently in anticipation of change, it would be theoretically possible to guess with some degree of certainty the resultant states that would ensue as a consequence of those change factors that it encompasses and those that encompass it. Yet again such results can be categorized as being either "expected" or "unexpected," falling into another two-state categorization scheme. More complex scenarios can be seen purely as combinations of this. Oversimplification maybe, but, given the fundamental elegance of such models, it is not surprising that a number of branches of traditional science are experiencing a growth toward their use to describe natural dynamics such as speciation—the study of why a single species splits in two—and the mathematics indicates that far from being a surprising phenomenon, it would be very odd if behavior like speciation didn't occur in systems of any real complexity. It appears to be a result of exactly the same process that filled the Universe with matter and that created subatomic particles, planets, and ultimately humans. Strange as it may seem, neutrons, butterflies, electrons, and elephants in some way owe their diverse characteristics to a principle that dictates much of what happens in the physical world. This principle is known to scientists and mathematicians alike as "symmetry-breaking," or "bifurcation" in some special cases, with similar phenomena happening naturally all over the place [2].

Symmetry is a regularly used term, often interpreted to mean "balance" or perhaps "harmony," or sometimes even "beauty." A mathematician or physicist sees the same attributes in symmetry, but defines the idea this way: "Something has symmetry if one or more of its properties remain unchanged when some other property is changed" [79]. A group of 10 identical objects possesses symmetry—line them up and it's impossible to know if any or all of them have switched position in the line. But if the line were composed of five objects that had one shape followed by five that had another, some of the symmetry is broken by observable variation. Swapping numbers five and six, for instance, would produce an obvious change. From this point of view, the definition of a species is simply that it is symmetric and speciation is then just a form of symmetry-breaking. With this in mind, mathematicians and physicists can apply their existing theories of symmetry-breaking. These describe how, why, and when symmetries will typically break up into subgroups—species in this case [2].

But what has symmetry-breaking got to do with the Web? Quite simply it demonstrates that binary mechanics are fundamental to a huge range of systems, not just those seen to be classically discrete like modern-day computer applications. Where once only the smooth and slippy features of evolving life were obvious, now scientists are beginning to realize that higher orders of Boolean classification are at play. This is especially true in systems that dynamically change over time, as is the case with both the advancement of the Web and the evolution of all living things.

The phenomenon of symmetry-breaking was first discovered in 1923 by Sir Geoffrey Ingram Taylor[4] when he investigated an aspect of fluid dynamics known as hydrodynamic "symmetry paradox." Since then, work in this area has concluded that, generally, when a system overly encounters stress, it loses symmetry [63]. If one were to heat a flat dish of oil uniformly from below, for example, at a certain critical temperature, its surface's uniformity is broken by the onset of a complex pattern of convection cells. These are typically hexagonal, with a few pentagons thrown in, and all much the same size—a phenomenon referred to as Rayleigh–Bénard convection [19]. So the overall symmetry breaks down. Add more heat and further systems of patterns appear until the oil's surface eventually descends into a chaotic frenzy of complex change.

---

[4]Sir Geoffrey Ingram Taylor was a physicist, mathematician, and expert on fluid dynamics and wave theory. He has been described as "one of the greatest physical scientists of the twentieth century" [104].

Bifurcation is a particular form of symmetry-breaking in which both possible outcomes of the breaking are represented. It is therefore analogous to situations where a particular entity or process splits or forks in two, as opposed to merely diverting off via one of the two possible available routes. This is a characteristic that plays a key role in how complex systems get organized. In early cosmic evolution, for instance, it was the phenomenon responsible for the virtual lack of antimatter in our Universe. As such, it has an intrinsic place at the table of dynamic systems such as the evolution of life and the advancement of the Web. Together with complexity, nonlinearity, fractals, and power laws,[5] bifurcation plays an essential part in the understanding of how a whole organism grows from a single cell into a multicellular life form.

Over longer periods of time, the mathematical picture of bifurcating systems highlights at least three "universal" phenomena: The first is that when a system first bifurcates, as in speciation, it usually splits into precisely two distinguishable types, thus following Boolean principles. To see three or more is a rare, mainly transitory phenomenon. The second is that the split occurs very rapidly, much faster than the usual rate of noticeable changes in characteristics. So, in birds, a significant change in beak length might happen within a few generations of a species, for instance, rather than by tiny increments over many generations. The third phenomenon is that the two new types or species will evolve in opposite directions: If one evolves larger beaks, the other will evolve smaller ones. And these evolutionary rules point to an interesting difference between the embodiment of natural, real-world systems and virtual architectures like those commonly found in mainstream digital systems like the Web. Whenever natural systems have successfully appeared and proved sustainable, both their purpose and the associated "hardware"—flesh, bones, and so on—needed to support them have seamlessly combined into one unit. That's why wings generally fly, mouths eat, and specific sections of the brains only process language: a specific tool for a specific job. You would not, for example, therefore expect a wing to be capable of flight and diagnosing color blindness, yet this is the heritage of our modern computerized world.

SYMMETRY IN SYSTEMS

There are some things common to almost all systems which are overly familiar almost to the point where they are routinely overlooked. In truth at least one of these aspects is so profoundly important that the fact that we take it for granted is profound in itself. And the property in question is, of course, continuity—or "symmetry," to be more scientifically precise. But why should we be concerned with symmetry in systems?

"In the first place, symmetry is fascinating to the human mind, and everyone likes objects or patterns that are in some way symmetrical. It is therefore interesting

---

[5]A power law relationship between two scalar quantities x and y is any such that the relationship can be written as $y = ax^i$ where a (the constant of proportionality) and k (the exponent of the power law) are constants.

that both natural and man-made systems often exhibit certain kinds of symmetry in the objects and conditions we find around us. Perhaps the most symmetrical object imaginable is a sphere, and nature is full of spheres—stars, planets, water droplets in clouds, and so on. The crystals found in rocks also exhibit many different kinds of symmetry, the study of which tells us some important things about the structure of solids. Even the animal and vegetable worlds show some degree of symmetry, although the symmetry of a flower or a bee is not as perfect or as fundamental as is that of a crystal [59]."

But the main concern here is not with the fact that the objects of nature are often symmetrical. Rather, it relates to the even more remarkable symmetries of a given problem space like the entire Universe, or the Web itself. There is a need to focus on the symmetries that exist in the basic laws themselves which govern the very manifestation of the systems in which they occur. This raises the question, How can a physical or abstract law be symmetrical?

The problem of defining symmetry in systems is an interesting one. One explanation came from Hermann Weyl,[6] the substance of which is that "a thing is symmetrical if there is something that we can do to it so that after we have done it, it looks the same as it did before." "So, for example, a symmetrical vase is of such a kind that if we reflect or turn it, it will look the same as it did before" [59]. Further definitions can also be found in the broad field of natural science, pointing to "symmetry as immunity to a possible change" [63], meaning invariance to change or transformation. In such ways the concept of breaking such symmetries therefore covers both types of change possible on an object or system—namely singular change, as in divergence or branching, and multiplicity of change as in bifurcating or "splitting" phenomena.

But again, what has this got to do with systems like the Web? Many would argue that the Web is an amorphous blob without any form, so how can it be considered to be symmetrical in any way? The answer to this is really twofold. First, the Web is known to exhibit structure at just about every level, some of which is certainly symmetrical but is not immediately apparent. Second, it is not the notion of "physical sameness" that is the important characteristic of symmetry in computer systems; rather, it is the fact that it is an observable facet of continuity. It tells us when things are the same, regardless of whatever interactions systems take part in or whatever variables they transform. If symmetry is preserved, then quite literally nothing detectable has changed in a system, and without change it is impossible to distinguish either the system from its environment or the various parts that make up its whole. It is as if the system or its parts do not exist.

Without symmetry-breaking, things are quite literally unobservable and so invisible to everything around them. For such reasons, symmetry-breaking is prolifically apparent everywhere in the world of computing, being found beneath almost all

---

[6]Hermann Weyl was a German mathematician who published technical and some general works on space, time, matter, philosophy, logic, symmetry, and the history of mathematics. He was one of the first to conceive of combining general relativity with the laws of electromagnetism. While no mathematician of his generation aspired to the "universalism" of Henri Poincaré or Hilbert, Weyl came as close as anyone [105].

data and programming structures [63]. For example, programmed loops are spiral time symmetries as are self-referencing hyperlink chains. Simple conditionals can be viewed as symmetry breaking. Argument defaulting is a form of overloading[7] where the symmetry is the preservation of some argument types. Furthermore, information and software patterns are also created as a result of symmetry-breaking in all of these cases [63].

The truth is clear: All systems are full of symmetry, and meaningful change cannot take place without that symmetry being broken. So at a most fundamental level the Web again shares a core property common to the natural world.

---

[7]The idea in computer programming of allowing the same definitions to be used with different types of data (specifically, different classes of objects), resulting in more general and abstract implementations.

CHAPTER 4

Natural Structures for Man-Made Machines—Curvature in Information and Computation

If, in some cataclysm, all scientific knowledge were to be destroyed, and only one sentence passed on to the next generation of creatures, what statement would contain the most information in the fewest words? I believe it is the atomic hypothesis (or atomic fact, or whatever you wish to call it) that all things are made of atoms—little particles that move around in perpetual motion, attracting each other when they are a little distance apart, but repelling upon being squeezed into one another. In that one sentence you will see an enormous amount of information about the world, if just a little imagination and thinking are applied.

—Richard Feynman

ENGINEERING PROBLEMS

Traditionally in Information Technology, hardware and software have not developed in tandem. Hardware manufacturers most often design their products to be as multipurpose as possible, whereas Software Engineers, on the other hand, typically reside at the opposite end of the spectrum, striving to make their solutions as specific and exact as they can. So, a long-standing compromise has grudgingly been accepted by all concerned. Square pegs shall fit into round holes as long as they are big and smooth enough! This, of course, has never been the way in the natural world, evolution has seen to that. We are in the business of engineering; not the same thing, or is it?

To investigate this disparity further, it is again necessary to strip back the concepts involved and look at the fundamental axioms entailed. "These are facts or assumptions that we take as self-evident and hence feel no need to try and prove from simpler principles" [88]. From these, simple models can be constructed that allow objective comparisons between the measurable realities of the natural world and the supposedly unnatural concepts of virtual phenomena like Web Life.

ARROWS EVERYWHERE—GRAPH THEORY AND FEYNMAN-LIKE DIAGRAMS

So what physical contortions might the wires, gates, and circuits of modern computer systems resemble if they conformed to the expectations of natural evolution rather than the designs of precision engineering? To help with this problem, conceptual graphs, similar to Feynman diagrams[1] found in quantum mechanics, can fortunately be used as a means of expressing the fundamental concepts and patterns concerned. Such graphs are not, however, those found in the two- and three-dimensional coordinate geometry taught in school. In such graphs, points are generally linked on a rectangular coordinate system to show the relationship between two variables, typically denoted as x (abscissa) and y (ordinate). Such graphs are more correctly referred to as Cartesian Graphs[2] and are not the type we shall be discussing here. Instead a more generalised form of graph will be adopted in which the concepts of abscissa and ordinate are dispensed with. This frees the notions of 'location' and 'association' in an abstract graph space.

Such graphs are typically used to show how particular, or possible, aspects of a system relate or change, capturing interconnections or transitions[3] between a system's individual elements or states in a graphical form.[4] Several variations of these diagrams exist (Figures 4.1 and 4.2). In one valid form the steady state of any system can be drawn as a line or arrow, generally referred to as an arc, edge, or vector, between two points or nodes, often drawn as circles if at all. Alternative representations can choose to use the reverse convention, using nodes to represent steady states or elements and lines to represent transitions or relationships between them. Lines can thereby represent a "step" [59] in the characteristic(s) of the underlying area being studied. In their sparsest forms, like Feynman's schematics, such diagrams describe the interaction between two facets of a system as a quantified outline of their interaction.

Graphs using lines between nodes imply that the transitions involved are not directional and hence can be reversed within a given model. Graphs containing arrows instead of lines imply explicit directionality. At the start of any such an arrow, the point at which a system last became stable is hence represented, and at its tip the point at which the system ultimately changes condition is also shown. Systems undergoing spontaneous or self-generated broken symmetry through bifurcation can therefore be described using the graph shown in Figure 4.3, with transformation

---

[1]Also (rarely) referred to as Stückelberg diagrams or (for a subset of special cases) penguin diagrams.

[2]The modern Cartesian coordinate system in two dimensions (also called a rectangular coordinate system) is commonly defined by two axes, at right angles to each other, forming a plane (an xy-plane). The horizontal axis is labeled x, and the vertical axis is labeled y. In a three-dimensional coordinate system, another axis, normally labeled z, is added, providing a sense of a third dimension of space measurement. The axes are commonly defined as mutually perpendicular to each other (each at a right angle to the other). (Early systems allowed "oblique" axes—that is, axes that did not meet at right angles.) All the points in a Cartesian coordinate system taken together form a so-called Cartesian plane [106].

[3]For all intents and purposes, "transitions" can also be viewed as a trajectory as in Feynman's original thinking.

[4]More formally referred to as a grammar.

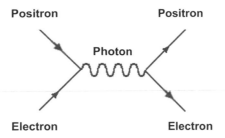

Figure 4.1. A typical Feynman diagram.

into all possible states—namely expected or unexpected outcomes—being shown as two further arrows. In such graphs the steady-state duration of any arrow is of little concern and may, for our purposes, be considered as trivial.

Induced bifurcation obviously needs one further arrow to represent the external impetus providing the root cause of change—as shown in Figure 4.4. This can be considered as an extension to the above Y-shaped pattern, thereby creating a more encompassing graph. This is capable of describing both spontaneous and induced bifurcation via the inclusion of an optional fourth leg: Basic relationship patterns can hence be shown in this way, but it is important to understand that these are mostly less exciting than the higher levels of structure they can be used to construct. These include more familiar constructs like sequences, clusters, hierarchies, and ontologies.

At this point it is important to mention two further properties of bifurcation as typically represented using graphs. First, bifurcation is traditionally considered to represent a fork or splitting structure in a system, but this is not necessarily always the case. What if one or both of the resultant outcomes of bifurcation were eminently untenable? That is to say that bifurcation was indeed valid, but its life expectancy was essentially zero for whatever reason. In such circumstances the above pattern can also be seen to cover a further type of characteristic common in systems. This is the concept of generalized change or deviation, including the ultimate termination, or halting, of any given system. Second, it should be understood that graphs merely provide a mechanism for representing relationships between things. In the above examples, arrows are used to show the association between contiguous states of a given system over time, but that is not necessarily their only use. Graphs can also be used to describe associations that are spatially dependent as well. They could, for

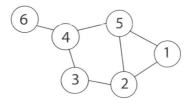

Figure 4.2. A typical graph with six vertices or nodes and seven edges.

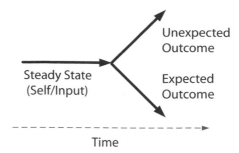

Figure 4.3. A state-based axiomatic directed graph showing spontaneous bifurcation.

instance, quite legitimately be used to model this sentence, replacing the spaces with edges and the words with nodes in a given graph. This thereby signifies that all the information contained combines together into a literal sequence of value to the reader. It is a fact that graphs, and graph theory specifically, describes relationship that is important. That they can be applied to describe both temporal and spatial relationships is essential when looking for common patterns across both real-world and virtual systems such as the Web.

RELAYS AND SWITCHES BY ANY OTHER NAME

None of the above discussions should come as a surprise to those familiar with the basics of computer architecture. The X- and Y-shaped patterns presented in Figures 4.3 and 4.4 may have been introduced on the premise of behaviors like a single species of animal splitting in two, but closer scrutiny should also reveal that they describe two of the most basic components in all digital computer systems, namely switches and relays. This range of observed occurrence may appear broad to the point of being mistaken and irrelevant, but, in truth, the underlying patterns at work are ultimately the same.

This is a blunt, yet overwhelmingly powerful, assertion. A relay is nothing more than a special type of switch that opens and closes under control of another circuit.

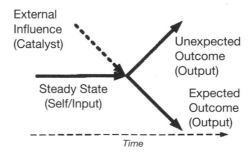

Figure 4.4. A state-based axiomatic directed graph showing induced bifurcation.

It is therefore one of the most important components types in just about all digital systems. In fact the processing units of all digital computers are, in essence, nothing more than vast banks of relays and simple switches, digital circuits that allow logic, and arithmetic to take place using binary encoded information and instructions.

In 1937 Claude Shannon produced his now famous MIT[5] Masters thesis that showed how relays could be arranged to form units called logic gates, thereby implementing simple Boolean operations, a work for which he has been called "the father of information theory." This concept, of utilizing the properties of electrical switches to do logic, is the basic concept that underlies all electronic digital computers, and Shannon's thesis became the foundation of practical digital circuit design when it became widely known among the electrical engineering community during and after World War II. However, standard electronic relays were too slow and unreliable a medium to make practicable the construction of large-scale general-purpose digital computers. So it was the development of high-speed digital techniques using vacuum tubes that made the modern computer possible. These were then later superseded by the invention of the transistor in 1947. Transistorized computers are hence normally referred to as "Second Generation" and dominated the late 1950s and early 1960s. By using transistors and printed circuits, a significant decrease in size and power consumption was achieved, along with an increase in reliability. The high-speed computers we see today are hence "Third-Generation" machines being based on integrated circuit technology. This is a form of electronics that allows many millions of transistors to be compacted into extremely small components, or microchips, using materials like silicon or gallium arsenide.

So the most basic elements and patterns at play in our modern-day digital computers are also prevalent across the natural world as well. Whether in the tiniest detail of the world smallest microprocessor, or in the lofty diversification of an entire species, underlying "X-" and "Y-"shaped patterns can be found. But this is not rocket science, because all the aforementioned patterns are simply a direct consequence of change. And without change the various features of any system would not be apparent, rendering them invisible and, for all intents and purposes, nonexistent. To put it simply, without the basic patterns of deviation such as switching, our Universe would not be here at all. This makes the contrived forks and branches of computer systems appear not so unnatural after all—yet another similarity providing evidence in favor of Web Life. But this is not the end of the similarities, by a long shot. Likenesses involving collections of these basics are plentiful also.

DIFFERENTIATION THROUGH DIVERGENCE

Everyone knows that relationships can take many forms, but it is less obvious that all relationships must obey one inescapable rule—specifically that anything partaking in a relationship has to form part of a wider collection of at least two, not necessarily distinct, things that differ in at least one way, be that via characteristic or state. For example, an otter can have a relationship with a fish because one may consume the

---

[5]Massachusetts Institute of Technology.

other. Similarly, both fish and otter could, conceivably, consume themselves and thus change their state from "whole" to "part" or even "living" to "dead." Furthermore, collections of elements connected by some relationship only come in two basic types, mathematical sets and sequences. In sets the order of constituent elements is unimportant, while order is paramount in sequences. Sets are therefore the most encompassing type of collection, because sequences can also be viewed as a special type of set—a "well ordered" set[6] to be mathematically precise [71].

Remembering the mathematical complexity of the Web and the four basic ingredients of computation, it is essential to connect the notion of aggregation with that of the relationships between the various elements involved. This is because only through the process of aggregation can complexity be cultivated, relying primarily on the effect of compounded relationships as its feedstock. Furthermore, from the perspective of life, the idea of complex sequences of association, in particular, is vital, providing the capability to define elegant and extremely powerful forms of rule.

Mathematically, sequences are ordered aggregates based on a particular and continual type of progression. These progressions are often complex, and under rare but not statistically implausible circumstances, systems incorporating such types of complexity can spontaneously form in self-organizing ways. Thus, given the right conditions, credible macro-level processes of evolution can take hold.

But this is a grossly superficial statement, so what reasoning might be proposed to associate sequential representations, discrete digital systems like the Web, and the notion of life itself?

It is no secret that significant portions of both the natural and digital world rely heavily on the notion of sequential association. Time is sequential, for example, with each consecutive second following its predecessor in a well-understood fashion. In a similar manner, traffic lights change, apples fall to Earth, and the threads of a computer program hang together. Furthermore, "take a well-defined sequence of operations and the concept frequently referred to as an algorithm is formed" [43]. But these are just examples. To address the real issues at hand, once again we must expose the underlying mechanics involved.

When thinking of the syntactical composition, or grammar, of any arbitrary "string" of information, the normal representation called upon involves a straight-line directed graph like the one in Figure 4.5. This shows a chain of ordered elements, one after another. Unfortunately, however, this depiction is somewhat deceptive, because sequences do not always follow a straight course.

For a sequence to form, there are basically only two requirements; first, that one or more elements are present and, second, that these elements are arranged in some particular order. This may initially appear straightforward, but there is a catch. For elements to exist in the first place, they "must be distinguishable from one another, be 'different' in some way by either variation or modification" [44]. Mathematically, this difference[7] is brought about by the breaking of at least

---

[6]Well-ordered sets are those in which all elements are arranged in definable order and have a recognizable first element of that order. Mathematically, this means that such sets have both cardinal and ordinal qualities.

[7]A single transition or trajectory from all the possible transitions available.

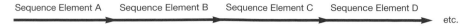

Sequence Element A   Sequence Element B   Sequence Element C   Sequence Element D

etc.

Figure 4.5. A directed graph incorrectly showing a pseudo-physical representation of a sequence of basic elements.

one symmetry across a similar characteristic found in the elements. Such symmetry-breaking creates noticeable boundaries within a sequence, allowing ordered relationships to form. Simply put, element difference plays a key role in the very notion of sequence—an obvious yet extremely important property across all systems' theory as will be shown shortly. When we add the capability to switch between different ordering schemes, the potential to compose extremely complex and elaborate systems of rules, processes, and information is formed, a fact that should be overly familiar to all those used to chasing information on the Web.

This essential notion of inter-elemental differentiation, or invariance, is often overlooked when thinking of sequences, but it is nevertheless always present. The arrowheads in Figure 4.5 perform such a task for instance, but these are merely graphical shorthand added for convenience and are of little real use when considering anything other than hypothetical ideas. Such breakpoints can be represented using a myriad of other forms, and in real-world systems they result in a countless number of noticeable characteristics across a myriad of properties. Physical structure and shape, weight, texture, color, electrical potential, and so on, are all a result of aggregated elemental differentiation. Without such differentiations, no evidence of progressive change would ever be apparent and two neighboring elements in such change might as well be considered as being one continual same. Again they would simply be unobservable to the point of nonexistence. To avoid invisibility, it is important that a means of differentiation is present; that symmetry is broken in other words. How this differentiation is actually manifested is a secondary consideration, important for other reasons.

But why labor on the notion of sequence and especially on its importance in natural complexity? The answer ultimately lies in the basic requirements for such a concept. Think of the bare essentials of a sequence again and remember that they simply equate to a list of objects, events, or concepts, arranged in some orderly, well-defined fashion. Simple sequences therefore provide examples of a consistent, single-attribute, single rule imposed uniformly across a set of more than one member. This one-dimensional linearity further provides a path between extreme regularity and extreme complexity because each successive element in a sequence must be absolutely as expected across at least one universal feature. This thereby creates at least one predictable attribute of the whole through many smaller asymmetries of its parts. It may appear surreal, but it is this regularity of asymmetries that is key, often creating new levels of symmetry from lower levels of breakage. Sequences hence depict regularly divergent themes, chains of expected asymmetric progressions leading to higher orders of organization, no matter how complex they may be.

RELATIONSHIPS AND TWISTING SEQUENCES

Now we will refocus on the basic structures produced by symmetry-breaking, again using graphs. This time, to simplify representation, let's remove the arrowheads and create a scenario where external influences are not needed to instigate change. Let's also insist that all cases of change are as expected. By doing this, two of the legs in the "X"-shaped graph introduced in Figure 4.4 become redundant—namely those needed for induced symmetry-breaking and unexpected outcomes. In this way the observable transition between subsequent sequential elements can be shown as one line veering away from the other along a straight tangential trajectory. This produces a much less contrived differentiation pattern, with the angle of the tangent between the two lines marking change boundaries and hence outlining the break in symmetry present.

Using this graphing technique produces a characteristic "kink" or "bend" between neighboring edges, or associations (Figure 4.6). And when more and more edges are added, this pattern ultimately forces the sequence's structure to twist round a curved path. This has a profound effect because, in essence, it makes it equally relevant to think of sequences as being curved rather than straight.

This now allows a number of provocative similarities of form to be studied. The reduction-intensive worlds of mathematics and computer science might love straight lines, for instance, but the natural world also has inbuilt preference for all that is curved as well. Now that the notion of sequence can be used to assimilate both, in specific contexts, the links between computation and natural phenomena such as life can be shown to be much closer than one might at first expect.

GROWTH SPIRALS, FIBONACCI PROGRESSIONS, AND OTHER SEQUENTIAL PATTERNS

In collections where rule dictates not only the position of elements within a group, but also the size of those elements, highly regular spiraling structures are often produced. Not surprisingly, because of their grand simplicity, such schemes are popular in the nature world and, also being fractal, have a direct link with many higher orders of complex phenomena. In particular, one such arrangement, known as a Fibonacci sequence, appears to play an interesting, if not crucial, part in the way that

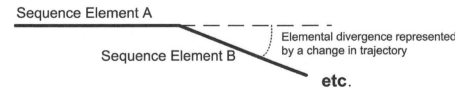

Figure 4.6. Element-to-element change in a sequence, producing a characteristic "kink" or "bend."

certain parts of the physical world hang together. This comprises a series of natural numbers corresponding to a particular ratio between successive elements and has fascinated many generations and cultures. Its corresponding mathematical equation can be shown as

The Fibonacci Sequence Formula

$$F(n) = \begin{cases} 0, & \text{if } n = 0 \\ 1, & \text{if } n = 1 \\ F(n-1) + F(n+2) & \text{if } n > 1 \end{cases} \tag{4.1}$$

In other words, starting with 0 and then 1, the next Fibonacci number is produced by adding the two previous Fibonacci numbers together. The first Fibonacci numbers for $n = 0, 1, \ldots$ are hence $\{0, 1, 1, 2, 3, 5, 8, 13, 21, 34, 55, 89, 144, 233, 377, 610, 987, 1597, 2584, 4181, 6765, 10946, \ldots\}$.

This sequence was first described by the Indian mathematicians Gopala and Hemachandra in 1150, who were investigating the possible ways of exactly packing items of length 1 and 2 into containers. In the West it was first studied by Leonardo of Pisa, also known as Fibonacci, to describe the growth of an idealized population of rabbits. So the progression also describes the number of pairs in the rabbit population after n months if it is assumed that:

- In the first month there is just one newborn pair.
- New-born pairs become fertile from their second month on.
- Each month every fertile pair begets a new pair.
- The rabbits never die.

Suppose that in month n we have a pairs of fertile and newborn rabbits and in month $n + 1$ we have b pairs. In month $n + 2$ we will consequently have $a + b$ pairs because all a pairs of rabbits from month n will be fertile and produce a pairs of offspring, while the newborn rabbits in b will not be fertile and will not produce offspring.

The term *Fibonacci sequence* is also applied generally to characterize any function g where $g(n + 2) = g(n) + g(n + 1)$. Such functions are more precisely those of the form $g(n) = aF(n) + bF(n + 1)$ for some numbers a and b so the Fibonacci sequences form a vector space with the functions $F(n)$ and $F(n + 1)$ as its basis.

Of particular interest, the Fibonacci sequence L with $L(1) = 1$ and $L(2) = 3$ is referred to as the Lucas numbers. This sequence was described by Leonhard Euler in 1748. The significance of the Lucas numbers $L(n)$ lies in the fact that they have the equivalence of raising ϕ to the nth power, where ϕ is an interesting irrational constant commonly referred to as "the golden ratio."

Phi' (ϕ), as a Mathematical Formula

$$\phi = \left(\frac{1}{2}(1 + \sqrt{5}) \right) = \frac{1}{2}(L(n) + F(n)\sqrt{5}) \tag{4.2}$$

Phi (ϕ) is approximately "1.618034 . . ." and was named after Phidia the Greek sculptor [45] by the mathematician Mark Barr. It was later christened the "golden" mean ratio or the "divine proportion" by Western culture. Consequently, two quantities are said to be in the golden ratio if the whole is to the larger as the larger is to the smaller (Figure 4.7).

Shapes and patterns defined by the golden ratio have long been considered aesthetically pleasing in the West, reflecting nature's balance between symmetry and asymmetry and the ancient Pythagorean belief that reality is a numerical reality, except that numbers were not units as we define them today, but were expressions of ratios. The golden ratio is still used frequently in art and design. Not only is it an essential ingredient to many naturally occurring formations, but it is key to many fractal spiral structures and is itself a fractal, as can be seen when it is written in the form of a continued fraction. From the bone structure of human beings to the seed pattern of a sunflower and the familiar spiral of a snail's shell, the Phi proportion is there, underlying the progressive dimensions demonstrated (Figure 4.8). Plato went so far as to call the Phi ratio the "key to the physics of the cosmos."

Series corresponding to progressions like the Fibonacci sequence can easily be shown as a spiralling graph. This group also contains a number of other spiraling geometries closely related to natural phenomena and in particular growth cycles. The logarithmic or "growth" spiral, for example, is a spiral whose polar equation is given by Eq. (4.3):

A Growth Spiral's Polar Equation

$$r = ae^{b\theta} \tag{4.3}$$

Here r is the distance from the origin, e is the angle from the x-axis, and a and b are arbitrary constants. The logarithmic spiral is also known as the equiangular spiral and the spira mirabilis. It can be expressed parametrically as in Eq (4.4).

Parametric Equations for Logarithmic Spirals

$$r = \cos \theta = a \cos \theta e^{b\theta}$$
$$r = \sin \theta = a \sin \theta e^{b\theta} \tag{4.4}$$

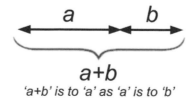

Figure 4.7. The golden ratio represented as a line divided into two segments a and b, such that the entire line is to the longer a segment as the 'a' segment is to the shorter 'b' segment.

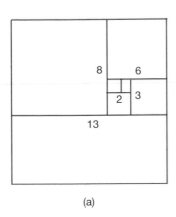
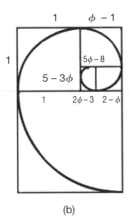

(a)   (b)

Figure 4.8. A tiling with Fibonacci number-sized squares that can be used as a closely approximated framework for a "golden" or spiral (seen in part b).

The logarithmic spiral can be constructed from equally spaced rays by starting at a point along one ray, and drawing the perpendicular to a neighboring ray. As the number of rays approaches infinity, the sequence of segments approaches a smooth logarithmic spiral (Figure 4.9).

Such spiral structures were first studied by René Descartes[8] in 1638 and later by Jakob Bernoulli,[9] Bernoulli was so fascinated by the spiral that he had one engraved on his tombstone—although the engraver did not draw it true to form—together with the words "eadem mutata resurgo" ("I shall arise the same though changed").

Logarithmic spirals are symmetrical in that they are self-congruent under all similarity transformations—scaling them gives the same result as rotating them. Scaling by a factor for 2π, for example, gives the same as the original, without rotation. They are also congruent to their own involutes, evolutes, and the pedal curves based on their centers.[10]

We see logarithmic spirals every day, from the natural growth curves of plants and seashells to the optimal curve for highway turns. Peer into a flower or look down at a cactus and you will see a pattern of logarithmic spirals criss-crossing each other. This elegant spiral pattern is called phyllotaxis, and it has mathematics as simplistically beautiful as its given name [26].

---

[8]René Descartes, also known as Cartesius, was a French philosopher, mathematician, and part-time mercenary. He is noted equally for his groundbreaking work in philosophy and mathematics. As the inventor of the Cartesian coordinate system, he formulated the basis of modern geometry (analytic geometry), which in turn influenced the development of modern calculus [107].

[9]Jakob Bernoulli, also known as Jacob, Jacques or James Bernoulli was a Swiss mathematician and scientist. His masterwork was Ars Conjectandi (the Art of Conjecturing), a groundbreaking work on probability theory. It was published eight years after his death in 1713 by his nephew Nicholas. The terms Bernoulli trial and Bernoulli numbers result from this work and are named after him [108].

[10]For more information see references listed at http://mathworld.wolfram.com/LogarithmicSpiral.html.

Figure 4.9. Various ray configurations leading toward a smooth spiral.

One reason why the logarithmic spiral appears in nature is that it is the result of very simple growth programs that can often be depicted as follows:

- grow 1 unit, bend 1 unit , followed by . . .
- grow 2 units, bend 1 unit , followed by . . .
- grow 3 units, bend 1 unit , and so on . . .

Any process that turns or twists at a constant rate but grows or moves with constant acceleration will generate a logarithmic spiral [26].

But why this emphasis on spirals in nature, and what has this got to do with the Web? There really is no hidden motive here. The point is merely to demonstrate that sequential structures are just as prolific in natural systems as they are in those made by humans. A sublimely obvious fact beyond any doubt, but it is commonly misunderstood that all of these natural systems are computationally just like the Web. They take in matter—which inherently contains information—as well as energy and transform it for their own purposes. And just as on the Web, where certain chains of hyperlinks have been designed to convey extremely specific concepts, so it is the way in the natural world. All species grow and mature in highly specific ways as the very name suggests. Furthermore, their growth processes involve biological instructions which themselves employ specific types of sequence.

There are certain types of physical sequence that are more suited to growth tasks than others. These are sequences that can achieve the maximum amount of effect with the minimum amount of effort. In essence, they are "tuned" for the task in hand, compressing the maximum amount of capability into the minimum amount of material. That's why ratios like Phi are so important, being an essential part of the geometry of such highly tuned formations. They are quite literally key to natural reduction processes.

L-SYSTEMS

Remaining with the notion of growth systems and comparisons with man-made look-alikes, an equally similar cellular automata program will generate phyllotaxis—arrangements like the leaves on a plant's stem—as well as a number of other natural-looking structures based on ratio-based sequences. Such automata fall under the general heading of L-systems and are particularly good at describing fractal structures that need to be "grown," like plants.

L-systems were invented in 1968 by the biologist Aristid Lindenmayer as a formal way of yielding a mathematical description of plant growth. They are remarkably algorithmically compact, which is especially impressive when one considers the infinite fractal detail they can describe [24].

Since L-systems describe growth, they comprise a special "seed" cell and a description of how new cells can be generated from a previous iteration, or "generation," of cells. As one might expect, the nomenclature of L-systems leans toward mathematical vocabulary, so the seed cell is actually referred to as an axiom and, for a particular L-system, all growth starts from the same axiom. The descriptions of how to grow new cells from old are known as production rules. For example:

$$\text{Axiom:} \qquad B$$

$$\text{Production Rules:} \quad B \rightarrow F[-B] + B$$
$$F \rightarrow FF$$

There is no need to worry about what the symbols mean, since the main concern is only how to "grow" things with an L-system. The rules in such systems specify a simple rewriting scheme that involves taking the axiom and substituting as many of the symbols as possible. After performing the substitution on the axiom, another set of symbols is produced and the same substitution regime can be applied on these and so on (Table 4.1).

The length of the resultant string hence grows dramatically at each step. But what does the string represent? By itself, the string means absolutely nothing, but in the context of a device that can interpret each symbol as a simple instruction, the string represents the blueprint for a fractal structure. For example, one such interpreting device can be found in the cellular machinery of plants and animals. In algae and most multicelled organisms it is known that individual cells can specialize in how they reproduce. Therefore Figure 4.10 shows how a hypothetical algae strain might grow, as specified by the production rules outlined above, and nicely illustrates that simplistic computer technologies can very easily be used to simulate growth patterns prevalent in the natural world.

Initially the algae starts with a single B cell. At some point in the future this would reproduce as specified by the $B \rightarrow F[-B] + B$ rule. Next the resulting B cells and the single F cell could each divide again—producing the third generation—but notice that the F cell reproduces according to the $F \rightarrow FF$ rule.

In such a way it is easy to see that cell specialization combined with growth rules specific to each cell type can result in some interesting and amazingly natural

Table 4.1. Resulting L-System Structures

Depth	Resulting Structure
0	B
1	$F[-B] + B$
2	$FF[-F[-B]] + F[-B] + B$
3	$FFFF[-FF[-F[-B] + B] + F[-B] + B] + FF[-F[-B] + B] + F[-B] + B$

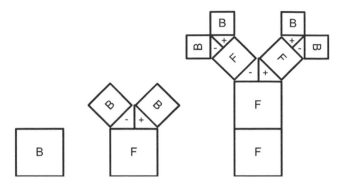

Figure 4.10. Resulting L-system structures (graphical).

growth patterns. It is also easy to see how larger computational systems like the Web can both easily incorporate growth-like algorithms and be subject to growth-like development processes.

INFORMATION COMPRESSION AND MAXIMIZATION IN BIOLOGICAL SYSTEMS

As Johannes Kepler[11] once said "Nature uses as little as possible of anything" and in such respects it is lazy, very lazy. It's a fact of life, quite literally. From a survival standpoint, evolutionary waste of any kind sooner or later points toward demise and is ultimately the reason why Phi, Fibonacci-like spiral structures and all forms of fractal are prevalent in nature. All contribute to mechanisms through which maximum effect and minimum waste can be achieved from minimum input. Phi, for example, appears often in the structural dimensions of plants, and Fibonacci progressions appear in the spirals of seed heads, leaf arrangements, and petal distributions, all being circumstances where information compression and reuse are vital to maintain the overall efficiency of their parent organism. Just as in modern relational database technologies where designers strive to drive out redundancy of information via a process known as "normalization," so too nature uses mechanisms like Fibonacci for the same purpose.

Nevertheless, for the sake of completeness, it is worth mentioning that these naturally efficient frameworks, although prevalent in certain kinds of natural systems, are not inherent across all physical systems known to spin, spiral, or twist. However, even across such a broad range of phenomena, there are still a number of generalized underlying themes that relate to a variety of regular progressions between elements. Fibonacci spirals are just one type of logarithmic spiral, for example, and in such spirals the space between consecutive elements grows exponentially at a fixed

[11]Johannes Kepler, a key figure in the scientific revolution, was a German astronomer, mathematician, and astrologer. He is best known for his laws of planetary motion, expounded in the two books *Astronomia Nova* and *Harmonices Mundi* [109].

positive rate. The spirals of galaxies follow another scheme, but again the pattern is based on some sequential rule of progression.

As Ron Knott, former lecturer in Mathematics and Computing Science at Surrey University, points out [25], Phi is nevertheless known to play an important and specific role in systems designed to arrange objects with maximum spatial efficiency. The problem of optimally arranging a collection of similarly shaped objects into any particular confined space usually depends upon the shape of the objects in question. Square objects, for example, arrange most closely in a square array, whereas round objects organize better in a hexagonal arrangement. So why doesn't nature favor these schemes? Seeds are often circular in cross section, again for the purpose of energy conservation during growth, so why don't we see hexagonal arrangements on seed heads?

Although hexagonal symmetry may well be the most efficient layout for circular seeds, it doesn't provide an effective solution to the problem of how to position leaves around the stem of a plant or how to pack flower heads on the same organism. What nature seems to do is to try and use the same pattern across as many of the structural schemes of the whole organism and its parts as possible, thereby minimizing the amount of information needed in an overriding scheme for growth. It hence opts for compromise schemes that provide best fit across all the physical attributes requiring representation during development cycles, simplifying design rules and extracting as many features as possible from the same, reoccurring set of instructions. Nature is minimalist by necessity, selecting arrangements and structures that maintain their efficiency as an organism continues to grow—a tall order for a single process, but one that nature, nonetheless, has mastered many times over during the course of evolution thus far.

Botanists have shown that new plant tissue grows from a single tiny group of cells, called the meristem, right at the tip of the plant's extremities. There is a separate meristem at the end of each branch or twig where new cells are formed. Hence new cells are only created at such growing points, leaving more mature cells to expand with growth further down the stem. Most often, new growth develops in a spiral fashion, as if the stem turns by a fixed angle in order to mark out some kind of boundary before a new cell appears as part of an iterative expansion of growth—the same mechanism shown in the theoretical discussion on the formation of sequences in abstract graphs, outlined earlier. Through this the amazing thing is that a single fixed angle can produce an optimal design no matter how big the plant grows, a fact proved in 1933 by Douady and Couder, two French mathematicians. So, once an angle is fixed for a leaf, say, that leaf will least obscure the leaves below it and be least obscured by any future leaves above it. Similarly, once a seed is positioned on a seed head, the seed's position in the overall head will move away from the center in a straight line, pushed out by other new seeds but still retaining the original angle on the seed head. No matter how large the seed head grows, the seeds will always be arranged uniformly on the seed head.

It should come as no shock to learn that the fixed angle of turn is frequently Phi. The most efficient scheme for maximizing collective exposure to light is when there are Phi leaves per turn amongst the leaves involved, each casting the least shadow possible on its neighbours. This also gives the optimum exposure to falling rain so that water is directed back along the leaf and down the stem toward the roots, and it also provides the best possible exposure to attract insects for pollination. The whole of the plant seems to produce its leaves, flower head petals, and then seeds based on the golden number.

In order to examine the reasons behind Phi's popularity in organism growth, a basic concept needs to be outlined. It must be understood that rotating the parent assembly though 0.6 of a full turn is exactly the same as turning 1.6 turns, 2.6 turns, or even 10002.6 turns since the position of the resulting point plotted along any given axis from the center of the turn has the same value in at least one plane. Hence the whole number part of any given rotation can be ignored for practical purposes. Given this observation, the various fractions of a revolution that are best placed for arrangement patterns can be explored, and it turns out that simple fractions are not the best of choices. If one examines the case of exactly half a turn per seed, for example, a two-armed distribution is formed and the seeds involved use the space available in a very inefficient manner indeed, fanning out in a straight string-like configuration (Figure 4.11).

A circular seed distribution would, of course, be much more preferable, providing greater physical strength and thus a greater ability to withstand harsh environmental conditions or predatory attack (Figure 4.12):

In the Figure 4.12, 0.48 turns per seed and 0.6 turns per seed have been used, respectively, producing a distribution that spirals out via two arms and an equally spaced arrangement of five arms. Both are still somewhat wasteful in terms of unoccupied space, so what happens when values closer to Phi are used?

With less concise rotational values, like 0.61, the arrangement of seeds is better but still leaves large gaps between those nearest the center of the resultant arrangement. This is also the case when the values 1.61 . . . , 2.61 . . . , n.61 . . . , and so on, are used. Furthermore, the exact same configuration is produced when n.39 rotations are used, corresponding to exactly the same rotational fraction in the opposite direction. In fact it turns out that any number which can be written as an exact ratio, a rational number in other words, will always produce a less-than-optimal distribution. If any rotational angle comprising the division of two natural numbers, p and q, is used, then the pattern formed will comprise q straight arms, the seeds being placed on every pth arm.

Irrational numbers, or those that cannot be concisely expressed to a finite number of decimal places, it transpires, provide some of the best rotational angles for optimum seed placement, and this group includes such illustrious constants as Phi, e and Pi (π) as well as their multiples. e, which approximates to 2.71828 . . . , produces a distribution with 7 arms since it involves a turn per seed value of just over 5/7. A similar representation is also seen with π, also producing 7 arms, approximating closely to 1/7 turns per seed.

Figure 4.11. Seed distribution created by 0.5 turns per seed.

(a)   (b)

Figure 4.12. Seed distributions created by (a) 0.48 turns per seed and (b) 0.6 turns per seed.

Using such irrational angles produces distribution patterns with low level space wastage, but for the very best arrangements specific types of irrational are needed. These correspond to numbers that never really conform to rational approximations and comply instead with a mathematical principle known as continued fractions.

A "general" continued fraction representation of a real number is one that corresponds to the formula:

A "General" Continued Fraction

$$x = a_0 + \cfrac{b_1}{a_1 + \cfrac{b_2}{a_2 + \cfrac{b_3}{a_3 \cdots}}} \tag{4.5}$$

where $a_0, a_1 \ldots$ and b_0, b_1 are integers.

Continued fractions provide, in some sense, a series of best estimates for an irrational number. Functions can also be written as continued fractions, providing a series of better and better rational approximations [30]. Continued fraction representations for well-known constants have long been investigated. When they can be expressed in closed form, they have the ability to provide approximations to irrational numbers within any desired degree of precision. They also provide high rates of convergence, thereby reducing the number of iterations needed to compute the desired irrational to any desired degree of precision. As a member of this elite group of numbers, Phi has the distinct honour of being the slowest to converge of all continued fractions, taking 26 iterations to converge to 10 decimal places. It is hence the most irrational of all continued fractions, ultimately providing the reason as to why Phi is so prevalent in the arrangement of seed heads and nature in general [25]. It is the optimum irrational constant for use in mechanisms aimed at reducing waste in distributions of arbitrary elements over the dimensions of both space and time.

To continue this theme, geometric orders based around Phi are just one small subset of fractals representations known to be highly efficient at compressing a

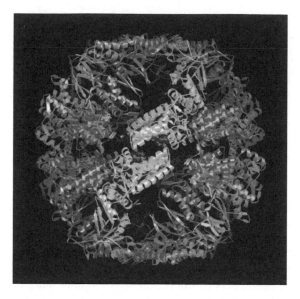

Figure 4.13. A more indigenous conceptualization of the Web.

great deal of detail—perhaps infinite—into a small finite space. Such capability can also be seen as a highly efficient form of arrangement, as outlined above, being found in virtually every organism alive. For example, a great deal of the work performed by the human body involves circulatory functions that have the goal of moving something from one part of the body to another. This task, while simple to state, is in fact very complex and involves a delicate tradeoff between conflicting aims. If we could design a circulatory system from scratch, one requirement would be that our system would be capable of transmitting things from potentially any source to any destination. However, we would also want our circulatory system to have as small a volume as possible, since it is obviously not practical to make an organism that consists entirely of plumbing. Nature solves the problem by building circulatory systems with fractal geometry that achieves both of these goals. It ingeniously minimizes material requirements while maximizing functionality through the ubiquitous use of fractals [24].

So how does this discussion relate to the Web? Phi is one of the major keys to information and process efficiency in the natural world. It is a differentiator in one of nature's best computational patterns, if you will. Most of our man-made computational systems are also designed to be as efficient as possible, and although the Web does contain a huge amount of duplicity, at localized levels at least it is no exception to this rule. Furthermore, it is apparent that, like the Web, there are a large number of natural systems that store and process information in an "optimized" manner using long sequences of constituents strung together. In physical realms such structures often reoccur as rotating patterns of material or action. They are also seen at multiple levels within a given system or context. So it is the way with the Web too.

It is a well-known fact that in the majority the Web is constructed out of long, hyperlinked chains of information or process, and a number of studies have now also shown that the Web possesses a fractal structure from many different perspectives. These topics will be discussed in more detail later, but for now it is enough to appreciate that the Web is often misrepresented. The common conceptualization of its maelstrom of pathways is one in which straight lines are employed everywhere. From node to node, to region on region, a standard network model is presented in which the Web supposedly repulses at even the slightest notion of curvature.

But a more indigenous model is presented here, one which strives for greater affiliations with the complexities of the natural world and one which is sympathetic to coiling Fibonacci-like patterns like those above. As will hopefully be shown, in this model, it is more appropriate to think of the Web as a collection of swirling vortexes of information and transformation. In this model, curvature is king and straight lines are banished to a much lowlier status. And it is this model that will form as a major hub of discussion in later sections. Hence, from this point on, try to think of the Web not so much as a tight latticework of linkages, but more as a loosely arranged bag of entangled springs—a conceptualization not dissimilar to the type favored by scientists researching into protein folding.

DEGREES OF FREEDOM AND INFORMATION REPRESENTATION IN BIOLOGICAL SYSTEMS

Sequences corresponding to progressions like the Fibonacci sequence can be easily shown as a spiralling graph, but it must be remembered that these represent only one type of sequential arrangement. There are other, similar fabrications where the ratio between successive elements stays constant instead. Take, for example, common mechanisms for the expression of thought, of which this very sentence provides a perfect example. It is, in fact, also a sequence or "string." Rearrange any or all of its letters or symbols and other legible sentences may well form, but none will most likely convey exactly the same meaning to any designated reader within a specific context. Each letter, space, and punctuation mark plays an integral and orderly part in the whole, but none is more formally significant than the other in terms of their actual syntactic order. They could be typographically bigger, smaller, wider, or taller than each other, or have completely different colors, but this would not necessarily add any extra value to the overall validity, meaning, or purpose of the information to be conveyed unless specifically stated.

Now, imagine a scenario where each character in a sentence was indeed of exactly of the same dimensions and possessed exactly the same amount of informational content. Imagine also if it took approximately the same number of characters, all strung together, to convey one particular unit of meaningful information, a word of information with fixed length for want of a better description. In such circumstances the difference between the characters and words would not result in a spiralling graph, because such a configuration would imply the use of information units of differing sizes. Instead the informational equidistance between the units used would kink the sentence's graph out into something approximating a uniform arc—a curve for which the tangent of broken symmetry remained constant at character and word boundaries. This would thereby double back on itself, forcing either a two-dimensional circular or three-dimensional corkscrew structure; this is called a *helix*.

Anyone can try this simple concept for themselves: Take two small piles of drinking straws, both equal in number and length. Put one pile to one side for a moment and arrange the remaining straws one immediately after the other, maintaining the same angle between them as shown in Figure 4.14. Eventually a rough helical pattern of straws will appear. Now take the other pile and cut them down into a collection comprising lengths 1 cm, 2 cm, 3 cm, and so on. Arrange these as the first pile, but making sure that the shortest straw comes first, followed the next shortest and so on. When this arrangement is complete, a spiral will be formed instead of a circle or overlapping helix.

Thinking specifically of helical structures, for a number of decades biology has known of precisely one such system for information storage and processing. Leap of faith or not, but is it not a striking coincidence that the coiling structure just outlined looks remarkably like that found in both DNA and RNA, the biochemical blueprints used to store and provision the physiological makeup of all living cellular organisms? Add to this the fact that the elemental geometric patterns of both these natural helixes are also mirrored in higher levels of cellular physiology—namely the "X" and "Y" shapes present in the physical structure of chromosomes—and at the very least an intoxicating fractal-like scenario starts to unfold. Could it be that the instructions for life itself are more closely related to the simplistic asymmetric, binary representations of the digital world than currently thought?

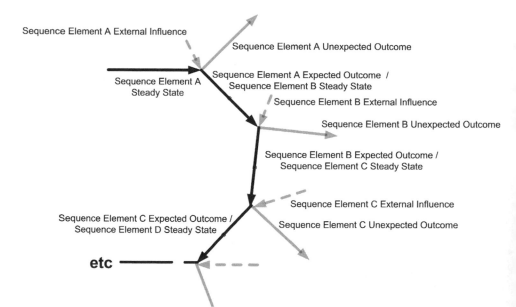

Figure 4.14. A two-dimensional directed graph showing a sequence of identically sized elements.

Certainly modern physiology appears to be warming to such ideas, recently coming to understand that they are not so far-fetched. It is well understood that curves provide some of the most economic structural geometries possible. Furthermore, many now appreciate that constructing such curves out of anything that has unit value must involve broken symmetry across all the units involved. So given nature's propensity for minimalism, its in-built preference for bundled coils of information and computation sequence should be clear. In short, that's why most low-level biological material comes curled up.

But there is more to this story than pure economy of structure. Efficiency of the content within that structure is important too, just as in man-made systems. An alternatively plausible interpretation of this might well be seen as reductionism. So in such respects both nature and humans share the same common constraints, both needing to engineer systems that embody efficiently purposeful units of content for the problems in hand.

For many decades, physiologists have well understood and respected the complexity of organic life, but it has only been relatively recently that experts have begun to realize the true enormity of the complexity involved. Now they are beginning to realize that it would be next to impossible for structures like DNA to hold the totality of descriptive information needed to express every aspect of a living being from conception through to death. It is now well understood that the location of

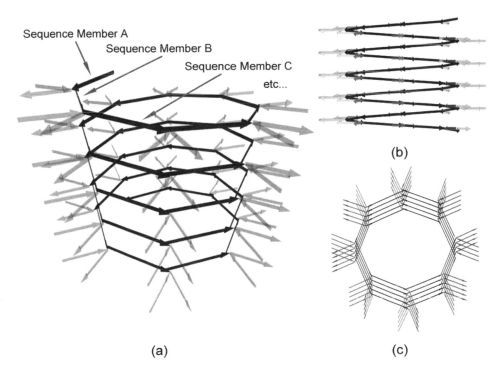

Figure 4.15. A three-dimensional graph showing a sequence (a–c) of linearly diverging elements.

every hair on our heads and every wrinkle on our skin, for example, cannot be expressed explicitly in our genetic makeup, yet still our bodily features consistently regenerate with relatively few cases of mutation during a normal lifespan. Skin cells die and are replaced, yet blemishes still appear in the same places and maintain the same discoloration. It is examples like this that point to the fact that some form of assistance is being given to our raw genetic code, some compression algorithm is working at different levels, but producing similar effect.

As already discussed, fractals are one such compression scheme that have been shown many times to possess an affinity for natural complex phenomena. In fact, several studies have already shown [3,8,9] that fractals are present in DNA, but these have been somewhat directed toward informational content. What has not been investigated properly yet, however, is the role that fractals might be playing in the overall physical structure of such biological systems as well—hence the curiosity behind the apparent reoccurrence of X and Y geometric patterns in complex information processing systems like physiology and the Web itself.

Based on the established existence of fractals elsewhere in DNA, for instance, it would not be unrealistic to expect such studies to unearth evidence that substantiated the existence of X and Y patterns, at least at gene and chromosome levels; such patterns being manifestations of the same overarching self-similar scheme of information organization—an essential part of the physiological compression of information perhaps. This is reinforced by trying to understand how DNA works within the life process. As has been shown earlier, X and Y are the fundamental patterns involved in switching structures of all kinds, be they natural or man-made. Hence it should be no shock to learn that early investigations into DNA undertaken by two French scientists unearthed the fundamental switching behavior of DNA as early as the 1960s. Working at the Institut Pasteur, François Jacob and Jacques Monod discovered that a small fraction of the thousands of genes arranged along the DNA molecule can function as tiny switches. Turn one of these switches on—by exposing the cell to a certain hormone to act as the triggering signal in an X-shaped relay—and the newly activated gene will send out a chemical signal to its fellow genes. This signal will then travel up and down the length of the DNA molecule and trip other genetic switches, flipping some of them "on" and some of them "off." These genes, in turn, start sending out chemical signals of their own (or stop sending them). So, as a result, still more genetic switches are tripped in a mounting cascade until the cell's collection of genes settles down into a new and stable pattern [67].

For biologists the implications of this low-level switching were enormous—so much so that Jacob and Monod later shared a Nobel Prize for it. It meant that the DNA residing in a cell's nucleus was not just a blueprint for the cell—a catalogue of how to make this protein or that protein. DNA was actually the foreman in charge of construction. In effect, DNA was a kind of processing unit, a molecular-scale computer that directed how the cell was to build itself and repair itself and interact with the outside. Furthermore, Jacob and Monod's discovery solved the long-standing mystery of how one fertilized egg cell could divide and differentiate itself into muscle cells, brain cells, liver cells, and all other kinds of cells that make up a newborn life form. Each different type of cell corresponds to a different pattern of activated genes [67]. In essence, DNA performs just as any computational system, striving for optimum fitness through consecutive generations of evolution.

A MORE DETAILED ACCOUNT OF DNA'S STRUCTURE

One might sensibly consider significant parts of the preceding discussions to be deliberately contrived. It is clear that uniform differentiation between the parts of any physically connected system will result in a structure that curves back on itself in at least one dimension, so why glibly construe that this should mimic the famous structure of DNA? Surely a circle in just one plane would do just as well if its circumference was great enough. Quite correct, a single planar circular structure would do just fine, but then this would also be the case with the molecular structure of DNA in vivo[12] if it were not for additional constraints imposed by the physical laws of molecular chemistry and the spatial confines of cellular biology.

DNA in its relaxed state usually assumes a right-handed 20-Å-diameter helix in which the nucleotide base planes are nearly perpendicular to the helix axis, with a vertical distance of 3.4 Å between them and 10 base pairs per helix turn, giving a "pitch" of 34 Å. Linear DNA in solution assumes this configuration because of its energy efficiency, pushing out into a third dimension purely as a consequence of the physical depth of the molecules involved and the rigidity of the molecular bonds between them. The physical chemistry of the situation enforces the practicality of this basic helical state; any deviation from this relaxed condition increases the energy of the DNA molecule and thus makes it less than optimally efficient. This situation is unacceptable in all but the most extreme of circumstances in nature.

The helix axis of DNA in vivo,[12] however, is also usually curved, rather than linear. This is a necessary condition, as the stretched length of the human genome is about one meter and needs to be "packaged" in order to fit into the nucleus of a cell. This compression increases the potential energy stored in DNA's structure and is used to drive reactions such as the unwinding events that occur during DNA replication and transcription. Too much stored energy is not necessarily a good thing though, and this problem is addressed by having DNA form the self-similar structure of supercoils, in which the helical axis of the DNA curves itself into a yet another level of coils. Such supercoiled structures are again one of nature's solutions to the problem of minimizing the excess energy, further following the tradition of reoccurring simplistic patterns to handle deep-rooted complex problems.

MORE EVIDENCE OF EFFICIENCY AT PLAY IN DNA AND HIGHER LEVELS OF PHYSIOLOGY

Optimal efficiency constants like Phi are not only found in high-level natural formations like seed heads, but are also significant in the dimensional properties of

---

[12]In vivo (Latin for (with)in the living). In vivo is used to indicate the presence of a whole/living organism, in distinction to a partial or dead organism or to a computer model.

both DNA and RNA. It has been shown that in B-DNA both pitch-to-diameter and diameter-to-offset are extremely close to the golden ratio. Here, pitch is the helical repeat, and offset refers to the vertical distance that forms the minor groove.

The Watson–Crick model, generally referred to as the double helix, consists of two helical chains coded round the same axis. These chains, excluding the bases,[13] are related by a dyad[14] perpendicular to the helix axis; thus the two chains are antiparallel as shown in Figure 4.16.

Furthermore, Phi is well known to play a key role in the geometry of a regular pentagon, as shown in Figure 4.17, given that the ratio of the diagonal of a pentagon to its side is 1 to Phi (1:Phi). A decagon is in essence two pentagons, with one rotated by 36 degrees from the other, and a cross-sectional view from the top of the DNA double helix forms a decagon, so each spiral of the double helix must trace out the shape of a pentagon.

To further glorify Phi's illustrious credentials, it also is considered to be the basis of the segmentation of a well-built, "normal" human body. For example, the ratios of lower arm length to hand length, whole body to navel down, and so on, all equal Phi:1. From these examples it is easy to construct a case that strengthens the idea that the proportions of DNA should similarly be based on Phi.

For the purpose of this discussion, consider the local dimensions of the type-B double helix, which appears to be the most common form of DNA in chromatin.[15] Given that DNA is a right-handed double-helix-structure, there are three crucial dimensions that essentially determine its final form: the external width (diameter) of the double helix, the length of its period—that is to say the pitch, or the height of a representative "slice"—and the vertical offset of one helix from the other, which forms the minor groove.

The novel feature of this interpretation of Watson and Crick's structure is the manner in which these three basic dimensions are held together by the rule of the golden ratio. In particular the height-to-width ratio and the width-to-offset ratio are always very close to Phi, and since the ratio between height and offset is responsible for the unequal sizes of the major and minor grooves of B-DNA, it could be construed that the ratio between the grooves is Phi-like, too.

Although the crystal structure of a B-DNA dodecamer[16] has been refined to high resolution, it is too short and irregular to accurately estimate the pitch, diameter, and offset of the DNA molecule as a whole. However, the most recent and best refined X-ray fiber studies of long chains of B-DNA yield ratios of 1.6031 and 1.538, respectively, or approximately 1% and 5% less than Phi.

Thus can the dimensional abundance of constants like Phi teach us anything meaningful? The answer is a most definite yes, and in an obviously profound way. Such phenomena demonstrate that although complexity is undeniable in the natural world, there are fundamental laws working to tame it. Just like us, nature fights to control complexity in its systems and thereby stop them veering off into chaos.

---

[13]In chemistry, a base is the reactive complement to an acid.
[14]A general pair, consisting of two parts.
[15]Chromatin is the substance of a chromosome and consists of a complex of DNA and protein in eukaryotic cells.
[16]A group of thick oily hydrocarbons.

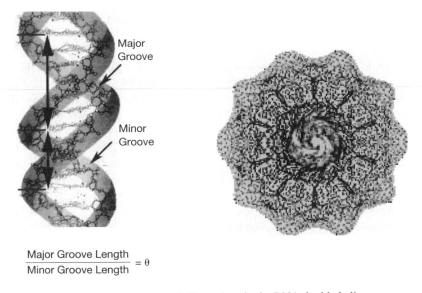

$$\frac{\text{Major Groove Length}}{\text{Minor Groove Length}} = \theta$$

Figure 4.16. Phi-related dimensions in the DNA double helix.

Physical absolutes like the second law of thermodynamics may well serve to deliberately push the Universe toward total instability, but this is counterbalanced at every level. So the natural world maintains its complex poise, right on the edge of chaos, the point at which interesting phenomena like life exist.

What is important to note here is that the laws that favor order are not as overt as their destructive counterparts. They are not contrived. Instead they are happy to hide behind emergent properties as a consequence of complexity itself. What is amazing for us in the case of the Web is that no matter how hard we try to manipulate its overall being, these laws are still overtaking our best efforts and shape it as we see fit. Today the Web does not represent the pristine, deterministic form that our information technologists might crave. Rather it has grown beyond such expectations and may now be venturing out into the domains of natural emergent beauty, that deep yet understandable beauty that comes with complexity.

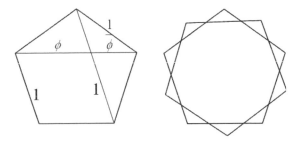

Figure 4.17. Phi-related dimensions in a singular pentagon and two overlaid pentagons.

BOOKS, BYTES, COMPUTERS, AND BIOLOGICAL SYSTEMS— AN ANALOGY

Now the point has been reached where it may be possible to start and tie all this material together more concisely. To summarize, a number of well-established ideas and a certain amount of grounded speculation have been aired so far, all of which are roughly intertwined as outlined in Figure 4.18. But by summarizing these concepts it is important not to get caught up in the practices of cargo cult science. "Such schools of thought never explicitly say what their ideas really are, but just hope that followers will catch on by all the examples of scientific integrity, a principle of scientific thought that corresponds to a kind of utter honesty—a kind of leaning over backwards" [46]. So what conclusions can be reasonably drawn up to this point and how are they relevant to the modern-day Web?

Certainly it is well known that both DNA and RNA contain essential information in the ontogeny of all living organisms. Furthermore, it is freely acknowledged that this information is stored sequentially. It is also known that at least one important dimension of DNA and RNA's helical structure is related to the optimizing constant Phi. Thus it is reasonable to conclude that Phi plays a leading role in systems where life has enough stability to sustain itself and enough creativity to deserve the name "life" [67]. What is of further interest, however, is the fact that both DNA and RNA are also known to contain information and instigate behaviors in accordance with fractal patterns, again pointing to the evolution of compression mechanisms intended to condense maximum complexity with minimum expenditure or effort. For example, intracellular processes instigate cascades of biological development with fractal characteristics—sequences of change that appear to contain more information than is present in their original genetic outline. Such cascades are irreversible in much the same way as hypertext forms one-way sequences of information on the Web. In such respects they are collections of unidirectional sequences working in tandem to achieve a set of broader aims: a program of instructions under any other name. Being sequential, every element of such progressions can be seen as an expected outcome from a binary discontinuity or a break in symmetry. This makes intracellular sequences inherently discrete from at least one perspective, again pointing to the comparisons with the computational systems in common use today. But once more this should come as no surprise because DNA and RNA are themselves also known to contain a form of digital information. "This is not a metaphor; it is the plain truth. It couldn't be plainer; life might as well be carrying around its genetic information on floppy disk [51]." Furthermore, it is known that ontogenetic mechanisms are highly regular, subdividing in much the same manner as the methods and schematics used in large-scale computer system design. For example, the human body contains approximately 100 trillion cells. Each cell contains a microscopic nucleus embracing two sets of the human genome, one set from the mother and one set from the father. In principle, each set includes some 60,000 to 80,000 genes on the same 23 chromosomes [41]. So one could quite easily compare a genome to a book or the design of an extremely large database system, a biological equivalent of the Web perhaps, or at the very least a highly complicated computer system. All are simply descriptions of some kind, encoded using differing alphabets, lexicons, and grammars. Furthermore, all are constructed from extremely similar, symmetry-breaking-based patterns, none more simple than the unassuming switch itself.

In addition, instead of chasing a formal definition of species, biologists are now going back to the more intuitive idea that organisms belong to the same species if they are effectively indistinguishable. The degree of similarity can be quantified by listing anatomical or behavioral features—an organism's sequence of characterizing qualities if you will—and observing how closely they match. And this is where symmetry comes into play again. The symmetry of an object or system is simply a transformation that preserves its structure. With speciation, the transformations are not rotations or flips, as with the symmetry of a sphere or hexagon, but are permutations—that is, shufflings of the labels employed in the model to identify the individual organisms.

None of this is speculation; it is the very bedrock on which modern physiology is laid. As far back as 1961, pioneers such as Jacob and Monod were comparing the most basic physiological ground rules with those now overly familiar in computer science. In fact their work was of such an undeniable standard that it was a revelation for all biologists [67]. In their work they showed that any biological cell contains a number of "regulatory" genes that act as switches and can turn one and other on and off. So cellular biology is quite literally concerned with a kind of biochemical computer. It is the computing behavior, the outright complex yet ultimately integrated and orderly behavior, of this entire system that somehow governs how one cell can become different from another: quite literally the mechanics behind all organic growth, mutation, and fundamentally the evolution of life itself. It is interesting to use an analogy and compare the information content common in biological systems to a kind of book and hence also to a computer system (Table 4.2).

To pick up the book analogy further, there are one billion "words" in the human genome, which makes it as long as 800 *Bibles* strung end to end. This makes the

Table 4.2. Physiological and Computational Comparisons

Biological Unit	Book Analogy	Computer System Analogy
Chromosomes	There are 23 chapters.	There are 23 subsystems.
Genes	Each chapter contains several thousand stories of genes.	Each subsystem contains several thousands artifacts, each being either a discrete program or data set.
Exons, Introns	Each story is made up of paragraphs, which are interspersed with advertisements.	Each artifact comprises content— either functionality or raw data, interspersed with labels identifying that content.
Condones	Each paragraph is made up of words.	All content is split up into words representing either individual data items or program instructions.
Bases	Each word is written using characters from a fixed alphabet.	Each word is split up into bytes from a fixed-size character set.

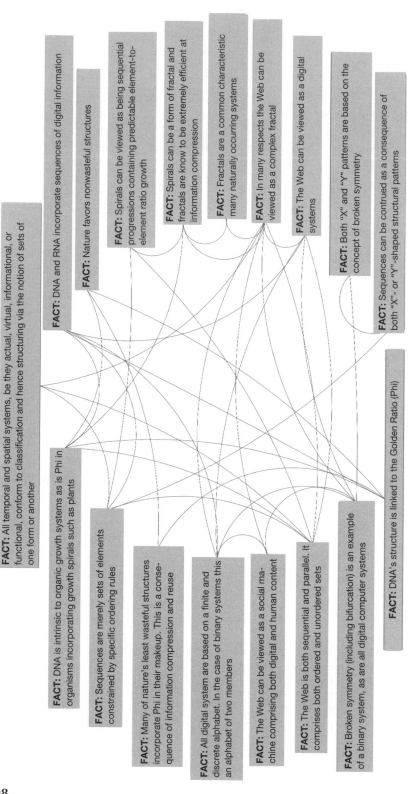

FACT: All temporal and spatial systems, be they actual, virtual, informational, or functional, conform to classification and hence structuring via the notion of sets of one form or another

FACT: DNA and RNA incorporate sequences of digital information

FACT: Nature favors nonwasteful structures

FACT: Spirals can be viewed as being sequential progressions containing predictable element-to-element ratio growth

FACT: Spirals can be a form of fractal and fractals are know to be extremely efficient at information compression

FACT: Fractals are a common characteristic many naturally occurring systems

FACT: In many respects the Web can be viewed as a complex fractal

FACT: The Web can be viewed as a digital systems

FACT: Both "X" and "Y" patterns are based on the concept of broken symmetry

FACT: Sequences can be contrued as a consequence of both "X"- or "y"-shaped structural patterns

FACT: DNA is intrinsic to organic growth systems as is Phi in organisms incorporating growth spirals such as plants

FACT: Sequences are merely sets of elements constrained by specific ordering rules

FACT: Many of nature's least wasteful structures incorporate Phi in their makeup. This is a consequence of information compression and reuse

FACT: All digital system are based on a finite and discrete alphabet. In the case of binary systems this an alphabet of two members

FACT: The Web can be viewed as a social machine comprising both digital and human content

FACT: The Web is both sequential and parallel. It comprises both ordered and unordered sets

FACT: Broken symmetry (including bifurcation) is an example of a binary system, as are all digital computer systems

FACT: DNA's structure is linked to the Golden Ratio (Phi)

Figure 4.18. Relationships between the concepts covered in prior sections.

genome a gigantic document, an information string of extravagant length, and it all fits inside the microscopic nucleus of a tiny cell that sits easily on the head of a pin!

The idea of the genome as a book or system of sorts is not, strictly speaking, even a metaphor. It is literally true. It is a collection of digital information written in a serialized, one-dimensional form. It is defined by a code that transliterates a small, fixed alphabet into a large lexicon of meaning through the order of their groupings. The only complication is that natural language books, written in English say, read from right to left, or the opposite direction in, say, Arabic, whereas some parts of the genome read from left to right, and some right to left, though never both at the same time.

Whereas the books humans read are written in words of variable length using letters typically from a 26-letter alphabet, genomes are written entirely in three-letter words, using only four letters: A, C, G, and T, which stand for adenine, cytosine, guanine, and thymine [41]. Also instead of being written on flat pages they are strung together into the familiar helical strands of DNA. This, of course, is where the opportunity for biological information storage lies, but instead of using just the two binary states 1 and 0, the information technology of living cells uses four states. "There is very little difference, in principle, between a two-state binary information technology like ours, and a four-state information technology like that of the living cell. In such respects the information technology of our genes is just as digital as that found in our everyday computer systems—a fact discovered by Gregor Mendel[17] in the nineteenth century, although he probably would not have put it quite like that" [51].

---

[17]Gregor Johann Mendel was an Austrian monk who is often called the "father of genetics" for his study of the inheritance of traits in pea plants. Mendel showed that there was particulate inheritance of traits according to his laws of inheritance [110].

CHAPTER 5

Positional Information and Scale-Free Networks

Nature uses only the longest threads to weave her patterns, so that each small piece of her fabric reveals the organization of the entire tapestry.

—*Richard Feynman*

A RIGHT PLACE FOR EVERYTHING

Other striking similarities can be found between the naturally occurring structures of genetics, metabolism, and life and those common to Information Technology. The late 1960s saw the start of a radically different approach to the understanding of the mechanics behind biological development. No longer were biologists just interested in the information stored in genes to describe the various cell types needed to create the diversity in living organisms, they also became interested in understanding why organisms develop with the right parts in the right places, in the correct proportions, more or less independent of the size of the whole [19]. The reason for this later became obvious when it was realized that there is nothing special about the substances, or cells, from which living things are made. "After all, living things, like every other macromolecular material thing in the Universe, are comprised of nothing more than a collection of molecules. What is special in living things, however, is that these molecules are put together in much more complicated patterns than the molecules of non-living things, and this assembly is done by following programmes, sets of instructions for how to develop. What lies at the heart of every living thing is not a "spark of life." It is information, words and instructions. If a metaphor is in order, don't think of fires and sparks and breath. Think instead of a billion discrete, digital characters, each with their own individual position in a much grander scheme. To understand life, don't think about vibrant throbbing gels and oozes, think about information technology" [51], and the more structure present, generally the better.

The term *positional information* was first introduced into the field of Ontogenetics—also known as developmental biology—by Lewis Wolpert in the late 1960s, without question being both a convenient and appropriate way of referring to the fact that cells seem to know where they fit within the holistic framework of an organism. Wolpert, however, also outlined a theory by which cells come by this knowledge. Positional Information, he proposed "is the main feature which determines the pattern of cellular differentiation, and . . . the pattern of differential information is universal. Essentially, a cell knows where it is, and this information specifies the nature of its differentiation."

So influential was Wolpert's work that it has recently been proclaimed as having changed the way we think about pattern formation in the embryo, thereby allowing new generations of molecular developmental biologists to frame their questions in a way that would give sensible answers. Beyond reasonable doubt, the notion of positional information has grown steadily since Wolpert's introduction, and the term has now become a staple phrase in the vocabulary of developmental biologists [19].

Further significant work from the likes of Christiane Nüsslein-Volhard[1] and Eric Wieshaus, into the embryonic development of *Drosphilia,* has shown emphatically that the precise position of cells along the anterior–posterior axis of such an organism is specified by a cascade of events, possibly starting with the presence, or level, of bicoid[2] *mRNA* in bicoid protein. From this initial instructional data set the intercellular developmental process is then further supported by increasing levels, or diffusions, of such a substance while new cells are developing. This model has been shown not to be universal, however. Chemical concentration is itself only a special case of the yet more general case. Cellular position could be represented by a set of genes, with additional genes being activated with an increase in distance in some higher-order pattern.

Nevertheless, the comparison has been made clear. Nüsslein-Volhard, Wieshaus, and Wolpert refer to the idea of an "initial instruction" to a lesser or greater extent, where we have a type of gene or protein that differs from the common understanding of such compounds solely as instructions for what cells should look like. This type of gene specifically conveys compositional information in relation to other parts of an organism as a whole. In such respects, the concept of Positional Information provides at least one proven answer to the question of how cells "know" where they are. It does so in a way that can scarcely be controversial: They know by virtue of their positional information.

WHAT IS INFORMATION ANYWAY?

The work associated with Positional Information also points to one commonly missed, yet essential, ingredient in the equation that makes information such a valuable resource in all forms of computation, be they natural or man-made: context. It is often misunderstood that the concept of data is quite different from that of information and is even further separated from that of knowledge.

---

[1]Christiane Nüsslein-Volhard is a German biologist who won the Albert Lasker Award for Basic Medical Research in 1991 and the Nobel Prize in Physiology and Medicine in 1995, together with Eric Wieschaus and Edward B. Lewis, for their research on the genetic control of embryonic development.
[2]A maternally transcribed gene in *Drosophila.*

But just what is information in the first place? Many interpretations exist but the term itself traces back to the Latin verb "informare," which for the Romans generally meant "to shape," "to form an idea of," or "to describe." The verb, in turn, supplied action to the substantive, "forma," which took various meanings dependent mostly on circumstance. The historian Livy[3] used forma as a general term for "characteristic," "form," "nature," "kind," and "manner." Horace[4] likened it to a shoe last,[5] Ovid[6] related it to a mold or stamp for making coins, while Cerio, amongst other uses, extended its use to include "form" or "species," specifying information as a philosophical expression denoting the essence or form of a thing as distinguished from its manner or content [29].

Regardless of its historic origins, to say that information differs from data is an indisputable fact. On its own, data is meaningless. The number 23031966 is worthless in isolation, for instance. Add some structure in the form of a couple of hyphens or slashes and its starts to make more sense, easily being recognizable as a date of some kind. But it is only when context is set and we are informed that this is actually someone's date of birth that the true value of the information being conveyed is realized. What Nüsslein-Volhard and Wieshaus demonstrated was, therefore, quite insightful—that is, that intracellular genetic processes provide a self-contained mechanism for making sense of the various elements needed to provide intrinsically informative systems. Descriptive and positional proteins provide the data and structural elements of the equation, while the surrounding chemical concentrations of such proteins provide the appropriate developmental context for the right cells to form in the right place at the right time. This inbuilt choreographed cascade of combining complexity results in the elegant and beautiful system we indifferently refer to as life.

Such concepts are obviously not new to Information Technologists though. For a number of decades, Data Analysts have been modeling information based on "X"- and "Y"-shaped patterns to engineer frameworks that need to fan out, and they use a form of incorporated positional information to achieve this. These are generally built using self-referencing schemes of data, with the inverted tree-like structure of a company's organizational chart providing a good example of the simplest type of this formation in common use. In Figure 5.1, for instance, the head of the company sits at the root of the tree, with their managers and subordinates laid out in successive orderly tiers of a hierarchy below them. This type of representation successfully models, for example, that a staff member could manage several other staff, but can only be directly managed by one manager.

---

[3]Titus Livius (around 59 B.C.–17 A.D.), known as Livy in English, wrote a monumental history of Rome, Ab urbe condita, from its founding (traditionally dated to 753 B.C.). Livy was a native of Padua on the Po River in northern Italy [111].

[4]Quintus Horatius Flaccus (December 8, 65 B.C.–November 27, 8 B.C.), known in the English-speaking world as Horace, was the leading lyric poet in Latin [112].

[5]In shoemaking, a last is a rounded oblong block used to approximate the form of the human foot used by a cobbler to help make or mend shoes.

[6]Publius Ovidius Naso (Sulmona, March 20, 43 B.C.–Tomis, now Constanta A.D. 17), Roman poet known to the English-speaking world as Ovid, wrote on topics of love, abandoned women, and mythological transformations [113].

Table 5.1. A Comparison Between the "Information Equation" in Information Technology and Ontogenetics

Field	Equation						
Information Technology			Data		Structure		Context
	Information	=	Characterizing Protein(s)	+	Positional Protein(s)	+	Presence of Specific Diffuse Protein(s) Concentration(s)
Developmental Biology							

Schemes like this are based solely on a "Y"-shaped pattern and work fine when the underlying hierarchy fans out in just one direction. When there is a need for expansion in more than one direction, however, problems occur immediately. In such cases an internal "many-to-many" relationship needs representation, one end of which describes expansion deeper into a formation while the other describes the same behavior in the opposite direction (Figure 5.2). This can model structures based on a mixture of both "X" and "Y" patterns, providing an important and advantageous transition from rigid hierarchies, into more expressive "networks" of information.

Hierarchies can typically only convey one type of compositional information, as demonstrated in Figure 5.1. Network organization, on the other hand, allows for the overlapping of multiple composition schemes, thereby providing information storage mechanisms with far richer descriptive capabilities. With the use of networks, for instance, it is relatively easily to model a scenario where staff members could manage multiple staff and, in turn, be managed by multiple staff members also (Figure 5.2). In other words the associative geometry of network structure is eminently extensible across multiple dimensions, whereas that of hierarchical structure is not.

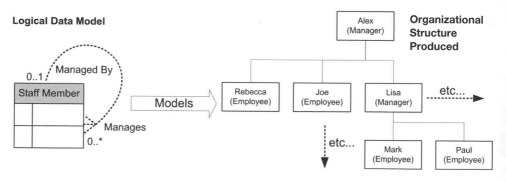

Figure 5.1. An example of a database entity relationship diagram (ERD) showing one-to-many hierarchical, recursive entity relationship.

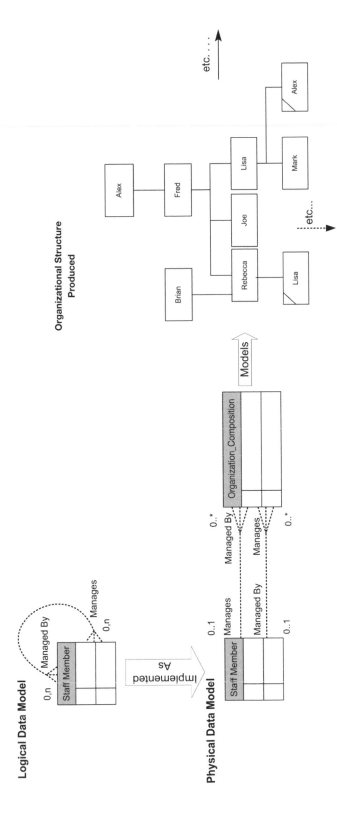

Figure 5.2. An example of an entity relationship diagram (ERD) showing a many-to-many network recursive entity relationship.

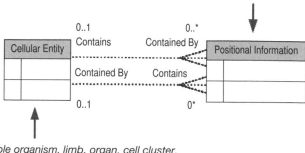

"**Where** and initially **when**"—*Whole organism, limb, organ, cell cluster, single cell type . . . etc.*

"**What**"—*Whole organism, limb, organ, cell cluster, single cell type . . . etc.*

Figure 5.3. An entity relationship diagram (ERD) providing a meta-model for multicellular organism composition.

Although logically such many-to-many networked entity models can be constructed using a single entity type, to "physically"[7] implement such a model needs an additional, separate entity if significant duplication of information is to be avoided—a theme that has again been aggressively promoted by natural evolutionary processes (Figure 5.3). This holds details of the overall structure being constructed—separated positional information in fact.

A BOW TO TIE COINCIDENCE TOGETHER

So it can be shown that self-referential structures with self-similar features can be constructed using relational data schemes like those outlined above. These in turn rely extensively on underlying "X" and "Y" patterns to create orderly collections of associated information.

From an organizational perspective it is interesting to note that such structures also appear to be emerging spontaneously at many levels on the Web. Recent studies [12] into the overall associative geometry of the Web have statistically analyzed tens of millions of websites and the hyperlinks between them. Through this research it has been empirically demonstrated that the Web is emerging as the outcome of a number of essentially independent and random processes that evolve at various scales. A striking consequence of this scale difference is that the structure of the Web is a pervasive and robust self-similar pattern, closely approximating to well-understood mathematical phenomena such as Zipf's Power Law [12]—an order coincidentally known to be present in DNA oligonucleotide sequences [14], and a number of sociological models.

---

[7]Here "physically" refers to the best method of actually programming such representation via relational database technologies.

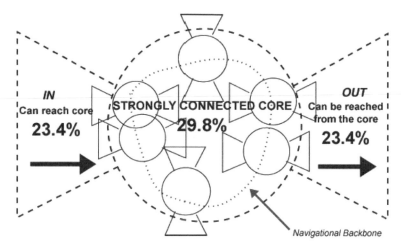

Figure 5.4. Similarly themed Clusters of Web content connected by the navigational backbone of the strongly connected core of the Web graph.

Even more compelling, these investigations point to a generic "bow-tie-like" model of the Web that is itself self-similar. This is not at all unlike the "X"-shaped pattern concept introduced in Chapter 4 and further highlighted in the types of relational data model shown above. Such bow ties comprise a central "Strongly Connected Core" (SCC), flanked by multiple input and output associations. These fan out in multiple directions to form the wings of the bow.[8] Not surprisingly, when the core of this model is examined in detail, it yields further levels of similar bow ties around smaller clusters of analogous Web content, only breaking down when insufficient volumes of materials are available, such as in the case of individual websites or even Web pages themselves.

One unexpected observation from this work has shown that central regions of individual bow-tie clusters are tightly connected together to form navigational backbones [13] (Figure 5.4). These represent almost a superstructure, off which lesser-used tendril routes dissipate and ultimately allow feedback for like entry and exit routes to and from a highway. This is not dissimilar to the concept of the sugar-phosphate backbone in DNA.

None of this is should appear outrageous; it is merely empirical evidence that the Web has an inclination to form information "hubs" at a number of levels. What is alluring, however, is that these act as concentration points for various types of information at varying levels of detail. In effect they are nodes in a fractal graph of the Web—points where symmetry breaks and the different facets of the Web meet. In such respects they quite literally represent the boundaries that produce the Web's fractal curvature.

---

[8]To be precise, this model also contains one further element, not shown here, representing totally unrelated Web content, but this is in the minority representing only 23.4% of the Web materials investigated.

WHY IS KEVIN BACON SO IMPORTANT?

The bow tie model is great in theory, but how useful is it and what premise leads to the expectation it will aid the return of useful information? Long the stuff of party games and folklore, the "small-world phenomenon"—the principle that people are all linked by short chains of acquaintances—has already been studied from an algorithmic perspective. These investigations have suggested that the phenomenon is pervasive in networks arising both in nature and technology [53]. Furthermore, it is clear that it has been a fundamental ingredient in the structural evolution of the Web. Over many trials using social systems, the number of intermediate steps in a successful chain was found to lie between five and six, a quantity that has since entered popular culture as the "six degrees of separation" principle.

Amusingly, Kevin Bacon, the Hollywood actor, has much to thank this principle for. A few years ago a trio of Pennsylvania college students with too much time on their hands came up with the game, "The Six Degrees of Kevin Bacon." Craig Fass, Brian Turtle and Mike Ginelli, wrote a letter to the then TV talk-show host Jon Stewart, who invited them on his show to demonstrate the game. From these humble beginnings, a website arose, a book was published, and a nationwide cult-fad was born. The game is based on a movie adaptation of the small world phenomenon, suggesting that we are all connected by six or fewer stages of circumstance or acquaintance. Fass, Turtle, and Ganelli took the concept one step further, noting how nicely Kevin Bacon could substitute for "separation" in the game. They hypothesized that he might also be the center of the Universe, at least when it comes to connecting actors.

Although never a major superstar, Bacon has been in a significant number of ensemble films, from *Diner* to *Apollo 13,* and the students discovered that if you use Bacon as an endpoint, you can link him in six degrees or less to almost any other performer. For instance, Kevin Bacon links to Kevin Costner in one swift link, both being in the movie *JFK.* Julia Louis-Dreyfus of American TV's *Seinfeld,* however, takes all six steps to make a chain, according to the book. She was in *Christmas Vacation* with Randy Quaid, who was in *Major League II* with Tom Berenger, who was in *Shattered* with Greta Scacchi, who was in *Presumed Innocent* with Harrison Ford, who was in *Raiders of the Lost Ark* with Karen Allen, who was in *Animal House* with Kevin Bacon.

The Kevin Bacon Game deliberately trivializes the underlying principle involved, but from this it is possible to suggest that, if it is indeed endemic to the Web and the right questions are asked, appropriate answers will be found quickly. In short, from a raw connectivity perspective the Web is a relatively small information space; so if the right questions are asked, then the right answers should be found without too much effort. Allowing searches to iterate into double figures suggests an act of diminished returns, and the principle provides an interesting control for limiting unnecessary process wastage.

SCALE-FREE NETWORKS

Mapping the Web in its entirety is an almost impossible task, akin to mapping a humongous maze. If it were possible to rise above such a maze, in a helicopter say, the task would be easy: One would simply draw the layout seen below. But there is no such means by which the Web can be observed. This is because its virtual existence does not directly correspond to anything we can understand in a material sense. So we must enter the maze and keep track of where it leads.

What a strange contrivance we have made for ourselves: We have built the Web, but we cannot easily tell exactly what we have built. Rather, we must investigate its form as though we were blind, feeling out its contours little by little. In 1999 Réka Albert, Hawoong Jeong, and Albert László Barabási of the University of Notre Dame in Indiana did exactly this, by sending a robot[9] into the maze of the Web and directing it to map out its virtual pathways [76]. The robot was a computer program that was instructed to enter a website and follow all its hyperlinks. These took the robot to an assortment of other websites, at each of which it would repeat the same process. On each outing the robot kept a record of the number of outgoing hyperlinks it encountered from each page.

To conduct this search for all 1 billion or so of the pages on the Web would have been far too much for the robot to accomplish. Instead, the researchers told their program simply to stay within the bounds of their university's many Web pages. This alone comprised a fine sample of some 325,729 HTML documents, interconnected by nearly 1.5 million hypertext links, and the researchers hoped that it would be sufficiently large and representative to act as a model of the Web as a whole [76].

As a result of this study, Albert and her fellow workers found that the probability distributions of both incoming and outgoing links in the graph their studies produced were dependent on power laws. Most pages had few links; a few had many; and each time the number of links was doubled, the number of pages with that many links decreased by a constant factor. The result is not obvious. Although one might intuitively expect fewer pages with many links than just a few, a power law is by no means the only relationship consistent with this. In fact, one might have expected the most plausible relationship to fit a statistically "normal" bell curve, with most pages possessing an average of perhaps three or four links. But the power law relationship says that there is no such preference—no scale to the connectivity of the network. A power law is scale-free [76].

A power law relationship between two scalar quantities x and y is such that the relationship can be written as in Eq. (5.1):

A Generalized Power Law

$$y = ax^k \tag{5.1}$$

---

[9]A robot in this sense is common parlance on the Web for a software program that is a software agent. A robot interacts with other network services intended for people as if it were a real person. One typical use of bots is to gather information.

where a is the constant of proportionality and k is the exponent of the power law, both of which are constants.

Power laws can be seen as a straight line on a log–log graph since, by taking logs of both sides, Eq. (5.1) is equal to Eq. (5.2):

A Power Law Expressed Using Logarithms

$$\log(y) = k \log(x) + \log(a) \tag{5.2}$$

Such power laws tell us that the Web is a special kind of small world network, one in which small average path lengths between two randomly selected nodes, coupled with a high degree of node clustering, combine to give a compelling criterion for connectivity: As the number of nodes in the network grows, the average path length increases very slowly.[10] Essentially it is relatively easy to get from one point in the network to another, no matter how large the network is.

The researchers at Notre Dame found also that a graph constructed to have the same power law distribution of connectivity, as they had observed for their section of the Web, does indeed show such characteristics.

So the Web is a small world and one in which its organization is very specifically characterized by a power law: by scale-free connectivity. Albert and her colleagues estimate that if the entire Web has the same structure as the Notre Dame University domain, then any two of its Web pages are separated by just an average of just 19 links. This is a somewhat larger span than in the 6 degrees common in types of social networks, but it is still a remarkably small number. This means that you can get from one extreme of the Web to another in fewer steps than it takes a normal man to run a hundred yards! From hand care to hacking, Homer Simpson to homeopathy, it's all just around the corner on the Web.

In fact, power laws seem to be a recurring pattern on the Web. Lada Adamic at the Xerox Research Centre has uncovered this kind of probability distribution in the number of pages per website, for instance. Furthermore, in 1998 she and her collaborators discovered that users who surf the Web also obey power-law statistics. Surfing is the common alternative to using search engines such as Google directly. You find a website that looks as though it might contain the information you want and then follow its hyperlinks to other pages until either you find what you are looking for or you conclude that its is not out there at all.

Most users will happily surf not just from one page to another but from site to site. But Adamic and her colleagues considered only the surfing pathways that surfers take within single sites. They were interested in how "deep" people go— how many clicks they follow, on average, before quitting the site. By looking at various data sets—the behavior of over 23,000 users registered with the service provider AOL, and visitors to the Xerox website, for example—they found that the probability distribution function of the number of clicks on a site obeyed a power law, or something very close to it [76].

---

[10]To be more mathematically precise, the characteristic path length is proportional to the logarithm of the number of nodes.

But what does a scale-free network actually look like? In a random graph most nodes have roughly the same number of connections and the structure looks relatively uniform throughout—as exemplified in the graph shown in Figure 5.5a. In a scale-free network, however, most nodes have only one or two links, yet a small but significant proportion are highly connected—as illustrated in Figure 5.5b. Thus the structure is very uneven, almost "lumpy," seemingly dense or pinched in some places but sparse in others [76]. It is these highly linked nodes that provide the shortcuts, the backbones that make the Web such a small world.

THE WEB'S BODY MASS

Not only are the ontology and topology of the Web scale-free, but it also turns out that the underlying infrastructure of the Internet also subscribes to such organization. This makes the Internet more like a natural body than anyone could have guessed. Such organizations are most often compared with the brain, and perhaps with some justification. Steven Strogatz and Duncan Watts at Cornell University have shown, for instance, that the pattern of connection in the neural network of the parasite nematode worm *Caenorhabditis elegans* displays the characteristic features of a small world network, having large clustering characteristics and small characteristic path lengths between neurons. Even more astonishing is the fact that Barabási and his colleagues have uncovered a still more vital network in the cells of a wide range of organisms that support a striking analogy with the scale-free Internet [76] or Web.

But how does this tie in with wider definitions of life? Perhaps the deepest principle of life is metabolism: The conversion of raw material from the environment into energy and the molecules that cells need every moment of their existence. Cells need access to a variety of building blocks: Our own cells, for example, are supplied with amino acids, sugars and lipids for food, as well as vitamins and mineral nutrients, water, oxygen and other essential substances. They use enzymes to re-

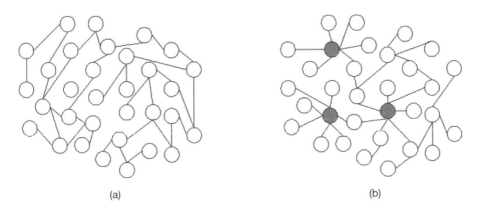

(a)   (b)

Figure 5.5. Examples of (a) random and (b) scale-free graphs.

arrange the atoms in these molecules to form new enzymes, nucleic acids, hormones, energy-rich molecules, and so on. The sequence by which useful raw material is converted into useful molecular form is called a metabolic pathway. Almost without exception, these pathways are not linear but instead branched and interlinked. They are literally a collection of "X" and "Y" structures purposefully strung together. A single raw material such as glucose is reconfigured or fragmented in many ways. The energy-rich molecules made during the breakdown of this sugar are used to power many other metabolic processes. So metabolism defines a large network of chemical reactions in which particular molecular substances can be regarded as nodes, and reactions (usually catalyzed by enzymes) can be considered as the links between one node and another [76]. Although it may not be apparent at first, from a structural point of view, this essential life-support system is exactly the same kind of networked support framework as found in the Web's relationship with the Internet—one simply feeds the other, just as metabolism feeds consciousness (Figures 5.6, 5.7).

In one stream of research at the University of Notre Dame, Barabási and his colleagues looked at the metabolic networks of 43 different organisms ranging from bacteria to plants to "higher" life forms like the nematode worm. They found that the connectivity distribution function in every case was scale-free, because the probability of a node having a certain number of links followed a power law. This implies that there are a few highly connected hubs in the network which play a crucial role in holding it together, as also predicted by IBM's bow-tie model of the

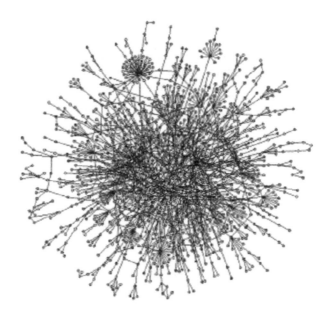

Figure 5.6. A part of the yeast metabolic network. The nodes represent molecules either supplied to or manufactured by the network, and the links are defined by the enzymic chemical reactions that convert one molecule into another.

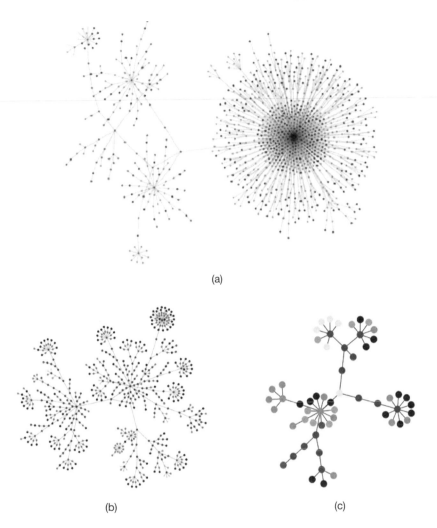

Figure 5.7. The graph structures of (a) Boingboing.net, (b) Wired.com, and (c) Google.com, respectively [86]. These show a striking resemblance to yeast's metabolic network shown in Figure 5.6.

Web. Many of the molecules representing these hubs reflect life's common evolutionary origins.

The scale-free structure of metabolic networks makes sound evolutionary sense, because it makes metabolism relatively insensitive to small incidences of random failure. If one or two enzymes are faulty, perhaps due to a genetic defect, this weakens or even severs the corresponding linkages in the associated metabolic graph. While this can have harmful consequences for certain biological functions, it need not, in a scale-free network, break up the whole entanglement and make life impossible. Therefore, scale-free networks can be considered as good "engineering," certainly on nature's part, wrought by trial-and-error explorations of options that are natural selection [76].

DNA AS AN ONTOGENETIC DATABASE

Returning to simpler models for supporting self-referencing, self-similar data structures, such as those found in relational databases, an interesting resemblance to biological information systems can be found.

As already shown in Figure 5.2, a suitable outline data model for the richly descriptive compositions of self-referencing data networks requires two discrete entities and two discrete types of association to effectively store its data and associative content. So, perhaps this provides evidence as to why DNA is itself also a structure comprising two parts.

DNA's famous structure is a double, rather than single, helix, with its intertwining being supported by two distinct types of base pairings—namely, purine–adenine always pairing with the pyrimidine–thymine and the pyrimidine–cytosine always pairing with the purine–guanine. So, it a case of doubles almost everywhere, with pairing being the name of the game.

Amazingly, the rules of base pairing state that if the sequence of nucleotides on one strand of DNA, are "read," the complementary sequence on the other strand can be immediately deduced; an extremely similar mechanism to that used in relational database technology, where similar "keys" form the basis for navigation around the information stored.[11] Furthermore, it is obvious that the Web is a network of information, a fractal network database in fact, that establishes itself around a navigational backbone of sorts, connecting one cluster of information to another. So, is it not remarkable that DNA has also long been known to possess such a backbone? This is a sugar-phosphate scaffold around which more complex proteins weave their biochemical blueprint and along which amino acids travel to extract this information during cell replication. Perhaps we, noncoincidentally, are acting as the Web's amino acids in a surreal mimic of nature's own biochemical workings!

Conjecture maybe, but yet still more evidence supports the idea of DNA as a structurally efficient database constructed from asymmetric linkages within a broader self-similar pattern. In itself, DNA's physical composition does not immediately present the recognizable characteristic of any fractal, but, as already highlighted, there have been studies suggesting that the placement of certain proteins along its length does indeed correspond to fractal patterns [8,9,14]. Furthermore, it may not be too far-fetched to construe that DNA is, in truth, merely a constrained form of progression, in much the same way as a spiral, and is therefore simply a fractal trying to break free. Therefore, from at least one perspective the notion of DNA as a purposeful fractal composition is not in the least fanciful. DNA surely cannot specify, for example, the vast number of bronchi, bronchioles, and alveoli or the spatial structure of the resulting tree in the lungs, but it can, however, specify a

---

[11]For further information see resources such as http://www.opensourcetutorials.com/tutorials/Databases/PostgreSQL/practical-database-design-part-1/page2.html as a basic introduction.

repeating process of bifurcation and development. Such processes suit nature's purposes [3].

In the 1980s, Chaos Theory brought to life a new kind of physiology, built on the idea that mathematical tools could help scientists understand global complex systems independent of detail. Computer Science too is based on mathematics, currently less formally chaotic in most circumstances certainly, but nevertheless stemming from similar roots. Twenty years ago it would have been almost impossible to find the word "fractal" in any physiology book, but today it would be hard to find a core textbook without it [3]. Researchers have found fractal and chaotic characteristics in the most unexpected of physiological circumstances; in the fibrillation of the heart, in the irregularity of cancer cell growth, and in the symptoms of some psychological disorders, to name but a few. So why not in the very instructions for life itself? Why would it be so strange if the structure of DNA were shown to conform to the compressed, self-similar realities that describe the diverse nature of most of our Universe and appear a cornerstone of the Web's evolution as well?

BACK TO GÖDEL—COMPRESSION, KEYS, CATALYSTS, AND RESTRICTORS

Refer back to the concept of Gödelization introduced early in Chapter 3, where both information and process can be converted and condensed into a single natural number. Hence it is possible to see how both can be treated in exactly the same formal manner—that is, being coded into the same mathematical form within a particular computational context. And, interestingly, a similar coding also takes place in a genetic context, in the process by which DNA is converted into protein by transcription and translation, some of which is further used to synthesise new strands of DNA [38].

In his book, *Gödel, Escher, Bach: An Eternal Golden Braid,* Douglas Hofstadter discusses the relationship between the coding of information into numbers, so that mathematical operations can be performed on them, and the coding of DNA into proteins, so that proteins can in turn produce or restrict the production of more DNA. He refers to such notions as "Strange Loops," which in common parlance can be seen as just self-reflexive, self-referential or recursive constructs.

As one might expect, when looking for such occurrences in genetics, some rather complex and perplexing scenarios can be found, for within the intricacies of the genetic encoding scheme are several instances of such strange loops. Hofstadter presents one exquisite example when he points out the reflexive nature of a palindromic sequence of DNA—a sequence where one strand of the double helix reads the same as the opposite strand in the reverse direction (Figure 5.8).

This configuration can be visualized as a stack of genetic information where the end of one strand matches the beginning of the other in the structure. At first sight this might not seem significant, but it shows the underlying mathematical beauty behind information storage in a strand of DNA that most geneticists take for granted. In fact, resent research has started to highlight the frequency, rather than the peculiarity, of palindromic sequences in DNA. For example, the P1 palindrome in the

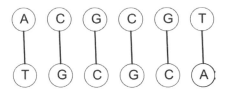

Figure 5.8. The palindromic nature of a sequence of DNA.

human Y chromosome could easily be considered to be as long as half the complete works of Shakespeare, and it's 99.97% accurate. The best guess as to why it's there is because Y chromosomes live alone and there's no chance to check their spelling against a partner. For this reason they possibly have to check gene spelling against themselves on the other arm of the palindrome—just one case of a recent discovery that's got little apparent mathematical significance, but quite a lot of "linguistic" importance.

The fact that is really interesting is that these palindromes are the sites at which restriction proteins—chemical structures that restrict or chop up DNA—act and slice nucleic acid. In nature these destroy foreign DNA that invades the cell. In the laboratory they are used extensively for genetic engineering, to construct new strands of DNA by cutting up two different strands of DNA and combining them together. Therefore these sites are essential for the survival of an organism, providing reference points essential to low-level survival processes. They show that the very mechanics of life itself are based on a simple self-similar concept, not only because of the nature of palindromic sequences, but also because of the self-referential, if not fractal, nature of transcription–translation–replication processes.

What is just as interesting here is that the cellular processes in which DNA partakes are known to utilize proteins as both information carriers and information processors. Hence DNA both embodies the machinery of the cell and the information it needs to act upon to affect change. It is literally a self-contained computing device. Yet from a biochemical position there is no distinction—a protein is just a protein. In such a way any interaction of protein with protein could be interpreted in one of thee ways; as data combining with data, process transforming data, or process interacting with process. Indeed all computational models are covered in a clean and concise manner when considering unification of the material involved via Gödelized encoding.

Nevertheless, even this is not the most fascinating of comparisons between digital and genetic worlds. There are many intracellular processes that are highly specific. They do not just occur as a result of any old protein interacting with another. Such processes must be triggered in a highly precise manner, needing the presence of another particular protein to promote their state through transition to create further proteins as part of a broader cellular process. One protein, or set of proteins, must act as a specific catalyst, as it were, a key to unlock the specific potential of another. Just as in the computational world of relational data, a specific packet of information—an individual protein type in this particular instance—points the way to the next logical element in a chain. In such a manner, cascades of genetic information are transcribed, relational data is retrieved, cellular processes are spawned, and abstract functions are computed. All are the same, really the same, when one examines the true nature of computation from the sufficiently high vantage point offered by Gödel's theorem. Thus biological cells compute using proteins in much the same way as a personal computer uses programs and data, or even the way the Web uses Web Services and websites. All are but different interpretations of the same picture, at different scales and using different materials.

What's more, all such systems can be represented in their simplest form using foundational "X"-shaped geometric patterns. In the case of genetic systems the catalysts present are proteins known as enzymes and the proteins they catalyze are known as substrates. Enzymes are a very special kind of protein with a very precise chemical definition.

A true catalyst in chemical terms substantially reduces the energy barrier that exists between atoms and that allows the atoms to get close enough to react and form a bond with one another. An enzyme, like all strictly defined catalysts, is therefore said to lower the energy of activation of a reaction, but the catalyst is not changed in any way in the process—rather like a conduit—a path through which reactions occur. All catalyst-like things do this. Therefore, when the atoms of protein molecules are acted upon by enzymes, an identical reaction occurs as would have occurred without the enzyme, but the energy slope required to overcome the proximity barrier is much, much smaller than would have been true without the enzyme's help (Figure 5.9). The structure of the enzyme is such that atoms of molecules can get close enough to interact, but the energy required to allow this closeness is relatively small—like going into an empty cupboard with someone relative to going into an empty auditorium with someone. The chances of interaction within the closet are greater than the chances within the auditorium—less energy being required to move around to increase the chances of bumping into one another.

Enzymes are very particular as one might expect in patterns requiring specificity. They won't catalyze just any old reaction, only those which are suited for that enzyme. This selectivity is essentially because of the fixed shape and size of the enzymes reaction zone and gives rise to a "key and lock" analogy. So again there is an extreme reliance on physical structure further down the fractal scale of living sys-

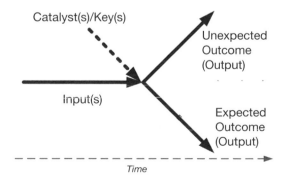

Figure 5.9. Catalytic inducement in an X-shaped axiomatic directed graph.

tems. Such sites may comprise only a tiny part of the entire enzyme's structure, but all of the structure is necessary in order for the site to be shaped correctly. And, only a select few molecules from any single enzyme will fit into this site. Therefore, there are thousands of different enzymes required in order for the thousands of different molecules within a living cell to engage in reactions. It is for this reason that a change in a gene—commonly referred to as a mutation—which encodes the enzyme's structure can result in a dysfunctional enzyme and lead to an inability of a cell to function properly.

There are many more instances of genetic and computing concepts coming together: An organism's genome can itself be uniquely encoded into a binary number, and arbitrary operations can be performed on it. For instance, enzymes and substrates could be encoded as binary functions which represent the activation or inactivation of an enzyme in the presence of a given substrate. The possibilities are endless and mind-boggling. Therefore it should be realized that the concept of encoding pervades throughout the genetic system and in turn throughout every living organism, thus being an overwhelming and characterizing attribute of life. This is particularly noticeable when formal language concepts are applied to DNA strands. A "string" of DNA can be formally specified by a grammar and can be parsed according to a set of productions, just as one would parse a natural or programming language string [38].

This all comes back to analogous models of computation and information. When described from extremely high-level perspectives, life is simply an information processing system, as is the Web, or any pocket calculator for that matter. This is not rocket science, but it is surprising that so many parallels exist between the artificial computer systems made by man and those fashioned by nature. This is especially true in the case of highly complex computer systems that are information-rich—a perfect depiction of the Web if there ever was one.

CHAPTER 6

Evolution through Engineering

The workings of evolution run so contrary to our normal intuitive assumptions about the world that there's always a fresh shock of understanding.

—*Douglas Adams, The Salmon of Doubt*

SOME KEY QUESTIONS STILL REMAIN

Regardless of the evidence so far, the challenge still remains: Why should one want to compare the World Wide Web with the chaotic self-similar lattices of the natural world and the structure of DNA? Surely they are all unconnected and dissimilar? Don't be fooled, quite literally, they all share aspects of a strikingly similar nature. It is undeniable that most modern digital computers are based on various binary schemes for data storage and algorithm construction, for instance. Central to such schemes are the concepts of broken symmetry, bifurcation, and two-state logic. Furthermore, DNA and RNA use similar schemes in the application of their quaternary alphabet of nucleotide bases. And it is also common knowledge that the largest man-made computer system in existence today is the World Wide Web, a complex maelstrom of concepts and communities that engulf, overlap, and intertwine in an unimaginable number of ways. The Web also sits on top of the Internet, the world's largest switching network, a mind-blowing coincidence when one considers that it has been known for more than 30 years that the ontogeny of genomic systems relies on exactly the same large-scale switching principles and that both the Internet and the Web exploit positional information technologies as part of their core protocol.[1]

But there is still more. The Web has been demonstrated to be a huge fractal bow-tie-like database, and it potentially shares this distinction with the conceptual way that DNA stores its own information. In addition, it is indisputably complex and self-similar across varying concentrations of interrelated content. Hypertext associations between apparently dissimilar Web resources may appear random under isolated inspection, but when they are considered within the context of wider communities, their power law association becomes apparent.

---

[1]Domain Name Services and Internet Protocol.

MEMES AND UNIVERSAL DARWINISM

The fact that the Web does not look like the double helix of DNA is irrelevant. It is merely a collection of concepts, connections, languages, and protocols that do not contain any notion of physical embodiment. Its deliberate separation from its Internet infrastructure sees to that by such a disconnection one could quite easily argue that the Web is simply a huge entangled map of coil-like graphs bounded by graphs. Unlike natural systems, the Web has had the rather good fortune not to be concerned with such physical practicalities. Even so, here too power laws have been observed [15], providing evidence that even the Internet itself is more physically akin to a hugely interconnected fractal architecture than not.

But all of this has little to do with mainstream thinking on how life evolved, has it not? Again don't be fooled. Classical Darwinian theories might well be tightly bound to material assets such as skin and bone, but more recently accepted ideas are not. In 1976 Richard Dawkins presented a far more ethereal update to accepted thinking on evolution. In this he outlined the idea of "selfishness" in genes [89], promoting the notion that they act only for themselves and therefore only replicate for their own good.

Dawkins also introduced the important distinction between "replicators" and their "vehicles." In the most obvious sense, one might expect his replicators to be the genes themselves, but this is not necessarily the absolute truth. It is the information held within them that is more the real replicator, and the gene's physical structure is simply its carrier. A replicator is hence anything of which copies can be made, and this includes completely virtual capital such as idea's, concepts, and even absolutely abstract information. A vehicle is therefore the entity that interacts with the environment to undertake or assist the copying process [78]. So, in a Web context, any concepts embodied in Web content can be seen as being replicators, and both human beings and software can be seen as being their vehicles.

Genes are, of course, replicators in a more holistic sense, selfish replicators that drive the evolution of the biological world. Nevertheless, Dawkins believes that there is a more fundamental principle at work. He has suggested that wherever it arises, anywhere in the Universe, be that real or virtual, "all life evolves by the differential survival of replicating entities." This is the foundation for the idea of Universal Darwinism, which encompasses the application of Darwinian thinking beyond the confines of biological evolution [78].

At the end of his book *The Selfish Gene,* Dawkins asked an obvious, yet provocative, question: Are there any other replicators on our planet? The answer, he claimed was "Yes." Staring us in the face, although still drifting clumsily about in its primeval soup of culture and technology, is another replicator—a unit of imitation [78].

This is an important leap because it raises evolution above a level needing physical contact, thereby making the Web an eminently suitable place for universal evolution to take place. In his search for further explanation, Dawkins stumbled, however, needing a name for the concept he had just invented—that is, a noun that conveyed the idea of a unit of cultural transmission, or unit of imitation. In the end he settled on the term "meme" from a suitable Greek root, a name inspirationally chosen for its likeness to the very word "gene" itself.

As examples of memes, Dawkins suggested "tunes, catch-phrases, clothes fashions, ways of making pots or of building arches." He mentioned specific ideas that catch on and propagate themselves around the world by jumping from brain to brain. He talked about fashions in dress or diet and also about ceremonies, customs, and technologies—all of which are spread by one person copying another [78]. In truth, although he would not have realized it at the time, Dawkins had captured the very essence of the Web, a virtual memetic framework that would evolve just as all natural life had done before it.

In a very short space, Dawkins laid down the foundations for understanding the evolution of memes. He discussed their propagation by jumping from mind to mind and likened memes to parasites infecting a host in much the same way that the Web can be considered. He treated them as physically realized living structures, and he showed that mutually assisting memes will gang together in groups just as genes do. Most importantly, he treated the meme as a replicator in its own right and thereby for the first time presented to the world an idea that would profoundly influence global society. If Dawkins were a gambling man, he would be very wealthy by now, because he had predicted the future of the Web before it was even born!

BOOLEAN LOGIC, REGULATORY NETWORKS, AND NEW FORMS OF LIFE

The currently fashionable notions of Grid Computing and Network Theory [6,7] aggressively position the Internet as a malleable and dynamic architecture of crisscrossing networks within networks and nodes within nodes. It can easily be viewed as an abstract self-similar mesh made up from nothing more than aggregates of "X"-derived patterns. In fact, network theory actually celebrates such crisscrossed connectivity when explicitly applied to the Web.

Recent research has demonstrated the Web to be a hugely complex aggregate of self-organizing interconnections with no central authority or meticulous design [7], and this decentralized, scale-free structure has unavoidable consequences for its evolution. Each time we are ready to "spin" a new set of connections on the Web, unable to escape its own laws, it creates this set based on the fundamental structural features of the myriad of connections "spun" before. Furthermore, it is the sturdiness of the laws governing the emergence of complex networks that is the key to their ubiquity. That's why Network Theory is equally at home describing such diverse systems as the interconnections behind natural language, the links between proteins in a cell, sexual relationships between people and the wiring diagrams of a computer chip [7].

For some time scientists, like Stuart Kauffman [17,18,52] have been interested in Network Theory, large Web-like networks, and the notion of life emerging from nonlife. In collaboration with colleagues, very much in an interdisciplinary environment, Kaufman has produced some groundbreaking work founded on concepts from areas such as chaos, complexity, and self-organized criticality.

So how does work like Kauffman's suggest that you might get emergent life out of the network that is the Web? To address this question, the raw properties of any arbitrary network must be considered first.

What makes a network? It's simple really. Only two types of component are really needed; the things to be connected and the actual connections between them. And how does any such network behave? This is the interesting part. The behavior of any arbitrary networked system is actually radically different depending upon the number of connections present. To demonstrate this, Kaufman's well-known analogy is often used:

Imagine a large empty room, on the floor of which a vast array of randomly placed buttons is laid out—10,000 or more say. Individual buttons can be connected in pairs by thread, but to start with no buttons are linked. This is definitely not a complex system in the everyday use of the term, but when threaded connections are added to this scenario the overall dynamic changes in a quite dramatic way. To demonstrate this change, start by connecting any two randomly selected buttons with a single length of thread, leaving them in their original position on the floor. Repeat this process a few times and if a button is chosen that happens to be already connected to others, just use the thread to connect it to another button as well. After this has been done a few times there will be a small amount of connectivity in the collection of buttons and the chances are that if you were to pick up any button from the floor, its connecting threads would only lift a few other buttons with it.

Make more threaded connections and eventually small random clusters of connected buttons will form that grow, slowly at first, in a linear fashion as the number of threads connecting pairs of buttons is increased (Figure 6.1). But when the number of threads approaches and then exceeds half of the number of buttons, the size of the largest cluster increases extremely rapidly—essentially exponentially—as each new thread is added. Very quickly a supercluster forms, a network in which the great majority of buttons are linked. Then the growth rate tails off, because adding more thread usually just increases the connectivity between the buttons already present in the supercluster [16].

This is a simple example of the phenomenon know as phase transition, which Kaufman likens to the way in which water undergoes change as it freezes into

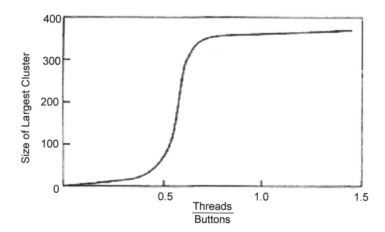

Figure 6.1. Phase transition in Kaufman's button network.

ice, these being two radically different manifestations of exactly the same base material.

Phase transition is a profoundly misunderstood and grossly underestimated symptom of evolutionary systems' behavior. It relates to all cases of systems where development goes unchecked and is even prolific in fields of complex human endeavor. Take, for instance, your average business project. At its inception it may be staffed with any number of personnel, all of whom understand their roles, responsibilities, and objectives well. Let the project run for a few months, however, throw in a couple more staff for good luck, and, no matter how competent the individuals concerned, the venture can easily become doomed to fail. Why? Quite simply because as the team members interact over time the number of connections between them increases and phase transition eventually occurs. What was once a simple piece of work suddenly becomes something quite different. Essentially, if the combined activity and understanding of the whole project team is not managed carefully, it can strangle its original purpose without having to try. This may not necessarily be a bad thing, given that the project's eventual outcome might actually exceed expectations. Nevertheless, it is almost certain that this unplanned outcome will be somewhat different from that originally expected.

But how does one link transitional emergent behavior with life or the Web? Again a compelling analogy comes to hand, relating back to the emergence of physical life on this planet some four billion years ago. For today's Web to play a part in this analogy, all you have to do is liken the resources present on the Web to the substances present in the primordial chemical broth from which life is believed by some to have originated. In this broth some substances acted as catalysts for the formation of other substances, so chemical A catalyzes the formation of chemical B. It is hard to see, given the variety of chemical raw materials around at the time, how this could not be the case, and even if the encouragement A gave to the formation of B was only small, it would still increase the concentration of B in the mix. Now suppose that the presence of B encourages the formation of C, C acts as a catalyst for the formation of D, and so on. Somewhere down the line, one of the compounds involved catalyzes the formation of A and you have a self-sustaining loop of interactions which in effect feeds off the raw materials available and makes more of the compounds in the loop, with the aid of energy from sunlight or heat from volcanic vents. There can, of course, be some other interactions: D might act as a catalyst for A as well as for E, and there may be some inhibitors as well. It is therefore easy to see how a network of connections between chemicals in the broth can arise, an autocatalytic network that sustains itself. This, argues Kauffman, is the way that life arose—as a phase transition in a chemical system involving a sufficient number of connections between nodes of the network [16].

A critical and pervasive feature of this argument is that like the emergence of a supercluster in the button and thread network, this is an all-or-nothing phenomenon. If the network is insufficiently connected, there is no life, but add one or two more connections and life becomes inevitable. There is no need to deliberately build a long chain of unlikely (chemical) events, one after another, in order for life to emerge, and there are no half-and-half states where you are not quite sure if the system is alive or dead.

This does not quite complete the picture, however. Although Kauffman knew that the very basic ingredients of life were involved in computation, he also understood that such computation was nothing like that undertaken by the simplistic devices that mainstream computer manufacturers produce. In the real cell, he realized, a great many regulatory genes could be actively switching biochemical processes at the same time. So instead of executing its instructions step by step, the way most man-made computers still do, the genomic computer executes most of its instructions simultaneously, in parallel. And if that were the case, he reasoned, then what mattered was not whether this regulatory gene activated that regulatory gene in some precisely defined sequence—that was a given as a consequence of higher-level patterns. What really mattered was whether the genome as a whole could settle down into a stable, self-consistent pattern of active genes. At most, the regulatory genes might be going through a cycle of two, three, or four configurations—a small number, anyway; otherwise the cell would just thrash around chaotically, with genes switching each other on and off at random. Of course, the pattern of active genes in a liver cell would be very different from the pattern in a muscle cell or a brain cell. But maybe that was just the point, Kauffman pondered. The fact that a single genome can have many stable patterns of activation might be what allows it to give rise to many different cell types during development [67].

Kauffman was also troubled by the normal tacit assumption that detail was everything. Bimolecular details were obviously important; he understood that only too well. But if the genome really had to be organized and fine-tuned to exquisite perfection before it could work at all, then how could it have arisen through the random trial and error of evolution? To Kauffman, this was like shuffling an honest deck of cards and then dealing yourself a bridge hand of 13 spades: possible, but not very likely. "It just didn't feel right," Kauffman has been quoted as saying. "If we had to explain the order of biology through lots of detailed, incredibly improbable bits of selection and ad hoc material, if everything we see was a hard struggle in the beginning, we wouldn't be here; it's as simple as that."

Kauffman was sure that there had to be more to it than that. "Somehow, I wanted it to be true that the order emerged in the first place, without having to be built in, without having to be evolved. I intentionally wanted it to be true that the order in a genetic regulatory system was natural, that it was quasi-inevitable. Somehow, the order would just be there for free. It would be spontaneous." If that were the case, he reasoned, then this spontaneous, self-organizing property of life would be the reverse side of natural selection. The precise genetic details of any given organism would be the product of random mutations and natural selection working just as Charles Darwin had described them. But the organization of life, the order, would be deeper and more fundamental. It would arise purely from the structure of the network and its switching capabilities, from computation itself and not the details [67]. Order, in truth, would rank as one of the great secrets of the Universe.

The irony of this discovery was that when Kaufman used the word "order," he was obviously referring to the same thing that other researches had found when studying complex systems. To them the order that Kaufman described was not the usual linear composition familiar to the traditional practitioners of "clean" science. No, this was something quite different; Kauffman's order was the "messiness" found in nonlinear systems—namely emergence, the incessant urge of complex systems to organize themselves into patterns. But then, maybe it wasn't so surprising that Kauffman was using exactly the opposite word, given that he was coming at the concept from exactly the opposite direction from other researchers like the economist Brian Arthur.[2] Arthur talked about "messiness" in systems because he had started from the cold and abstract world of economic equilibrium in which the laws of the market were supposed to determine everything as cleanly and precisely as the laws of physics—a world of linear fundamentals and expectations. Kauffman talked about "order" because he had started from the opposite end of the systems spectrum, in the entangled, contingent world of Darwin, in which there were no real known laws yet—just accident and natural selection. But both viewpoints essentially reached the same conclusion, in that complex nonlinear systems have a propensity to produce pattern and emergence, both fundamental and critical properties of high-order systems such as life. And by the same token it is not unreasonable to propose that the complex nonlinearity of the Web might develop patterns and emergence too, possibly as life.

There is obviously a great deal more to this argument, and it is also important to point out that Kauffman's ideas are both speculative and controversial. But not everyone is convinced by other ideas around life as an emergent property of complex systems either. However, Kauffman does put forward a persuasive package of elements in his argument, not least since all these elements fit the emergence of life into the same set of complex systems based on simple laws that are found so often elsewhere in the Universe. As Kauffman puts it, "life crystallizes at the critical molecular diversity because the catalytic closure itself crystallizes" [17].

Certainly, Charles Darwin didn't know about self-organization—matter's incessant attempts to organize itself into ever more complicated structures, even in the face of the incessant forces of dissolution described by the second law of thermodynamics. Neither did Darwin know that the forces of self-organization apply to the creation of living systems just as surely as they do to the formation of snowflakes or the appearance of convection cells in a hot pan of oil. So the story of life appears to be, indeed, the story of accident and happenstance, but it is almost certainly also the story of order: a kind of deep inner creativity that is woven into the very fabric of nature [67]. Perhaps if the likes of Kauffman had been alive in Darwin's time, the famous ideas behind works like *The Origins of Species* would have been far richer. As Kauffman himself later said in print, perhaps a more apt title for such a work might have been *The Origins of Order*. Whatever the origins of life, though, ideas involving networks, connections, and self-organizing criticality provide powerful new insights into the way that life operates once it has emerged.

---

[2]W. Brian Arthur is Citibank Professor at the Santa Fe Institute. From 1982 to 1996 he held the Morrison Chair in Economics and Population Studies at Stanford University. Arthur pioneered the study of positive feedbacks or increasing returns in the economy—in particular their role in magnifying small, random events in the economy.

BINARY BIOLOGICAL MACHINES

Kauffman and his team also undertook some much less controversial work into the way that biological cells work at the level of genes, providing the instructions that operate what is sometimes called "*the machinery of the cell*." This again pulls DNA back into the debate about Web life.

The relevant points that underpin Kauffman's investigations in this field are that genes act to control the machinery of the cell and, crucially, that genes can effect each other, with one gene turning another on or off—a binary switching system in short, identical to how discrete digital systems work. As such, the process of running a cell can be described in terms of a system with one node for each gene and also with connections between genes like the threads linking the buttons in Kauffman's famous analogy, or the hyperlinks in the matrix of the Web. With between 30,000 and 100,000 genes involved, one might expect that the problem of describing the behavior of such a system would be too complicated to solve. Undaunted, however, Kauffman and his colleagues investigated the behavior of such large networks via computer simulation, further taking into account the complication of feedback involved.

By applying the rules of Boolean logic, the team looked for the formation of stable patterns resulting from simple binary-based rules, and it indeed discovered a number of circumstances where large networks settle into repeating patterns, called, logically enough, "state cycles." These varied from cycles short enough to be noticed as a pattern through to progressions that might involve so many stages that one could wait the lifetime of the Universe and never notice any repetition. They also noticed cycles where systems might freeze into one particular state and never change thereafter. These state cycles, it was found, function as attractors, compelling systems' activity to change progressively toward them. In fact, in some cases state cycles turn out to be very powerful attractors, so that whatever state the system starts in, it very quickly moves toward one of these state cycles.

Kauffman and his colleagues argued that particular types of these cycles might be the key to cellular life, having found that in systems where just one input per node is applied, regardless of how many nodes there are and whatever the Boolean logic applied, nothing interesting ever happens. The system either develops into a very short state cycle or freezes up. If the number of connections to a node is greater than two, chaos reigns. There are attractors, but they have a huge number of states and they are also very sensitive to change. The only systems that behave in a way that is both complicated enough to be interesting and stable enough to be understood are those in which each node is connected to exactly two other nodes—corresponding closely to the foundational "X" and "Y" patterns discussed in Chapter 3. In this type of system alone, each state cycle has a length equal to the square root of the number of nodes. Even in a system with 100,000 nodes, a typical state cycle will be just 317 steps long. Better still, these state cycles are powerful attractors and if a system is set up in any random state, it quickly moves toward one of these cycles without being sensitive to small disruptions.

There's more. The same kinds of statistics apply to the number of different state cycles that can exist in such a system, although only in a more approximate way. In the kind of systems just described, there should be a number of different attractors approximately equal to the square root of the number of nodes present. With 100,000 different nodes, there will be about 317 different attractors. With 30,000, there will be about 173 different attractors. There are between 30,000 and 100,000 genes in the human genome and there are 256 different kinds of cell in the human body. Could it be that each cell type represents a particular state cycle for the human genome in which specific genes are turned on and others off?

To test this possibility, Kauffman has compared the number of genes and the number of cell types in different living organisms. Bacteria have only one or two different kinds of cell, for example, yeasts maybe three, the fruit fly 60, and so on. Kauffman has also shown that the number of cell types increases in approximate proportion to the square root of the amount of DNA present in the organism, and even though the genetic blueprints have not yet been obtained for every species, it seems a reasonable rule of thumb that the number of genes is proportional to the amount of DNA present.

The implications of this are, of course, profound. The same rules that govern linked piles of buttons and ultimately the workings of the Web are active in the cells of our own bodies. In simple terms there are a couple of hundred types of human cell because there are there are a couple of hundred state cycles which are attractors in the network of tens of thousands of genes interacting with one another in accordance with the rules of Boolean logic (Figure 6.2). And that's it, another secret of

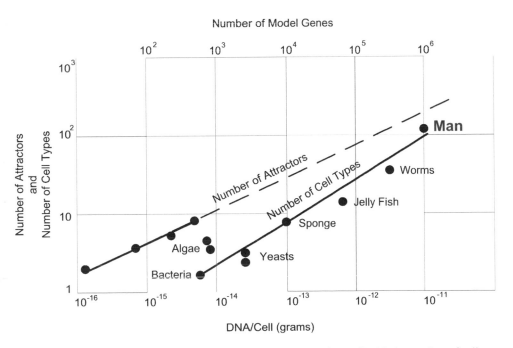

Figure 6.2. A log–log graph comparing the amount of DNA in a cell with the number of cell types for various organisms.

life at the level of cells. As Kauffman himself puts it, "we are the natural expression of a deeper order."

nK NETWORKS

In his work on the machinery of the cell, Kauffman used a greatly simplified network model for deliberate reason. With this he effectively reduced the multifaceted chemical signatures of the components involved in genomic interaction into the one-dimensional nomenclature of Boolean logic. He thereby created a study method that captured the behavioral essence of such hugely complex systems and allowed the detailed study of phenomena such as clustered behaviour and stabilisation effects.

Kauffman's approach used networks of varying size, containing n number of nodes, each with K number of inputs. For obvious reasons, such models are now referred to as "nK" networks, and their use proved critical to large parts of Kauffman's work. It was with such networks, for example, that he and his team discovered the relevance of setting $K = 2$ thereby creating patterns that were neither stable nor chaotic [58]. Such tools also highlighted the regulatory effect on coalescing systems of switching nodes based on two inputs—that is, networks made from Boolean "OR" and "AND" gates, which are logical axioms Kauffman chose to call "Canalizing Boolean Functions."[3]

But what principles allow $K = 2$ networks to exhibit such profound order? The answer appears to be that such arrangements develop a connected mesh, or *frozen core,* of elements, fixed in either an "on" or "off" state—a concept extremely similar to the Strongly Connected Core concept present in the Bow-Tie model of the Web [12] presented in Chapter 5. This creates spanning or "percolating," barriers of constancy which break the system into functionally isolated islands of unfrozen elements cut off from influencing one another by the barriers of frozen elements. What's more, the formation of these islands appears to be a sufficient condition for order in Boolean networks. Failure of a frozen core to percolate and leave such islands conversely appears to be a sufficient condition for chaos to thrive. Hence boundaries where frozen cores are just percolating and, more importantly, unfrozen regions are just breaking into unfrozen islands represent the phase transition between order and chaos. And it is at such boundaries that interesting phenomena like life appear.

Two related means of forming such percolating barriers are now recognized, the most prevalent of which is commonly known as "forcing structures." These types of formation generally account for the order seen in large, apparently random $K = 2$ networks, for instance, resulting in large interconnected matrices of elements which percolate across the entire arrangement. These often fall into a fixed state, leaving

---

[3]Generally a canonical form is a function that is written in the most standard, conventional, and logical way. In Kauffman's Boolean Networks, A canalizing rule is a Boolean rule with the property that one of its inputs alone can determine the output value, for either "true" or "false" input. This input value is referred to as the canalizing value, the output value is the canalized value, and we refer to the rule as being canalizing on this particular input.

behind functionally isolated islands of elements which are not part of the forcing structure [18].

It is therefore no coincidence that islands and boundaries are familiar themes on the Web. It is literally full of clusters and communities that insulate themselves for whatever reasons. But here again too, the dynamics of complexity can be seen at play as boundaries change over time. On the Web perpetual isolation is merely a misconception as evolutionary forces cause information, work, and social connectivity to continually reorganize.

"X" AS A CANONICAL SUPER PATTERN

Although Kauffman's work is without doubt significant, he appears to have been only mildly interested in the fundamental structural geometry of such networks, and here the immutable "X"-shaped graph pattern again looks to be particularly relevant. This can often be drawn as shown in Figure 6.3, with the steady state of a given system represented as a node rather than an arrow as originally described. Graphs of this type normally also show the input (i_1) needed to instigate such steady states and other stimulants ultimately used to trigger change (i_2), thereby using arrows to represent transitions between nodes as state points within a problem space. Such graphs also typically include both types of potential change, or output from a given node. These can be seen as both expected (O_1) and unexpected ($NOT\ O_1$) state changes, with unexpected outputs often relating to errors produced by the node.

An interesting and obvious characteristic of this pattern is that it can be used to model both forms of standardized Boolean logic. For instance, consider the set of mapped paths through this pattern, comprizing

$$\{i_1 + i_2 \rightarrow O_1, i_1 + i_2 \rightarrow NOT\ O_1, i_1 \rightarrow O_1 + NOT\ O_1, i_2 \rightarrow O_1 + NOT\ O_1\}$$

to be read as

Input 1 with Input 2, producing only Output 1,

Input 1 with Input 2, producing only NOT Output 1,

Input 1, producing Output 1 and NOT Output 1, and

Input 2, producing Output 1 and NOT Output 1

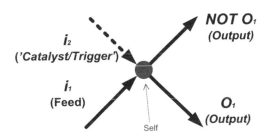

Figure 6.3. An alternative representation of the X-shaped axiom as a $K = 2$ network node.

This can not only be seen as mechanisms for representing both a singular Boolean logical OR gate (as in Kaufmann's nK networks) and a singular Boolean logical AND gate, but can also model Boolean characteristics in terms of both input and output—that is, patterns demonstrating both forking and switching characteristics, thereby making it a truly versatile and canalizing super pattern.

This is fine theory to be sure, but in practice its application is obvious. Quite simply networked systems founded on recurrent X-shaped patterns can not only provide all the basic parts needed for computing to take place, but are also well-suited to the construction of complex schemes balanced on the edge of chaos—systems such as the evolution of life itself. Scientists familiar with the messiness of biology have known this for some time now, but it has only been recently that those with more clinical backgrounds like computer science and physics have started waking up to the idea. In doing so, they are starting to realize the deeper implications of such patterns in large and complex connected systems. Perhaps today, if you could get the radical free thinkers from such disciplines together in debate about such matters, heads would quickly start to nod. There are simply too many similarities to ignore, and the reality may be dawning that complex computational systems like the Web have a tempting propensity to appear life-like.

AUTOCATALYTIC SETS

As an outcome of work like that of Stuart Kauffman, it has been realized that if the conditions in complex networks are right—in any given "primordial soup," as it were—then there is no need to wait for random reactions to occur at all. The constituents or agents involved should simply gravitate to form a coherent, self-reinforcing web of reactions. Furthermore, each constituent in the web should catalyze the formation of other constituents in the web, so that all the constituents steadily grow more and more abundant relative to constituents that are not part of the web. Taken as a whole, in short, the network should catalyze its own formation and in doing so be categorized as an "autocatalytic set" [67].

Kauffman was in awe when he realized all this. Here it was again: order for free, the distinctive "messiness" of complex emergent behavior. This was natural order arising through cleaner, more fundamental laws of the Universe, order that comes from molecular-like complexity involving high orders of interaction, manifesting itself ultimately as a system that just grows. The idea was, and always will be, indescribably beautiful.

But was this the real essence of life? Kauffman had to unfortunately admit that it was not, if one meant life as traditionally recognized in a biological sense. An autocatalytic set has no internal blueprint from which to build itself, no DNA to speak of, no genetic code, no cell membrane. In fact, it has no real independent existence except as a haze of constituents floating around in some particular space. Its fundamental nature is not to be found in any individual member of the set, but in the overall dynamic of the whole—that is, its collective behavior.

Even so, Kauffman believed that in some deeper sense, autocatalytic sets could be considered to be alive. Certainly, they can exhibit some remarkable lifelike properties. They can spontaneously grow, for example, and there is no reason in principle why an autocatalytic set shouldn't be open-ended, producing more and more constituents as time goes on—and constituents that are more and more complex. Furthermore, autocatalytic sets can possess a kind of metabolism. Constituents can take in a steady supply of "nourishment" in the form of other constituents circulating around them, and they can catalytically glue themselves together to form more and more complex compounds.

Autocatalytic sets can even exhibit a kind of primitive reproduction. If a set from one space happens to spread out into a neighboring space—in a flood say, to use a suitable analogy from the natural world—then the displaced set can immediately start growing in its new environment if the conditions are right. Of course, if another, different autocatalytic set were already in habitation, the two would intermingle in a competition for resources. And that, Kauffman realized, would immediately open the door for natural selection to purge and refine the sets. It is easy enough to imagine such a process selecting those sets that possessed the most appropriate fitness for the space, the landscape as it were. Eventually, in fact, it is easy to envisage the competitive process giving rise to a kind of DNA and all the other attributes we naturally associate with life. The real key is to get a set that can survive and reproduce. After that the evolutionary process would kick in and could do its work in comparatively short order [67].

This may appear like a lot of speculation, but not to Kauffman and his fellow workers. The autocatalytic set story was far and away the most plausible explanation for the origin of life that they had ever heard. If it is true, it means that the origin of life did not have to wait for some ridiculously improbable event to produce a set of enormously complicated molecules. It means that life could certainly have emerged from very simple ingredients indeed. Furthermore, it means that it had not been just a random accident, but was part of nature's incessant compulsion to resist entropy, its incessant compulsion to self-organize.

When Kauffman tackled the underlying mathematics of his ideas, the reality became obvious in that the number of reactions goes up faster than the number of polymers—connections and types of resource in the case of the Web. So, if there is a fixed probability that a polymer will catalyze a reaction, there is also some complexity at which that reaction becomes mutually autocatalytic. In other words, it was just like the genetic networks found in Artificial Life; and if any primordial soup passes a certain threshold of complexity, then it will undergo a peculiar phase transition. The autocatalytic set will indeed be almost inevitable [67]. And by such principles, if the conditions are right, the Web too is destined to "live."

This is not deliberate trickery. When one looks at the ideas behind autocatalytic sets, it soon becomes apparent that they have the potential to be ubiquitous across all complex systems, not just those restricted to biological classification. Autocatalytic sets can be viewed as webs of transformation amongst components in precisely the same way that the economy is a web of transformations amongst goods and services or the Web is a network of transformation of data and knowledge. In a very real sense the Web is an autocatalytic set—it is the archetypal definition of a system that consumes material—mostly unstructured information in this case—and converts it into something else, something much more powerful and useful.

CHAPTER 7

A Less-Than-Simple Matter of Boundless Organics

All the limitative Theorems of metamathematics and the theory of computation suggest that once the ability to represent your own structure has reached a certain critical point that is the kiss of death: it guarantees that you can never represent yourself totally. Gödel's Incompleteness Theorem, Church's Undecidability Theorem, Turing's Halting Problem, Turski's Truth Theorem—all have the flavour of some ancient fairy tale which warns you that "To seek self-knowledge is to embark on a journey which . . . will always be incomplete, cannot be charted on a map, will never halt, cannot be described."

—Douglas R. Hofstadter

OPEN WORLDS, FEEDBACK, AND CRITICAL SELF-ORGANIZATION

Now that similarities between the micro properties of living organisms and the Web have been investigated, it is time to consider macro-level similarities as well. Just as in naturally occurring physical systems where it can take millions of participating elements to exhibit noticeable impact on surroundings, it has been shown that the Web has now reached a size and complexity that could demonstrate a number of life-like macro properties. Statistics from studies like those that produced the Bow-Tie model of the Web have measured its connectivity to be between 29.8% and 76.6%, depending upon the strength of connectivity measured—a range whose median teeters just over the 50% limit needed for phase transition to take place and superclusters to form. Furthermore, both the Bow-Tie model and the notion of "X"-shaped base patterns ultimately revolve around the concept of binary connections between nodes and the capability for switching to take place, the essential property found by Kauffman in his huge, "life-like" networks.

Now, ask any anthropologist about the critical conditions needed for life and two recurring themes appear: first, that any evolutionary life process must be self-controlling, providing justification in itself for itself, and, second, that it cannot be wholly insular. Such systems must be open to external influence and be powered from a plentiful source of energy or impetus. As most systems do not possess such sources internally, they must therefore be driven from and by their environment in accordance with the second law of thermodynamics, the common term for such systems being "Open World." Add feedback to this concept, leading to transitional behavior, and one is faced with the notion of *"critically self-organizing open world systems."*

Classical thermodynamics states that closed systems are those that exchange energy but not matter with their surroundings. Living organisms, in contrast, are open systems that exchange both energy and matter with their surroundings. This crucial difference allows living organisms to keep their internal state constant via a flux of matter and energy through the pathways between their internal components, regardless of scale [20]. So it may not be too extreme to paraphrase and say "for chance to have a chance, for time to be more than an illusion, and for history to be the site of aleatory[1] emergence, systems must be open" [29]. Even so, in order to understand the true nature of open systems our natural affinity to closed order must be examined first.

The identification of the principles governing intrinsically stable systems can be traced back to a discovery that occurred over three centuries ago. In 1686, Sir Isaac Newton presented the conclusions of his *Principia* to the Royal Society in London. While his formulation of the basic laws of motion and the definition of pivotal concepts like mass, acceleration, and inertia marked a milestone in the history of science, it was his identification of the universal law of gravitation that had the most distinguishing impact both within and beyond the world of modern science.

The third book of his *Principia* discusses universal gravitation and bears the significant title "The System of the World." In the course of describing this system, he not only transforms the understanding of the natural world but also claims to define the logic of stable systems wherever they occur. For Newton, there was actually only one system in the world, and it is governed by absolute universal laws that make natural processes potentially transparent and predictable.

At a distance of more than three centuries, it is difficult to appreciate the enthusiasm with which many greeted Newton's theories. In the words of Alexander Pope's memorable couplet:

Nature, and Nature's Laws lay hid in night:
God said, Let Newton be! And all was light!

The conviction that the order of the natural world can be rationally comprehended makes it possible to believe that disorder and chaos are merely apparent and can be finally explained in terms of order.

There is, however, a high price to be paid for the apparent transparency and predictability that Newton brought to science. "Classical Science," as so many modern philosophers have pointed out, emphasizes a "dead and passive nature, a nature that behaves as an automaton which, once programmed, continues to follow the rules inscribed." Newton's vision of the world is in effect a machine governed by continuously linear abstract rules, often analogized to a mechanical clock, tick tocking for eternity. It is a mechanical device made up of separate parts organized by a design that is not implicit in the parts or its workings as such.

[1]Dependent on chance, luck, or an uncertain outcome.

Through such an analogy, it is easy to see how Newton's ideas helped to inspire and power the Industrial Revolution. By means of Newtonian principles, the world became a place within the reach of most human intellects, offering viewpoints easily amenable to the tools of reduction and structuralism. In this ideal and simplistic realm, "natural" motion is constant and always directed in a straight line—a world of which Euclid would be proud. Irregular motion, curvature, and angles are out of place in such a world, being dismissed as nothing more than a distraction from accepted thinking. Such worlds are intrinsically stable, if somewhat descriptively restrictive, simplistic, and "uninteresting."

Nevertheless, from such relatively simple positions, it is possible to derive the fundamental characteristics of inherently stable systems. While Newton was primarily interested with systems in the physical Universe, his analysis can be widely appropriated to interpret all "systems," be they real or abstract. Fundamentally, stable systems are hence:

- **Closed:** Once established, they are not amenable to outside sources of influence, be they based on either energy or information.

- **Deterministic:** The internal laws of the system function universally and cannot be broken. Effects are proportionate too and can be accurately predicted from their causes.

- **Reversible:** The laws governing such systems apply to both temporal directions. As a result of this reversibility, time appears to be inconsequential.

- **Operate at, or near, equilibrium:** The closure of the structures and the reversibility of their governing laws incline a stable system to the state of inertia. Forces and counterforces, as well as actions and reactions, tend to balance each other and change only occurs between equilibrium states.

- **Parts are independent of each other and are hence externally related:** The whole is the sum of its parts. Since independent parts are not fundamentally changed by their position in the whole, the whole can be reduced to the parts that comprise it without compromising the definition or individual function of those parts.

Though intended to be universally descriptive, Newton's mathematical formulae can only describe relatively simplistic natural systems and are, in truth, woefully inadequate for explaining the descriptive features of complexity, or systems classically categorized as operating far from equilibrium.

Newtonian systems are inherently mechanical, having a distinctive trait where self-subsistent parts are joined by the imposition of external relationships. Since differences between parts remain indifferent to each other even when bound together, a composition, mixture, or aggregate of parts is merely a "formal totality," which involves nothing more than a "semblance of unity." Neither mechanical combination nor mechanic assemblage exhibits any genuine unification or real integration.

In contrast, an organism, like a beautiful work of art, is a self-organized entity. Rather than imposed from without, order in an organism emerges from within through a complex interplay of parts, which in the final analysis constitutes the definition and activity of the whole. According to the principle of "intrinsic finality," "an organized natural product is one in which every part is reciprocally both end and means."

Since means and end are so intertwined and mutually constituted, the parts of an organism do not point beyond themselves to external orders, but constitute their own purpose. In this way an organism exhibits inner teleology or purposiveness without purpose—that is, purposiveness without a purpose other than itself. In contrast to mechanical, stable assemblages, organisms are integrated wholes that display systemic unity. This unity presupposes a systemic structure that differs from mechanical systems in important ways, and it is precisely these differences that separate the Information Revolution from its Industrial predecessor.

Based on such definitions, the Web can most definitely be considered as organic, rather than mechanic. It maintains a relatively constant composition by continually taking in nutrients from its environment and returning excretory products [20] in the form of cumulative information and services. Not only is it being externally fed from mankind's inquisitive and compulsive need to share experience and knowledge, but it is also receiving energy indirectly from our global electrical grid via the Internet's underlying infrastructure. From this perspective, one could easily consider it to be analogous to a parasite, and a greedy one at that. Without mankind to serve its every need, it would surely perish. But herein can be found one huge conundrum: If the Web is the only member of a truly new and living species, what evidence exists to support this proposition?

Surprisingly, some might offer evidence that the Web has evolved noticeably already since its original inception, advocating that it has undergone a kind of speciation at least once so far. When the Web was first truly born, at the CERN laboratories in the early 1990s, it was a loose collection of largely academic papers associated via hypertext links. Very slowly it expanded but was still dependent on raw natural language text as the bedrock for its associations. From this starting position the likes of search engine technologies flourished and the entire e-commerce revolution was sprung. Nevertheless, for some, this was not enough. The Web's associative muscle, they felt, was not strong enough to spawn the next generation of Web technologies. So by the end of the 1990s, work began to enhance the Web's core architecture based on modern mathematical and linguistic thinking. This was intended to increase the accessibility of the meaning contained within the Web's content and added much rigor to the overall Web concept. For such reasons, this new extension to the Web became recognized in its own right as the Semantic Web: The Web had split in two.

Many still consider the Semantic Web to be a relatively new class of Web technologies, but this is sadly a common misperception. The technologies involved have been available for over seven years, making the Semantic Web a relatively old man in IT terms. Yet still it has not seen mainstream adoption. Why is this so, especially given the meteoric rise of its forerunner?

The Semantic Web was always intended to complement and strengthen the traditional Web, but in fact it has actually developed along a tangential path to date with only limited applicability. A number of very fine and worthy Semantic Web languages and tools have been developed, but almost none have crossed over into

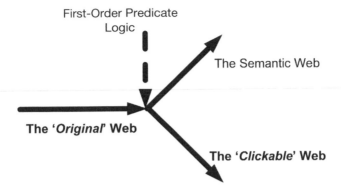

First-Order Predicate Logic

The Semantic Web

The '*Original*' Web

The '*Clickable*' Web

Figure 7.1. The first speciation of the Web.

mainstream Web world. The Web has, it appears, undergone a form of bifurcation, catalyzed by the introduction of ideas based on mathematical formalisms such as first order predicate logic[2] (Figure 7.1). From that splitting point, one variant of the Web continued to develop along the lines of increased natural language strength—a Web variant some now refer to as the "mainstream" or "clickable Web," while the other has headed off down a path based on mathematical principle, strong reasoning, and provable semantics. This is not to say that Semantic Web does not have its place in the new and brave world of the Web, quite the contrary, it is already searching out its own destiny in areas like Bioinformatics and Software Engineering. Only time will tell if it will ultimately recombine with the mainstream and prove this argument incorrect.

GÖDEL, INCOMPLETENESS, AND MAINTENANCE THROUGH CHANGING BOUNDARIES

Closed worlds may well be a precondition for stability in systems, but open worlds are unquestionably an essential ingredient in life processes. The workings of a car engine and the grinding of stone against stone in a windmill are both examples of good old-fashioned stable linearity, being precise and well-defined in their making from the very outset. These are relatively simple processes, elegant almost, being easy to implement and control. So surely nature must gravitate toward such standards by default; after all simple is best, correct? True, but again the intricate workings of the Universe can be deceptive. They appear to demonstrate a natural propensity to veer away from the clean-cut and stable. Our world is not naturally a perfect and simple place where boundaries are an absolute, rather imperfection and openness to change, it seems, are part of our fundamental existence.

The idea of imperfect logic dates as far back as the ancient Greeks. Epimenides, the celebrated Greek poet, lived in Crete during the sixth century B.C. and is reputed

[2]First-order logic (FOL) is a system of mathematical logic, extending propositional logic.

to have created the oldest of logical paradoxes by stating that "all Cretans are liars." Being a Cretan himself, this statement implied hidden reflexive complications and outlines a dilemma in logic that has occupied the minds of many noteworthy philosophers for centuries. In 1931 Kurt Gödel wrote an influential paper on such matters entitled "On Formally Undecidable Propositions in Principia Mathematica and Related Systems." Though he eventually became a professor of mathematics, Gödel always remained interested in philosophical problems. Born in Moravia in 1906, he studied at the University of Vienna, where he took part in the discussion group that became known as the famous Vienna Circle. Among those Gödel met in this elite group were the philosopher Rudolph Carnap and the mathematician Kurt Menger. Their discussions introduced Gödel to a broad range of problems in philosophy and mathematical logic, immersing him in the writings of many well-known philosophers. Gödel did not share the philosophical outlook of the Vienna Circle but quickly realized the similarities between the self-referentiality involved in the investigation of language through language and the mathematical formalization of mathematical systems.

While Gödel's work on imperfect logic is directed specifically against arguments advanced in *Principia Mathematica,*[3] its implications extend far beyond any particular mathematical dispute. In 1910 Bertrand Russell[4] and Alfred North Whitehead[5] announced that they had derived all mathematics from logic without any contradictions. Intrigued by this claim but not convinced of its validity, the well-known mathematician David Hilbert issued a challenge to prove its credibility in a lecture delivered in 1930. Is it possible, he asked, "to demonstrate rigorously—perhaps following the very methods outlined by Russell and Whitehead—that the system defined in *Principia Mathematica* was both consistent (contradiction-free), and complete (namely that every true statement of number theory could be derived within the framework drawn up in *Principia Mathematica*)?" If the propositions put forward by Russell and Whitehead could be shown to be both consistent and complete, the age-old dream of logic and mathematical certainty would be a reality and the

---

[3]The *Principia Mathematica* is a three-volume work on the foundations of mathematics, written by Alfred North Whitehead and Bertrand Russell and published in 1910–1913. It is an attempt to derive all mathematical truths from a well-defined set of axioms and inference rules in symbolic logic. The main inspiration and motivation for the *Principia* was Frege's earlier work on logic, which had led to some contradictions discovered by Russell. These were avoided in the *Principia* by building an elaborate system of types: A set has a higher type than its elements, and one cannot speak of the "set of all sets" and similar constructs which lead to paradoxes (see Russell's paradox).

The *Principia* only covered set theory, cardinal numbers, ordinal numbers, and real numbers; deeper theorems from real analysis were not included, but by the end of the third volume it was clear that all known mathematics could in principle be developed in the adopted formalism.

The questions remained whether a contradiction could be derived from the *Principia*'s axioms, and whether there exists a mathematical statement that could neither be proven nor disproven in the system. These questions were settled by Gödel's incompleteness theorem in 1931. Gödel's second incompleteness theorem shows that basic arithmetic cannot be used to prove its own consistency, so it certainly cannot be used to prove the consistency of anything stronger [114].

[4]Bertrand Arthur William Russell, 3rd Earl Russell, was an influential British logician, philosopher, and mathematician, working mostly in the twentieth century [115].

[5]Alfred North Whitehead was a British-American philosopher, physicist, and mathematician who worked in logic, mathematics, philosophy of science, and metaphysics [116].

boundaries of modern science would be firmly grounded. But Gödel proved once and for all the impossibility of this vision by showing that "all consistent axiomatic formulations of number theory include undecidable propositions."

Gödel's theory extends the paradoxes of self-reflection, which he first encountered in the debates about language in the Vienna Circle, to number theory and information theory in general [29] and can be easily illustrated by the following mind-twisting, self-reflexive conundrum, commonly referred to as the Liar's Paradox:

The sentence below is true.
The sentence above is false.

which can also be written as

I am lying now.

or

This statement is false.

The problem with the paradox is that it seems to show that even the most cherished common beliefs about truth and falsity actually lead to a contradiction. Statements can be constructed that cannot consistently be assigned a truth value even though they are completely in accord with relevant grammars and semantic rules. Consider the simplest version of the paradox, the sentence "This statement is false." If one supposes that the statement is true, everything asserted in it must be true. However, because the statement asserts that it is itself false, it must be false. So the hypothesis that it is true leads to the contradiction that it is true and false. Yet one cannot conclude that the sentence is false because that hypothesis also leads to contradiction. If the statement is false, then what it says about itself is not true. It says that it is false, so that must not be true. Hence, it is true. Under either hypothesis, one ends up concluding that the statement is both true and false. But it has to be either true or false—or so our common intuitions lead us to think—hence there seems to be a contradiction at the heart of our beliefs about truth and falsity.

However, the fact that the Liar's Paradox can be shown to be true if it is false and false if it is true has led some to conclude that it is neither true nor false. This response to the paradox is, in effect, to reject one of the most common beliefs about truth and falsity: the claim that every statement has to be one or the other. This common belief is called the Principle of Bivalence.

The proposal that the statement is neither true nor false has given rise to the following, strengthened version of the Liar's Paradox:

This statement is not true.

If it is neither true nor false, then it is not true, which is what it says; hence it's true, etc.

This again has led some to propose that statements can be both true and false, a concept known as Paraconsistent Logic.

So powerful and surreal is such insight that still today it causes much debate on even the most leading edges of mathematically rooted fields. In the Semantic Web community, for example, discussion regularly consumes the attention of those involved to establish whether data used to describe data—metadata in other words—can also be classified as data itself. But one thing is known, in that "a theory has to be simpler than the data it explains, otherwise it does not explain anything. The concept of a law simply becomes vacuous if arbitrarily high complexity is permitted" [88]. At some point it has to be contained to be of any purposeful meaning.

The proof of Gödel's Incompleteness Theorem hinges upon the capabilities of a formally self-referential mathematical statement, a singularly difficult task to accomplish. In fact it took an act of genius merely to connect the idea of self-referential statements to number theory. Gödel uses a statement that approximates to the Liar's Paradox to prove his claim around "undecidable propositions." Looping self-reflection, hence, becomes strange when, in turning back on itself, it generates irresolvable paradoxes. And this is where the Web comes in, because it too is a self-reflective system at a number of levels.

The consequences of Gödel's proof are profound and apply to all systems that conform to the ideas presented in Russell and Whitehead's work. It thereby points to incompleteness and uncertainty as being unavoidable attributes of all apparently complete and consistent systems. In other words the concept of absolute and unquestionable understanding of any stable or closed system may, under particular types of inspection or context, be a fallacy. Essentially the concept of closed systems is a complete misnomer, and all systems are in fact open in at least some sense.

Such ideas state that the Universe is not naturally the domain of closed boundaries, but instead it is a never-ending expanse of folded realities. It is only within the confines of such folds that we are fooled into simplistic security, because stability settles to points of apparently measurable and predictable order. Nevertheless, should the condition of whichever such fold transgress any of its boundaries and break its own symmetry, then transition into different rule sets may be an unpredictable consequence—unpredictable, that is, purely as a result of the complexities on either side of the transition itself. In Gödel's mind at least, therefore, it seems that emergence, through transition, is the real meta-order of everything around us, before us and after us. So self-reflexive systems like the Web are more normal than not. Uncertainty is the only certainty there is in the Universe, and therefore it is an unavoidable consequence whenever symmetry is broken. When one thing comes to an end and another thing starts, uncertainty is apparently nature's ever-present witness, as can be seen in Figure 7.2.

But all is not lost. For those who believe that the depths of complexity can, some day, be proved ultimately fathomable, there is no need for a concept such as uncertainty, so perhaps a greater truth for future use may well be that "the only true certainty in the Universe is complex certainty!"

It is important to understand precisely what is at stake with the notion of undecidability. Since undecidable propositions cannot produce expected outcomes in de-

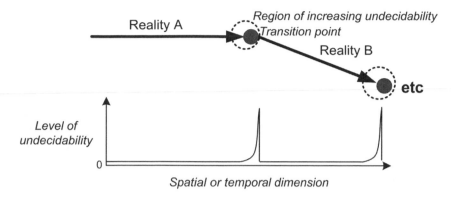

Figure 7.2. Levels of undecidability in systems structure.

terministic forms of binary logic, they leave no room for speculative exchange involving logical argument, and structuralism cannot be used to understand them. But this does not mean that undecidables simply lack binary structure and formal association. If this were true, then undecidables would clearly be considered outside the structure and context of any truly tangible system. They would be included in an oppositional existence, thus being part of a system they were supposed to exclude. Such structuring would make the undecidable determinant and thus decidable, hence destroying the very basis of its proposition.

Undecidability therefore forms a kind of boundary that systems need even if it interrupts their reflective self-relation. It obstructs the decisive definability of all systems as an indiscernible externality, being neither fully excluded nor fully included. This "outside" which is "inside" exposes the openness of every system that seems to be closed.

Cognitive philosopher Douglas Hofstadter[6] calls such paradoxical reflexives "strange loops." As examples Hofstadter points to Gödel's proof of unprovable mathematical axioms as well as to the seemingly ever-rising notes in a Bach canon, or the endlessly rising steps in an Escher staircase. In his book *Gödel, Escher, Bach: An Eternal Golden Braid,* he states: "The 'strange loop' phenomenon occurs whenever, by moving upward (or downward) through the levels of some hierarchical system, we unexpectedly find ourselves right back where we started."

Life and evolution entail the necessary strange loop of circular causality—of being tautological[7] at a fundamental level. You can't get life and open-ended evolution unless you have a system that contains that essential logical inconsistency of

---

[6]Douglas Richard Hofstadter is an American academic. He is probably best known for his book *Gödel, Escher, Bach: An Eternal Golden Braid* (abbreviated as GEB), which was published in 1979, and won the 1980 Pulitzer Prize for general nonfiction [117].

[7]An empty or vacuous statement composed of simpler statements in a fashion that makes it logically true whether the simpler statements are factually true or false—for example, the statement "either it will rain tomorrow or it will not rain tomorrow."

circling causes. In complex adapting processes such as life and the Web, evolution and consciousness's primary causes seem to shift as if they were optical illusions. So, part of the problem that humans have when trying to build systems as complicated as our own biology is that in the past we have insisted on a degree of logical consistency, a sort of clockwork logic that blocks the emergence of autonomous happenings. We unconsciously try to block such emergence when it is within our reach, threatened by our lack of complete control and comprehension. But, as Gödel showed, inconsistency is an inevitable trait of any self sustaining system built out of consistent parts. And as our grip on the Web in its entirety slowly slips, Gödel's work also points to more emergent destinies in its path.

Gödel highlighted, amongst other things, that attempts to banish self-swallowing loopiness are pointless, because, in Hofstadter's words, "it can be hard to figure out just where self-referencing is occurring." When examined at a conceptual level, every part appears legitimate, but when the lawful parts are combined into a larger whole contradictions arise.

AN ABSTRACTIONLESS UNIVERSE

While an undergraduate medical student at Dartmouth College, Stuart Kauffman had a vision that somewhat contradicted the thinking of his peers at the time. As Kauffman remembers it, he was standing in front of a bookstore window daydreaming about the design of a chromosome. As he stared in the window, he imagined a book, a book with his name on it, a book that he would write in the future.

In his vision, the pages of the book were filled with a web of arrows connecting other arrows, weaving in and out of a living tangle. It was the icon of the Web today, although he would not have known this at the time. But the mess was not without order. The tangle sparked mysterious, almost cabalistic, "currents of meanings" along the threads. Kauffman discerned an image emerging out of the links in a "subterranean way," just as recognition of a face springs from the crazy disjointed surfaces in a cubist painting.

As a medical student studying cell development, Kauffman saw the intertwining lines in his fantasy as the interconnections between genes. Kauffman suddenly felt sure that out of that random mess would come inadvertent order—the architecture of an organism. Out of the chaos would come order for no reason: order for free, the complexity of the points and arrows generating a spontaneous order with its own pecking order of associations and classifications. But this was something of a nauseating proposal for his more conservative contemporaries. That systems could produce their own order flew in the face of traditional reductionist principles. Systems were not supposed to do such things, that was for science and technology to do, defining whatever boundaries and thresholds it considered best fit the requirements of human comprehension and design.

Although a cornerstone of many modern systems' modeling methods, the imposition of artificial boundaries can be counterproductive in some circumstances. Such techniques employ rigorous categorization as a deliberate tool to disarm the very character of complexity itself, segregating particular elements or concepts at specific levels of abstraction. A good example of this surely comes from the field of physical chemistry, where the concepts of compounds, elements, atomic partials, and subatomic particles have gradually permeated their way into popular understanding and modern language. It is hence common knowledge that certain types of element will or will not react with other types to produce recognised compounds. Furthermore, the role of electrons in such reactions is considered to be well understood, yet this understanding is lacking in detail in many texts. For instance, the role that specificity plays across boundaries is not always addressed—that is, which specific electrons are involved in some reactions.

Carbon, for example, can react with oxygen to produce the common molecule carbon monoxide. Most chemists would define its structure using the chemical formula $^-C \equiv O^+$, therefore satisfying the valence, or electron-sharing requirements, of both the elements involved. This representation is, in fact, a form of generalization not only on the part of the specific electrons involved, but also because it is certainly a hybrid of three chemical structures. The model is deliberately simplified for convenience, deeming that enough information is represented to understand the overall relevant detail. It sacrifices minor specifics for the sake of the greater good associated with a broader classification.

In such ways there is a common tendency to gravitate toward the security of knowledge embodied in categorization for the sake of categorization, choosing to pay little attention to the power of direct boundless association at the risk of forsaking clarity of focus.

Approaches to addressing complex problems by discarding apparently irrelevant detail may be pragmatic, but experience has shown a number of times that such brevity is often a false economy. Part of the problem in mankind's inability to understand true complexity has been that we have insisted on a degree of logical consistency in our analysis, a sort of clockwork logic that blocks the emergence of autonomous and apparently inconsistent events or things. But as the mathematician Gödel showed, inconsistency is an inevitable trait of any self-sustaining system built from a collection of consistent parts [21] and is hence inherent in many complex problems and phenomena.

To eliminate inconsistency is a sure way of blocking the path of true understanding. This is because inconsistency implies a clear propensity for crossing boundaries, no matter how indecipherable those boundaries might be. Likewise, crossing boundaries also implies distinction between the various parts of any given system. But this produces a paradox; how can any part be fully understand, even if its actuality is obvious, when its very edges are unclear? This has been a debilitating proposition for most until very recently. Even entertaining the slightest possibility of such a concept would once have been seen as unthinkable and impractical, but today computerization is making it possible to go beyond natural levels of comprehension and associative cognition. The use of artificial boundaries between apparent abstractions in problem spaces like the Web may be used as a useful framework to start the understanding process, but beyond that we could, and should, allow raw computer power loose in the gaps in between. On the Semantic Web today, for instance, the concept of abstractionless association is accepted and there is nothing to stop a direct and formal association between a gross generalization of information—a metaclass—and a specific instantiation of an element from a much lower order of definition. The subject of "modern medicine" could quite legitimately, therefore, be formally associated with the writings of the Hippocrates, yet modern medicine is clearly a high-level classification and Hippocrates is clearly just one example of an individual in the huge class of all the individuals who ever walked the earth. Even so, through the very act of making this assertion a thin slice of structure is automatically added to the information imparted. What's more, by applying some simple association rules, a lot of similarly related data, and some very powerfully computing power, it is not too far-fetched to think of a scenario where all medical knowledge could be derived by the process of association. Starting with just one known fact about Hippocrates—the fact that he is related to modern medicine in some distant way, for example—it would be quite feasible to let a computer algorithm automatically generate the structure behind the vast body of information eventually retrieved, thereby generating one huge corpus of medical information.

The real point to be made is that the organization of the Web is not precise, just as Gödel predicted in any real complex system. It contains few boundaries that serve any real purpose across all possible uses, and in such respects it is almost overtly organic. The categorizations it does contain blur from one to another as if by a process of blunt osmosis rather than sharp crossover. Furthermore, this blurring is self-reflexive and self-organizing in much the same way as found in all living organisms.

Such self-organizing systems are apparent and abundant in nature. In 1961 François Jacob and Jacques Monod[8] discovered one such example in the function behind the classification of the regulatory gene, whose function is to turn other genes on. In one breath this revelation blew away all hopes of immediately understanding DNA and life by the simple process of classification. The regulatory gene set into motion the quintessential cybernetic dialogue: What controls genes? Other genes! And what controls those genes? Other genes! And what . . . an ever-extending ladder or hierarchy of interaction and association [21], and one where distinction between types is both essential and irrelevant at the same time, depending upon your perspective? Jacob and Monod's regulatory genes reflected a spaghetti-like vision of governance—a decentralized network of genes steering the cellular network to its own destiny—again a model not unlike that of the modern-day Web, a Web which might perhaps have its own similar destiny!

Just as the discovery of regulatory genes painted a self-reflexive image of holistic description, so a similar repeating cascade of descriptions can be associated with the Web. The raw data of the Web may predominantly live in the seemingly banal HTML documents of an incalculable number of websites, but there are already popular mechanisms in place to portray higher-level description of the information contained; data about data, or metadata in the idiom of geek-speak. But this concept strangely loops back on itself with ease. Data about the weight of a book, for example, may be seen as useful information to a librarian, but it is not essential to their core duties—it is metadata in other words, but to a courier company it represents es-

---

[8]François Jacob and Jacques Monod originated the idea that control of enzyme levels in all cells happens through feedback on transcription.

sential facts, turning magically from one form of data into another. Just as beauty is in the eye of the beholder, it transpires that definition is in the hands of the consumer in the case of data. Data is metadata and vice versa—or data is data is data, to put it in more simplistic terms. Again classification is both all and nothing depending upon perspective and application. It is a self-sustaining loop of mutual description on which the Web thrives.

SELF-SUSTAINING, SELF-ORGANIZING SYSTEMS

In 1991, a young Italian Scientist, Walter Fontana, showed mathematically that a linear sequence of function *A*, producing function *B*, producing function *C*, could be very easily circled around and closed in a cybernetic way into a self-generating loop, so that the last function was the co-producer of the initial function. When Stuart Kauffman first came across this work, he was elated with its beauty, proclaiming "You have to fall in love with it! Functions mutually making one and other. Out of all function space they come gripping one and other's arms in an embrace of creating!" Kauffman called such an autocatalytic set an "egg," stating that "An egg would be a set of rules having the property that the rules they pose are precisely the ones that create them. That's not really crazy at all."

To get an "egg," there is a need to start with a huge pool of different agents or constituents. They could be varieties of protein pieces or fragments of information or computer code. If they are left alone to interact upon each other long enough, they will produce small loops of "things-producing-things." Eventually, if given time and freedom, the spreading network of these local loops in the system will crowd upon itself until every producer in the circuit is a product of another, until every loop will be incorporated into all other loops in a massively parallel interdependence. At this moment of catalytic closure, the web of parts suddenly snaps into a stable new game: The system sits on its own lap with its beginning resting on its end and vice versa. It has folded in on itself to create its own looping reality. A familiar story perhaps? Exactly, because the "web of parts" in this description might as well be the World Wide Web for all intents and purposes.

Life began in much the same way, jumpstarting into existence as a complete whole, much as a crystal suddenly appears in its final form—though miniature—from a supersaturated solution: not beginning as a vague half-crystal, not appearing as half-materialized shadow, but wham, all at once, suddenly emerging. "Life became whole and integrated, not disconnected and disorganized," writes Kauffman. "Life, in a deep sense, crystallized."

He goes on to say that his research hopes are, "to show that self-replication and homeostasis—basic features of organisms—are natural collective expressions of polymer chemistry. We can expect any significantly complex set of catalytic polymers to be collectively autocatalytic," hinting at his compulsion for inevitability again. "If my model is correct, then the routes to life in the Universe are boulevards, rather than twisted back alleyways." In other words, given the possible complex chemical permutations we have in the real world and, likewise, the complex computational capabilities of the digital world, both real and artificial life is inevitable, and certainly the Web appears to be providing enough computational elbowroom to achieve the latter.

"We've got to get used to dealing with billions of things!" Kaufman once preached to an audience of scientists. Huge multitudes of anything are different, certainly different in most imaginable ways from the pitifully small quantities that mankind can comfortably juggle within the normal confines of our meager brains. The more elements involved in any given system, the exponential potential for interactions where one triggers the manufacture of yet another. Hence, at some point, a collection loaded up with an increasing diversity and abundant number of elements will reach a threshold where a certain number of those elements will spontaneously align into a self-supporting loop. They will form an auto-generated, self-organizing, self-sustaining network of connected pathways. As long as energy flows in, the network will "hum," and the loop will remain.

Kauffman is not alone in his intuition, suggesting notions of invention-begats-invention-begats-invention to cultural evolution and then on to much greater goals. He is quite frank about it, clearly identifying the desire of his ambition: "I am looking for the self-consistent big picture that ties everything together, from the origin of life as a self-organized system, to the emergence of spontaneous order in genomic regulatory systems, to the emergence of systems that are able to adapt, to non-equilibrium price formation which optimizes trade amongst organizations, to this unknown analogue of the second law of thermodynamics. It is all one picture. I really feel it is. But the image I'm pushing on is this: Can we prove that a finite set of functions generates an infinite set of possibilities?"

Such questions raise the concept quite rightly referred to as a "Kauffman machine," a well-chosen set of functions and data that connect into an auto-generating ring and produce an infinite stream of more complex functions. Nature is full of such machines. An egg cell producing the body of a baboon is one, for example. An evolutionary machine generating a fruit bat from a blob of bacteria over a billion years of constantly adjusted natural computation is another. This may more correctly be referred to as a Von Neumann machine, because John Von Neumann himself posed the same question in the early 1940s, starting the field of Ontogenetics in a feverish frenzy of academic interest. He also wondered, "Can a machine make another machine more complex than itself?' Whatever it is called, the question is the same: How does complexity build upon itself?"

Certainly the growth of complexity really does have something to do with far-from-equilibrium systems, like the Web, building themselves up and cascading to higher and higher levels of organization. It's as if they are eternally trying to climb the ladder of an ever-richer hierarchy of existence—atoms, molecules, autocatalytic sets, and so on. The key thing is that once higher-level entities emerge, they can also interact amongst themselves. A molecule can connect with a molecule to make a new molecule in much the same way that low-level computational objects can interact. In fact, all self-organizing complexity is really analogous to chemistry.

The source of chemistry's power is simple variety: Unlike quarks,[9] from the subordinate and "cleaner" regions of physics, atoms can be arranged and rearranged to

---

[9]Quarks are one of the two basic constituents of matter in the Standard Model of particle physics.

form a huge number of structures. The space of molecular possibilities is effectively limitless. The second source of power is reactivity: Structure A can manipulate structure B to form something new—that is, structure C.

Of course this insight leaves out lots of things like rate constants and temperature dependence, which are crucial to the understanding of real chemistry, but that's intentional. The contention here is that "chemistry" is a concept that actually applies to a wide variety of complex systems, including economics, technologies like the Web, and even minds.

As John Von Neumann pointed out long ago, a piece of computer code leads a double life. On the one hand it's a program fragment, a series of commands telling the computer what to do. But on the other hand its just data, a string of symbols sitting somewhere inside a computer's memory. So, it is possible to think of defining a "reaction" between two programs: Program A simply reads in program B as input data, and then it "executes" to produce a string of output data, which the computer now interprets as a new program, program C.

Next, take a few zillion of these symbol-string programs, put them in a simulated pot where they can interact at random, and watch what happens. In fact, the results will not be unlike the autocatalytic models produced by Stuart Kauffman, but with some rather weird and wonderful variations. There will be self-sustaining autocatalytic sets, of course, but there will also be sets that can grow without bounds. There will be sets that can repair themselves if some of their component "chemicals" are deleted, and there will also be sets that adapt and change themselves if new components are added. There will even be pairs of sets that have no members in common, but that mutually catalyze each others existence. In short, the alchemy program suggests that populations of pure processes—symbol string programs in this analogy—are enough for spontaneous emergence of some very lifelike structures indeed [67].

What is really interesting with this is that once sufficient levels of complex interactions are reached, it ought to be true in general that autocatalysis occurs whenever the conditions are right—whether this involves molecules, economies, or the very Web itself. Once a sufficient diversity of objects has been accumulated at the higher level, a kind of autocatalytic phase transition takes place and an enormous proliferation of things can be found at that level. The proliferating entities then proceed to interact and produce autocatalytic sets at still higher levels. When one thinks about it, in fact, this upward hierarchical cascade is just another kind of self-organization, so how is the cascade shaped by selection and adaptation?

Perhaps, if one started with some founder set of constituents—molecules, companies, Web resources, whatever—they could potentially give rise to autocatalytic behaviors. Some of these behaviors would inevitably end up as being dead and meaningless, but if the "live" constituents can somehow organize themselves so that they don't make so many dead constituents, then the "live" constituents have a selective advantage. Add incentive to grow into the mix such, as in cases where positive feedback is prevalent and a sure-fire recipe for "lifelike" properties is created. Systems involving high technology, such as in the Web's case, provide a highly fertile environment for such conditions to occur. Restrictions like technology lock-in (discussed in Chapter 8) force an almost inevitable upward spiral of take-up and positive feedback. Furthermore, the overwhelming connectivity of the Web provides the perfect example of intertwined complexity on which further complexity can breed. It's plain to see that the ingredients are right and the cooker has been turned up to the right temperature. Now all that is needed is to sit back and watch for signs of emergence as the Web slowly cooks.

CHAPTER **8**

Emergent Intelligence and Posthuman Concepts

What magical trick makes us intelligent? The trick is that there is no trick. The power of intelligence stems from our vast diversity, not from any single, perfect principle.

—Marvin Minsky, The Society of Mind

WHY ON THE WEB?

At times the Universe can be a most confusing place. In fact, under all but the most insightful scrutiny, it can appear almost supremely paradoxical. At one extreme it clings to order as a fundamental constituent of its very fabric, while at it other it also embodies basic laws that constantly try to degenerate such order into chaos—physicists even have a word for it: entropy.

Ever since scientists like Ilya Prigogine[1] worked on the theory behind self-organization in complex systems, many academics have realized that a number of types of systems can be shown to employ self-regulatory mechanisms—not least of these in the area of economics, as pointed out by the eminent economist Brian Arthur.

Arthur was one of the first to realize that, in mathematical terms, Prigogine's central point was that self-organization depends upon self-reinforcement—a tendency for small effects to become magnified when the conditions are right, instead of just dying away under the effects of entropy. This is a familiar theme, also being precisely the same message made implicit in Jacob and Monod's work on DNA. Furthermore, this is a theme familiar to many an engineer who would know it under the term "positive feedback." This occurs in many contexts: Tiny molecular motions grow into convection cells, mild tropical breezes grow into a hurricane, and seeds and embryos grow into fully developed living creatures. Positive feedback

---

[1]Ilya Prigogine was a Belgian physicist and chemist noted for his work on dissipative structures, complex systems, and irreversibility. Prigogine is known best for his work on dissipative structures concentrated on thermodynamic systems far from equilibrium. His work in this field led to pioneering research in self-organizing systems, as well as philosophic inquiries into the role of time in the natural sciences. His work is seen by many as a bridge between natural sciences and the social sciences [118].

In his later years, his work concentrated on mathematical role of determinism in nonlinear systems on both the classical and quantum level. He proposed the use of a complex Hilbert space in quantum mechanics as one possible method of achieving irreversibility in quantum systems.

The Web's Awake. By Philip Tetlow
Copyright © 2007 the Institute of Electrical and Electronics Engineers, Inc.

seems to be an essential condition of change, of spontaneity, of life itself [67]. Furthermore, through the likes of Arthur's work, it has been shown to explain the liveliness, complexity, and richness of many global systems and their respective frameworks, not least of which are the real-world economy and the Web itself.

But there are still many more fundamental factors that lie at the heart of the reasoning as to why the Web might be such an opportune place for the evolution of a higher level of complexity. Take, for instance, the technological forces at work behind the Web, an aspect of its disposition that is plainly undeniable. This is an interesting area for somewhat unexpected reasons, because until a couple of decades ago the accepted notion was that technologies simply came at random out of the blue, fallen from heaven in celestial books of blueprints for making steel or silicon chips, or anything like that. Furthermore, such things were made possible by inventors—smart people like Thomas Edison[2] who sort of came by these ideas in their bathtubs and then added them to their books of blueprints. It was all very mystical. Strictly speaking in fact, technology was not even considered to be part of any economic model. It was "exogenous," delivered as if by magic by noneconomic processes.

More recently, however, there have been a number of efforts to model technology as being economically "endogenous," meaning that it is produced within an economic system itself [67]. This is an extremely relevant concept, especially given that Web-connected endeavors are so embroiled in the global economy that some have been the sole instigator in the emergence of many new economic frameworks. Taking an endogenous outlook on technology implies that the outcome of investment in research and development, however, is almost like a commodity. But this is not necessarily the entire story.

When one looks at economic history, as opposed to economic theory, technology is not really like a commodity at all. It is much more like an evolving ecosystem. In particular, innovations rarely happen in a vacuum. They are usually made possible by other innovations already in place. For instance, a laser printer is basically just a photocopier with a laser and a little computer circuitry added to tell the laser where to etch on the copying drum for printing. So a laser printer is possible when one has computer technology, laser technology, and photo-reproducing technology together. One technology simple builds upon the inherent capabilities of others.

In short, technologies quite literally form a richly connected matrix. Furthermore, most technological matrixes are highly dynamic. They can grow in a fashion that is essentially organic, as when laser printers give rise to desktop publishing software and desktop publishing opens up a new niche for sophisticated graphics programs. There is literally a catalytic reaction taking place, just as in Kauffman's autocatalytic Boolean networks.

Also, technology networks can undergo bursts of spontaneous evolutionary creativity and massive extinction events, just like biological ecosystems. Imagine that a new technology, like the automobile, is invented which outdates the horse as the primary mode of low-cost travel. Along with the popularity of the horse goes the primary need for blacksmiths, the pony express, the watering trough, the stables,

---

[2]Thomas Alva Edison was an inventor and businessman who developed many important devices, not least of which was the electric light bulb [119].

and so on. Whole subnetworks of dependent technologies and support systems collapse in what the economist Joseph Schumpeter called "a gale of destruction." But along with the automobile comes a new generation of change; paved roads, petrol stations, drive-by fast food chains, motels, traffic police, and traffic lights. A whole new network of goods, services, and associated technologies begins to grow, spawning cascades of evolutionary sequences elsewhere, each one filling a niche opened up by the redundant goods, services, and technologies that came before. The process of technological change is not just a mimic of natural eco-processes; it is again exactly like the origin of life itself.

Neoclassical economic theory assumes that systems like the economy are entirely dominated by negative feedback; the tendency for small effects to die away and have no lasting impact on the wider environment. This propensity has traditionally been implicit in the economic doctrine of "diminished returns" [67]. But, as has been realized in more recent times, there is also positive feedback, or "increasing returns" present as well, influences that bubble up and build each other leading to higher plateaus of stability. These not only help promote significant change such as trends, but also help to explain the lively, rich, and spontaneous nature of many real-world systems.

Certainly there are a number of circumstances where positive feedback is more likely to emerge than not, one prime example being in the take-up of technology by a population.

TECHNOLOGY LOCK-IN

There are obviously immense differences that positive feedback can make to a system like the economy. Take efficiency, for example. Neoclassical theory might lead one to believe that a free market will always choose the best and most efficient technologies, and, in truth, this is most often the case. Nevertheless, there are still plenty of examples where this is not necessarily true. Take, for instance, the case of the commonplace QWERTY keyboard layout, the one used on virtually every typewriter and computer keyboard in the Western world; the name QWERTY is spelled out by the first letter along the top row of keys. Although it is ubiquitous today, it is by no means the most efficient design for human typing. If fact, an engineer named Christopher Scholes designed its layout in 1873 specifically to slow typists down; the typewriting machine of the day tended to jam if the typist went too fast. But then the Remington Sewing Machine Company mass-produced a typewriter using the QWERTY system, which meant that lots of typists began to learn the layout, which meant that other typewriter companies began to offer QWERTY versions of their own machines, which meant that still more typists began to learn it, and so on and so forth. Through this process of positive reinforcement the QWERTY keyboard layout is now used by millions [67]. It is entrenched into our economic practices and social interactions and is essentially locked into the fabric or our existence forever. Positive feedback has catapulted it to be the standard, for all its flaws and weaknesses.

To reinforce this point, consider the Betamax versus VHS competition in the videotape market of the 1970s and 1980s. Even in 1979, it was clear that the VHS format was well on its way to cornering the market, despite the fact that many experts had originally rated its slightly inferior to Betamax technologically. How could this have happened? Simply because the VHS vendors were lucky enough to gain a slightly bigger market share in the beginning, which gave them an enormous advantage in spite of the technological differences. Video stores hated having to stock everything in two formats and consumers hated the idea of being stuck with obsolete video cassette recorders, so everyone had a big incentive to go along with the market leader. That pushed up VHS's market lead even more and the small initial difference grew rapidly—again a case of increasing returns [67] and a fine example of the propensity of how certain types of technology can lock in their users.

QWERTY keyboards and VHS video recorders are not isolated examples. Similar examples proliferate in the world of technology, and in fact increasing returns are anything but isolated phenomena: The principle applies to everything in high technology [67], and especially the highly connected framework of the Web. Without a doubt the types of positive feedback shown above are what is known as a "network effect," where more people are encouraged to join a network the larger that network becomes. So, the result is that the network grows more and more quickly over time.

Further examples of technology lock-in through network effects are, at times, overly obvious. Microsoft's Windows product is a fine case in point, for instance. The company spent vast amounts in research and development to get their first copy to market. The second copy cost it the company about $10 in materials and manufacturing. This does not undermine the quality or earth-shattering capabilities of the product. Windows is a piece of software that has undoubtedly changed the world, but the economic model on which it is developed is radically different from those of old. It's the same story in electronics, computers, pharmaceuticals, and even aerospace. High technology could almost be defined as "congealed knowledge." The actual marginal cost is close to zero, which means that every copy a company produces makes the actual product cheaper and cheaper to them. Furthermore, every copy offers a chance for learning: getting the yield up on microprocessors and so on. Hence, there is a tremendous reward incentive for increasing production—in short the system is governed by increasing returns [67].

Amongst the high-tech consumers, meanwhile, there is an equally large reward incentive for flocking to a standard. If an airline were in the market for buying a particular type of jet liner, for example, it would want to make sure that it bought a lot of them so that their pilots didn't need to be multi-skilled. By the same token, an office manager would try to purchase all the same kind of personal computer so that all the staff in their office could run the same software. The end result is that high technologies very quickly tend to home in to a relatively few standards: HTML and JavaScript on the Web, for example.

Now compare this with the standard bulk commodities of the old economic world. It is easy to think of products such as grain, fertilizer and cement, where most of the knowhow was acquired generations ago. In the new economy of the technology age, and especially the ultra-new economic world of the Web, the real costs are of land and raw materials, areas where diminished returns can easily set in. So these tend to be stable, mature areas that can be described reasonably well by standard neoclassical economic models [67]. The newer high-technology industries, like those associated with Information Technology, are light on such resources and heavy on positive driving forces that predict expansive take-up, quick standardization through lock-in, and high profitability. Essentially such industries are susceptible to self-promotion and cascades of change and development, driving their surrounding economies toward higher plateaus of stability. Furthermore, as lock-in takes hold and take-up rises, there are further benefits for the consumers. Technology not only initiates increased learning, but also drives other socioeconomic parameters like communication and productivity, thereby allowing individuals to reach further and in more efficient ways.

High technology is a powerful catalyst for both economic and social change, and the added connectivity provided by the Web is akin to pouring rocket fuel onto the fire. What is apparent today is that positive feedback in the extreme is taking place on a vastly macro scale like never before. Additionally, this change is taking place at an unprecedented rate, with one technology bouncing off the benefits of another and rapidly fertilizing the ground for new and better generations of technologies to come. This is literally a feeding frenzy of innovation and creation created from a writhing entanglement of positive feedback loops. Seldom has our planet experienced such an explosion of expansion and almost certainly never in such condensed timescales. Perhaps Stuart Kauffmann was more inspired than he thought, and this is indeed similar to the way that life emerged out of the primordial chemical soup some four billion years ago. And even if this vision is too adventurous, certainly the way in which society is going about its daily business is changing radically and new models are required to explain it.

SWARM BEHAVIOR

What is intelligence? No, it's a serious question; this is not just a simple matter of whether someone can understand the finer points of rocket science or brain surgery.

Table 8.1. Neoclassical and New Age Economic Comparisons

Neoclassical Economics	New Economics
Decreasing returns	Much use of increasing returns
Based on nineteenth-century physics and old-fashioned ideas on equilibrium, stability, and deterministic dynamics.	Based more closely on complex systems like biology and contemporary ideas based on structure, pattern, self-organization, life and cycles
Based on the assumption that no externalities are involved and all agents have equal abilities.	Externalities and differences become the driving forces, with systems constantly unfolding.
Elements involved in models are based around quantities and prices.	Elements in models are based around patterns and possibilities.
No real dynamics in the sense that everything is expected to remain at equilibrium.	Economy is constantly on the edge of time. It rushes forward, with structures constantly coalescing, decaying, changing.

In fact, it is not just a matter of human capability. Mankind's likely inclination might well be to consider intelligence as a solely human quality, but there are many different types of intelligence at play out there. It may be possible to narcissistically compare like with like forevermore, using contrived IQ tests, but such metrics will not work across all of the natural world. Just like complexity, intelligence works in many ways and at many levels, proving almost indefinable in many of its most authentic forms. Take, for example, the mind of the humble herring. Could such a creature outsmart the intelligence of any individual in their right mind? How about an ant, a bee, or a starling? Same question: How would any mortal fancy their chances? Easy one might think, but what if the rules are changed slightly. How about a shoal of herring, a swarm of bees, or a colony of ants? Could any individual construct their own skyscraper capable of housing several thousand of their brethren out of nothing more than dirt, for instance? That's exactly what a colony of ants can do, and to them it's one of the easiest things in the world. Furthermore, they are far from unique. It goes without saying that bees can produce great honeycombed hive structures and even our friend the herring can easily organize itself into a moving current of consensus, sometimes up to seventeen miles long—no problem for them perhaps, but for us as individuals a sure impossibility.

Even so, would one ever consider a bee to be the brightest of creatures? Its not, and that's just the point. There are certain types of intelligence that emerge as if from nowhere. They are created by the summation of tiny bits of capability, capability that on its own is inconsequential and nondifferential, but capability nonetheless. This works at lower levels in the main, but has just enough quirks, lumps, and bumps to fit precisely into a much greater, purposeful jigsaw of intellect—a jigsaw with no keystone, no ruler, or single manager. No master mind then in this collective puzzle, but still a puzzle that reveals a clear and concise picture once whole. A puzzle that is the norm in the realms of distributed intelligence.

"Where is the spirit of the hive . . . where does it reside?" asked an author as early as 1901. "What is it that governs her, that issues orders, foresees the future . . . ?" We are certain today that it is not the queen bee. When a swarm of bees decides to migrate to another location, the queen bee can only follow. The queen's offspring manage the election of where and when the swarm should settle. A handful of anonymous drone workers scout ahead to check possible hive locations in hollow trees or wall cavities. They report back to the resting swarm by dancing on its contracting surface. During the report, the more vigorously a scout dances, the better the site it is championing. Other bees then check out the competing sites according to the intensity of the dances before them and will concur with the scout by joining in the scout's jig. That encourages more follows to check out the lead prospects and join the commotion when they return by leaping into the dance troop of their choice [21].

It is uncommon to see a bee, except for the scouts that is, which has inspected more than one site. The bees see the message "Go there, it's a nice place." They go and return to dance, saying "Yeah, it's really nice." By compounding emphasis, the favorite sites get more visitors, thus increasing further visitors. As per the law of increasing returns, those with more votes get more votes and those with less vote's lose out. Gradually, one overwhelming multitude of agreement is reached and the hive moves as a whole [21]. The biggest crowd wins, end of story.

This is an election hall of idiots, for idiots, and run by idiots, and it works marvelously. This is true democracy at work and is the stuff of all distributed governance. At the point of cumulative departure, by the choice of the masses, the hive takes the queen and travels off in the direction indicated by mob vote [21]. This is a pressgang of natural consensus.

"The hive chooses" is the disarming answer of William Morton Wheeler, a natural philosopher and entomologist, who founded the field of Social Insects. Writing in his provocative 1911 essay "The Ant Colony as an Organism," in the *Journal of Morphology,* Wheeler claimed that an insect colony is not just an analogy of an organism; it is indeed an organism in its own right, in every important and scientific sense of the word. He wrote: "Like a cell or a person, it behaves as a unitary whole, maintaining its identity in space, resisting dissolution . . . neither a thing nor a concept, but a continual flux or process." The collective bee community that is the hive is a mob of several hundred thousand united into a purposeful singularity.

Distributed systems are systems made of a collection of entities: humans, technical systems (such as websites), insects, and so on, systems where decision and control are taken directly by these entities. The stereotypical example of a distributed and complex system would be a colony of ants, as already highlighted. Without any central coordination, such a collective will behave in an extremely coherent way indefinitely if left undisturbed in a suitable habitat. It can also show complex social reorganization in periods of difficulties. This leads to the observation that structural flexibility, fast reaction to external environment changes, and robustness appear to be the positive consequences of distributed systems.

Thus the functional constituents of distributed systems encode and react to the outside world without any global view of the system and without any central coordination. The global behavior and functionalities of their parent emerge from the culmination of local interactions. In some systems, local learning rules can further allow individual adaptation to the environment, resulting in better global behavior. If such systems are then capable of self-organization, their functions evolve over time so that they can respond better to the requests of their environment. So, in this sense, a complex self-organized system cannot be described as structurally stable.

The Web, too, is an organized assembly with no central authority. It is pushed and pulled in multiple directions, not by any direct order but by the overwhelming compulsions of consensus and positive feedback. In such ways it too adapts to and adopts from its environments as part of a co-evolutionary process.

But can the Web be said to exhibit intelligence, the type of "swarm intelligence" shown by the colonized worlds of insect life, for example? Most certainly. Just look at any number of trends spawned by Web culture so far. E-commerce, Internet dating, and blogging are all responses from the Web collective to the demands of its environment—us in other words. These are not just freak accidents, but are quite literally migrations of focus in just the same way as that which is demonstrated when a swarm of bees moves hive or a colony of ants constructs a sky-scraping nest. Some, however, might protest that such swarm intelligence is just cheating, because it's "not the same" as the intelligence referred to in the normal human contexts of psychology or sociology. No, sorry, this is just not the case, intelligence is intelligence no matter what form it comes in, just as ice and steam are both just water at heart. Swarm intelligence is merely a higher transitional state built upon the compounded contribution of many, many minds, whether each is as insignificant as that of a single ant or as Earth-shattering as Einstein's huge intellect.

ARTIFICIAL LIFE

Swarm intelligence and distributed systems may both be interesting subjects, but in isolation do such fields really highlight any distinguishing traits of life? In an attempt to understand the detail of such matters a new field of study, known as Artificial Life or A-Life for short, has emerged. A-Life aims to investigate the fundamental properties of living systems through the simulation and synthesis of life-like processes in artificial media.

Chris Langton,[3] one of the founders of the A-Life approach, defines Artificial Life as "a field of study devoted to (a) understanding life by attempting to abstract the fundamental dynamical principles underlying biological phenomena and (b) recreating these dynamics in other physical media, such as computers, making them accessible to new kinds of experimental manipulation and testing." While biological research is essentially analytic, trying to break down complex phenomena into their basic components, A-Life is synthetic, attempting to construct phenomena from their elemental units. A-Life complements traditional biological research.

Much of the focus in A-Life research is trying to understand high-level behavior from basic low-level units interacting according to very simple rules, in much the same way as work on distributed systems. One of the early works following this approach was John von Neumann's[4] research in the early 1950s. Von Neumann was primarily interested in whether an artificial machine could create a copy of itself, and so he wanted to invent a set of rules by which a computer could be programmed to produce an exact replica of itself—a clone for want of another term. As a tool he used a cellular automaton originally devised by Stanislaw Ulam.[5]

Briefly an automaton like Von Neumann's consists of a grid of artificial cells, similar to a chessboard, where each cell can exist in one of a finite number of states; for example, different colors of the cells could be used to represent different states. In addition, there is a simple set of rules which govern how a cell can change its state. The rules specify exactly how this can happen by reference to the states of its neighbors and the cell's own state. At each step of the program the states of all the cells are determined. As the program progresses, the cells constantly change their state and complex emergent patterns can be observed and studied. By way of interest, the most popular type of this algorithm is John Conway's "Game of Life."

[3]Christopher Langton was one of the founders of the field of artificial life. He coined the term in the late 1980s when he held the first "International Conference on the Synthesis and Simulation of Living Systems" (otherwise known as *Artificial Life I*) at the Los Alamos National Laboratory in 1987. He created the Langton ant and Langton loop, both landmark simple artificial life simulations [121].

[4]John von Neumann was a Hungarian-born mathematician who made important contributions in quantum physics, functional analysis, set theory, computer science, economics, and many other mathematical fields [122].

[5]Stanislaw Marcin Ulam was a Polish mathematician who helped develop the Teller–Ulam design which powers the hydrogen bomb, as well as a number of other important mathematical tools [123].

A cellular automaton has three basic characteristics:

- **Parallelism:** All states are updated simultaneously.
- **Locality:** The new state of any particular cell is based exclusively on its old state and the state of its neighboring cells.
- **Homogeneity:** The same set of rules are used for all of the cells.

A concept closely related to cellular automata is that of agent-based societies, not at all dissimilar to the ideas of natural collectives discussed earlier. In these an agent-based approach to simulation aims to represent individual actors or groups in a given system. Hence, each agent has a set of characteristics, or attributes. For instance, an agent representing a human could have attributes such as, age, job title, and so on, and obviously each agent may have different values associated with their characteristics. Agent-based systems are therefore often described as heterogeneous, as opposed to homogeneous, meaning that all agents are not considered as having the same values, but are different. To stress the individuality of the agents, many researchers prefer to use an "individual-based model" as opposed to an "agent-based model." So, agents may interact with each other and/or with an environment, and from these interactions macro-scale behaviors may eventually emerge.

Not surprisingly, agent-based models are widely used in the simulation of complex systems, having been applied in many different fields of research including entomology, economics, and anthropology, as well as in sociology, where the term "artificial societies" is applied to agent-based models of social processes.

In fact, the distinction between cellular automata and agent-based models is difficult to make. For example, a spatially explicit, grid-based, immobile agent model initially appears to be the same as a cellular automaton. However, cellular automata are always homogeneous and dense, because all cells are identical. A grid-based agent-based model might occupy only a few grid cells, and more than one distinct type of agent might live on the same grid. Hence, the widely accepted distinction seems to be whether or not a simulation is based on a dense and uniform dissection of the space, as in a cellular automata, or based on specific agents distributed within the space.

Swarm Intelligence (SI) is an Artificial Intelligence technique based around the study of collective behavior in decentralized, self-organized, systems, with the expression being introduced by Beni and Wang in 1989, in the context of cellular robotic systems or cellular robotic automata. Such techniques therefore demonstrate just how collective intelligence is not just isolated to the natural world and can be easily recreated in computational contexts as well. These may be deliberately contrived in the case of experiments like cellular automata, but the connection is clear: The Web can be as much a swarm as the buzziest collection of bees!

THE SWARM BEING THAT IS THE WEB

The Web has no start, no end, and no center. It has no elected leader, commandant, or marshal. It is just a horde of nodes connected to other nodes, a cobweb of linkages streaming out in every conceivable direction, constantly colliding and coiling together like a bag of freshly released springs. It provides a restless image fading at innumerable indeterminate edges. To summarize, it is a swarm of networked informational content to all but the most pedantically analytic.

The Web is the archetype, a constant displayed to represent all intelligence, all interdependence, all things economic, social and ecological, all communications, all democracy, all groups, all large systems. This image is certainly dangerous, being so compulsively illusive as to ensnare the unwary in its paradox of a shapeless indiscernible whole.

When Charles Darwin searched for a description at the end of his *Origin of Species*—a book that is one long persuasion about how species evolved from the conflicting interconnected self-interests of many individuals—he also found a notion of such a tangled web. He saw "birds singing on bushes, with various insects flitting about, with worms crawling through the deep Earth," and with the whole web of life forming an "entangled bank, dependent on each other in so complex a manner."

Today's Web, the web of global information, is the epitome of multiples just like Darwin's controversial discovery. Out of it comes a true swarm being, a mythical metaman of distributed existence, spreading itself over the entire planet so that no part can say, "I am I." It is simply a case of "this is this" for the Web. It is incomparably social and insuppressibly of many minds. It embodies both of the computer and of nature, of artificial and natural, and so it is a true amalgamation of both. But it is by no means perfect; in fact it deliberately craves imperfection. It bares all the faults and flaws of any network, as well as all the redundancy and ricocheting vectors (i.e., things going from here to there and back), and for good reason. Just as in the complex networks that form all natural organisms, the Web nurtures small failures in order that large failures don't occur as often. And it is this capacity to hold error rather than repel it that makes its distribution fertile ground for learning, adaptation, and evolution.

A network swarm is all edges and therefore open-ended any way one comes at it. In fact, in many ways, the network is the least-structured organization that can be said to have any structure at all. Yet, in other respects, it can be seen to possess extreme levels of formality and order. It is capable of infinite rearrangement and of growth in any direction without altering its basic shape, which is really no shape at all within the bound of recognizable limits, and in that sense alone it is fractal. Networks, like the Web, have the remarkable capability to absorb the new without disruption. As the Computer Scientist Craig Reynolds[6] is once quoted as saying, "There is no evidence that the complexity of natural flocks is bounded in any way. Flocks do not become 'full' or 'overloaded' as new birds join." How big a telephone network could be made? How many nodes can one even theoretically add to a network and still have it work correctly? These are questions that have hardly ever been asked [21].

---

[6]Craig Reynolds, an A-life and computer graphics expert, created the Boids artificial life simulation in 1986. Reynolds worked on the film Tron (1982) as a scene programmer and on Batman Returns (1992) as part of the video image crew [123].

Add to this the fact that network logic is sometimes counterintuitive. Suppose there was a need to lay a telephone line that would connect a select group of cities—perhaps Kansas City, San Diego, and Seattle for the purpose of illustration. The total length of the lines connecting those three cities is 3000 miles. Common sense therefore says that if you were to add a fourth city to this network, the total length of the cable needed would increased. But that is not how network logic works. By adding a fourth city, such as Phoenix, as a hub and running each of the lines from the other cities through that hub, the actual total length of the cable needed decreases to 2850 miles, or 5% less than the original quota. Therefore the total unraveled length of a network can be shortened by adding nodes rather than taking them away—a perplexing paradox, but one that is true nonetheless.

Network structures have their own logic, one that is out of phase with normal expectations, and this logic is quickly molding the culture of human living in the Web age. What we get from heavy-duty communication networks, the networks of parallel computing systems, distributed appliances, and distributed being is not only a network culture but a vast social machine—a social machine with a mind of its own, a swarm mind of moreness.

THE WEB'S CORE MEMORY AND ITS PLACE IN INFORMATION VALUE

A feature often associated with the concept of intelligence is memory—the ability of a system to retain information. However, a number of misconceptions are commonplace when relating this concept to the Web. For instance, it is often considered that the Web is just to one colossal memory bank, a global encyclopedia of virtual documentation that contains large sections of society's various accounts. But the Web is more than that. Not only does it carry vast quantities of explicitly specified dynamic data, but it also carries its own implicit positional information as outlined in Chapter 5. Its very structure behaves as a lattice memory adding multiple layers of richness to the information already present.

In much the same way as the early ferrite-core memories (Figure 8.1) used in computers during the 1950s and 1960s, the Web embodies structural information by the very location and connectivity of its various elements, and in turn their Universal

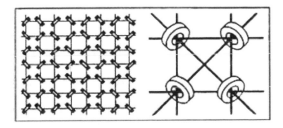

Figure 8.1. Ferrite-core memory.

Resource Indicators (URI's)[7] which pin them further down to a specific location on the global Web map. Core memories used small magnetic ceramic rings—the cores—to store information via the polarity of the magnetic field they contained; their location within the overall mesh of cores provided the address by which such information could be accessed. Through analogies like this, it soon becomes clear that the relative position and various interrelationships of each resource on the Web are essential if it is to be interpreted comprehensively and within all relevant contexts.

But there is more to this analogy of magnetism and memory, with the randomness of the Web's constitution potentially contributing greatly to its capability to remember. As we shall see in Chapter 9, spin glasses are a special kind of magnet that contains highly complex regions of competing magnetism. They are hence complex systems containing both positive and negative feedback in much the same way as the Web itself. This analogy is so powerful for the following reasons: An array of normal ferromagnets subject to a magnetic influence from the outside can store a memory—that's exactly what happens when audio tape is used to record a song, for instance. But this kind of tape can only store one memory at a time. In storing a new memory the old one is erased. A spin glass, however, can store many memories all at once, just like a neural network and like the brain, and it does so spontaneously, without being given any instructions. It is able to do this because a spin glass array of magnets and antimagnets has more than one "best" arrangement of magnetism. Each such best arrangement can get connected to a different memory and store it. In essence a spin glass's most energetically favorable states, its basins, correspond to a memory [80].

Correct interpretation of information on the Web is a real and significant obstacle to its progress. Just because information is available and can be accessed does not mean to say that it is accurate or of any relevant value to its consumer. At present the Web does not guarantee its own quality and will not underwrite any of society's failures as a direct result of our interaction with it. Research into provenance issues is hence focusing on areas such as trust and authority in information publication and retrieval on the Web. For instance, how can one ascertain if a reference unearthed, by say Google, contains valid and accurate information? Furthermore, even if the information contained is valid, how can the user know if the individual or organization that published it in the first place had any legitimate right to do so? Such concerns have led some to propose radically different models for querying the Web that do not just take into account its raw data content. In doing so the various attributes that could be taken into account when trying to achieve "total comprehension" of a particular Web resource may be outlined as:

- Internal Constitution:
    - *The resource's own content.* The actual data or program code contained within the resource itself, from both lexical and semantic perspectives.

---

[7]A Uniform Resource Identifier (URI) is an Internet protocol element consisting of a short string of characters that conform to a certain syntax. The string comprises a name or address that can be used to refer to a resource. It is a fundamental component of the World Wide Web. A URI can be classified as a locator, a name, or both. A Uniform Resource Locator (URL) is a URI that, in addition to identifying a resource, provides a means of acting upon or obtaining a representation of the resource by describing its primary access mechanism or network "location."

- *The resource's own metadata.* Information held within the resource specifically intended to describe it to other resources, like search engines. Again this can be interpreted under both lexical and semantic headings.

- *The resource's own content structure, grammar, or syntax.* How various subcomponents such as headings, paragraphs, images, and alike interrelate.

- *The resource's outbound links.* Information about the content that a resource chooses to link to.

- External Environment:

  - *Meta-descriptions.* In certain circumstances, for instance when using Semantic Web technologies like the Resource Description Framework (RDF), metadata can be created as a referenceable Web resource in its own right, implemented to provide enhanced descriptions of other referencable data or functionality held elsewhere on the Web. In such ways, URIs can now be used to describe URIs in a truly self-reflexive manner.

  - *The references made to a resource by other nonmeta resources—that is, inbound hyperlinks.* It makes sense that if someone wanted to find out about a stranger, but knew their friends well, they would make enquiries of these friends. And so it is the same on the Web. The names, locations, and descriptions of resources that have directly hyperlinked associations with a particular resource, or quote its URI, also provide legitimate clues as to the nature of any Web content.

Combine all these factors and a more elaborate interpretation of Web content can be formed, one in which structural and semantic interpretations play a key role.

As has been highlighted a number of times already, the various paths across the Web that lead to and from one particular point to another are integral to the Web's function, and memory is an essential part of this. But here again, not surprisingly, comparisons can be found with the natural world. The main storage medium inside willow seeds, ants, and all other living things may not be electronic, but it is electrochemical. It exploits the fact that certain kinds of molecule are capable of "polymerizing," which is simply the joining up of molecules into long chains of indefinite length. For example, "polythene" is made of long chains of the small organic molecule ethylene. Starch and cellulose are polymerised sugars. In fact, some polymers, instead of being uniform chains of one small molecule like ethylene, are chains of two or more different kinds of small molecule. As soon as such heterogeneity enters into the polymer chain, information technology and therefore memory becomes theoretically possible. If there are two kinds of small molecule in the chain, the two can be though of as representing 1 and 0, respectively, and immediately any amount of information, of any kind, can be stored, provided only that the chain is long enough. "Without a doubt this is a concept of awesome proportions, for there is enough information capacity in a single human cell to store the *Encyclopaedia Britannica,* all thirty volumes of it, three or four times over" [51].

But the miracle of chemical chains does not end with their use in memory. Like all good systems capable of Gödelization, sequences of chemicals can also constitute successive stages in some useful process, like the release of energy or synthesis of an important substance. In such cases, each step in the chain may need an enzyme. Different enzymes are needed for different steps in the chemical process. Sometimes there are two, or more, alternative chemical pathways to the same useful end. "Although both pathways culminate in the identical useful result, they have different intermediate stages, and they normally have different starting points" [51]; again an unusually similar scenario to common Web-based usage contexts.

THE APPARENT FAILURE OF ARTIFICIAL INTELLIGENCE

Since Alan Turing wrote his hugely influential article proposing the now famous Turing test[8] as a way of deciding whether a machine is conscious, most workers in the field of Artificial Intelligence (AI) have accepted, in effect, that if a machine can persuade a human observer that it is conscious, then it must be. But still, to this day, there are few advances from this community that even come close to passing the Turing test, leading skeptics to believe that the early promises of the AI movement are nothing more than speculative. As a case in point, the Loebner Prize for AI is the first formal instantiation of a Turing test and even though its has been running annually since 1990, its gold medal and grand prize of $100,000, which goes to the program that completely fools the judges, still remains unclaimed.

In a similar manner, it is also often pointed out that chemists have failed in their attempts to duplicate the spontaneous origin of life in the laboratory. This fact is used as if it constituted evidence against the theories that these chemists are trying to test. But actually one can argue that we should be worried if it turned out to be very easy for chemists to obtain life spontaneously in a test tube. "This is because chemists' experiments last for years, not thousands of millions of years, and because only a handful of chemists, not thousands of millions of chemists, are engaged in doing such experiments. If the spontaneous origin of life turned out to be a probable enough event to have occurred during the few man-decades in which chemists have done their experiments, then life should have arisen many times on Earth, and many times on planets within radio range of Earth" [51].

Such chemistry is a fitting comparison for the Web's development, because it too is the end result of many millions of small but significant contributions cumulated over many steps—"an immensely powerful idea, capable of explaining an enormous range of things that would be otherwise inexplicable" [51], rather than being the offspring of a few well-chosen experiments by experts. Furthermore, it must be remembered that the Web is also part of a huge social shift in mankind's communal behavior. Such cultural evolution is "many orders of magnitude faster

---

[8]The Turing test is a proposal for a test of a machine's capability to perform human-like conversation. Described by Alan Turing in the 1950 paper "Computing Machinery and Intelligence," it proceeds as follows: A human judge engages in a natural language conversation with two other parties, one a human and the other a machine; if the judge cannot reliably tell which is which, then the machine is said to pass the test. It is assumed that both the human and the machine try to appear human. In order to keep the test setting simple and universal (to explicitly test the linguistic capability of some machine), the conversation is usually limited to a text-only channel such as a teletype machine as Turing suggested [124].

than DNA-based evolution" [51], which tends to negate the need for evolutional gestation periods measured in lifetimes.

But even so, how could one propose that the Web is aspiring to "true life," given that by its very definition it is a social machine that is strongly artificial across significant parts? Obviously, such an observation is true, but it is also plainly clear that in a good deal of respects the Web is not in the slightest bit similar to the systems engineered by mainstream AI. Furthermore, there is significant reasoning to support the claim that the Web will never be able to pass Turing's test, nor should it need to. This is not because it is unwilling to face up to such a challenge, but is simply because this test is nowhere near suitable to assess the Web's bona fide capability for "consciousness." Turing's test is founded on a view of intelligence that requires comparison based on the dimensions of the singular human mind, but the Web is not comparable to such a model. It presents a kind of fuzzy logic created from an averaged bulk of facts, opinions, and publicly expressed emotions. It would be wrong, therefore, to ask the Web to hold a truly meaningful conversation based on first-, second-, or even third-person perspectives, but it would be perfectly acceptable to ask it for any number of profound answers amounting to its own unique and inspired point of view. Is this first person? No, because there are no people involved. Grammatical phraseology simply breaks down when applied in this way.

Again, should this unique view be considered as "personal" and hence embody consciousness appropriate to Turing's liking? That's one for the philosophers surely, but it does lead to a couple of interesting questions. For instance, can "bioelectrical" hybrid technologies be judged to possess consciousness, independent of any trial based on Turing's test, and does this proposition have any synergy with the field of AI? Common sense appears to say a strong maybe, but the jury is still out and will remain so for a long time yet. What is apparent, however, is that the Web is sufficiently different from other types of AI that have gone before, and in such respects it cannot be categorized, criticized, or stigmatized under the same banner.

POSTHUMAN PHILOSOPHIES AND COLLECTIVE CONSCIOUSNESS

It may well be acceptable to conclude that the Web is capable of independent intelligence, but it would be wrong to try and compare such capability with the overall notion of thought, at least in a truly human sense. Our minds carry a much richer range of facilities, ultimately finishing up in higher notions of self. From this it is easy to see why there seems to be an inbred compulsion in the human condition to try and understand our own existence. From many eras of human history comes evidence of attempts to make sense of what we are and how we relate to the world. We understand, for instance, how earlier humans saw the forces of nature being controlled by Gods, thereby determining human existence and subjecting us to their whim. By enhancing our technical capabilities, the story goes, we gained increasing confidence in our ability to exert control over these forces and thus learned how to impose our own will on nature. In the humanist period of western development, where science advanced and deities held less sway, it even became possible to think of ourselves, with all our intelligence and skills, as coming to dominate our fickle and violent world. Indeed, some thinkers came to believe that even the Universe is precisely tuned to the production of human existence—a theory latterly known as the "Strong Anthropic Principle."

Today the possibilities suggested by synthetic intelligence through technologies like the Web are deeply challenging to that sense of human predominance. These developments awaken deep-rooted anxieties about the threat to human existence from technology we cannot control or understand. Society knows that it is capable of creating entities that may equal and even surpass its natural capabilities, and it must seriously face up to the possibility that faculties like human thought may be created in nonhuman forms. While this is one of our deepest fears, it is also the holy grail of computer science. Despite the enormous problems involved, the development of an artificially conscious entity may likely happen within our lifetimes, if it has not happened already [40].

But it is not enough just to make such a snappy prediction. Rather than attempting to forecast future potential realities, it is often more prudent to investigate the obstacles that stand in their way in order to prevent their being. In such a manner the pessimist invariably produces stronger reasoning by deliberately looking to weed out the less plausible alternatives. So, based on such practice, what happens when the tables are turned and we ask what is preventing the Web from evolving into a higher level of collective consciousness? What is stopping it from just transitioning into one all encompassing global brain?

To start the list, there are three obvious candidates that currently work against any greater ambitions that the Web might have for itself:

- **The Web Presently Lacks Precision.** When you ask the Web a question about "flocks" for example, typically using a good search engine like Google, it has no real idea if you are referring to the collective noun for birds, sheep, or Arabian three-legged pterodactyls! In fact it does not really understand what you are talking about at all; the underlying technologies simply guess at what is being sought based on some reasonably substantial rules around the way natural language is composed. Through this inherent lack of clarity in its underlying architecture, the mainstream Web has little comprehension of meaning. It is semantically weak to be abrupt.

- **The Web's Dispersion and Diversity Actually Work Against It.** Two websites may complement each other perfectly, being genuinely capable of combining to produce a total that is greater than the sum of their individual parts, but if one is hosted in Japan and the other in Jordan and they don't know about each other's existence, how can this productive union ever be formulated? Even worse, if one is written in Japanese and the other in Hebrew or Arabic, what good would it do even if they did know of each other, because without some facility to interpret between them their coming together would again be meaningless. And this leads to a greater problem: What should be the common language of the Web? Should it be English by the very fact that it is the most prevalent tongue in the world? Consensus might say yes in this case, but there are much less obvious examples of language disparity on the Web. Take the interchange of data between various types of Web service, for example. The point is really that there are few dominant dialects on the Web today and that it needs more standardization in this area to increase its overall strength.

- **The Web Is Far from Being Independent.** There are still few stable technologies today that are capable of any true notion of "self." For this reason the Web is technically nowhere near to standing on its own two feet without mankind to directly support it. On its own it is not yet fully self-sufficient or self-organizing and is most definitively not fully self-aware. Even so the technical landscape is changing quickly, and it is becoming apparent that the changes needed for capabilities like pervasive self-awareness to occur are surprisingly small. This obviously leads to the conclusion that if the Web is truly evolving in a natural sense, it will become self-organizing in the very near future. In doing so, its combined computational power will increase dramatically in a very short space of time. Furthermore, if the Web's evolution is also being driven in a truly dynamic and complex manner, this change will be irreversible in a spectacular way according to the law of entropy. Technical advances like the Semantic Web, encompassing languages like OWL,[9] RDF, and SWRL, are helping the Web towards greater things already, along with much more human-focused tools like www.stumbleupon.com.

Even though it is right and proper to attempt to discredit overly ambitious posthuman views of the Web's future, there is nonetheless a growing mound of evidence pointing to credible, yet toned-down, versions of such potentials. To ignore these would be a major oversight.

THE PENROSE PARADOX

It may be worth introducing a little more skepticism to help balance out the arguments for and against the Web as a truly conscious entity. There are those who adamantly resist the notion of any algorithmic mechanism, like a computer system such as the Web, demonstrating life-like intelligence, with some having put forward significant and noteworthy points of view. In particular, the work of Roger Penrose must be marked out as a particularly fine example of weighty objection. Penrose has written several controversial works in which he argues that the known laws of physics do not constitute a complete system and that consciousness[10] cannot be explained until a new physical theory—what he terms Correct Quantum Gravity (CQG)—has been devised. He argues against the strong AI[11] viewpoint, concluding that the processes of the mind are not "algorithmic" and therefore cannot be dupli-

---

[9]OWL is an acronym for Web Ontology Language, a markup language for publishing and sharing data using ontologies on the World Wide Web. OWL is a vocabulary extension of RDF (the Resource Description Framework) and is derived from the DAML+OIL Web Ontology Language. Together with RDF and other components, these tools make up the Semantic Web project.

[10]In this case, Penrose specifically refers to human consciousness.

[11]Strong AI is a hypothetical form of artificial intelligence that can truly reason and solve problems; a strong AI is said to be sapient, or self-aware, but may or may not exhibit human-like thought processes.

cated by any sufficiently complex computer. This is based on claims that human consciousness transcends formal logic systems because things such as the insolvability of the halting problem[12] and Gödel's incompleteness theorem restrict an algorithmically based logic from traits such as mathematical insight. Nevertheless, Penrose's work was published in 1989, a good year before the Web came into existence, and therefore refers to computation in a much more "centralized" manner than that which can be envisaged today. However, he does directly concede that "it is true that we are concerned with matters of principle here, but it is not inconceivable that there might be some 'critical' amount of complication in an algorithm which it is necessary to achieve in order that the algorithm exhibit mental qualities." Because this is not at odds with Stuart Kauffman's work on emergent systems, then perhaps Penrose is, in fact, only an often misquoted and worthy philosopher on this subject, rather than an outspoken oppositionist.

It should be noted that Penrose's views on the human thought process are not widely accepted in scientific circles, however. According to Marvin Minsky,[13] because people can construe false ideas to be factual, the process of thinking is not limited to formal logic. Furthermore, AI programs can also conclude that false statements are true, so error is not unique to humans. Charles Seife,[14] another dissenter, has said, "Penrose, the Oxford mathematician famous for his work on tiling the plane with various shapes, is one of a handful of scientists who believe that the ephemeral nature of consciousness suggests a quantum process." Nevertheless, Penrose and Stuart Hameroff have constructed a theory in which human consciousness is the result of quantum gravity effects in microtubules. But Max Tegmark,[15] in a paper in *Physical Review E,* calculated that the timescale of neuron firing and excitations in microtubules is slower than the decoherence[16] time by a factor of at least 10,000,000,000. The reception of the paper is summed up by this statement in his support: "Physicists outside the fray, such as IBM's John Smolin, say that calculations confirm what they had suspected all along." We're not working with a brain that's near absolute zero. "It's reasonably unlikely that the brain evolved quantum behaviour," he adds.

But then again, Penrose's opinions are given some weight by the slow progress of work on AI. It cannot be denied that early proponents of this field grossly underestimated the difficulty of their task. Arthur C. Clarke placed HAL, his thinking,

---

[12]In computability theory the halting problem is a decision problem that can be informally stated as follows: "Given a description of a program and its initial input, determine whether the program, when executed on this input, ever halts (completes). The alternative is that it runs forever without halting."

[13]Marvin Lee Minsky is an American scientist in the field of Artificial Intelligence, co-founder of MIT's AI laboratory, and author of several texts on AI and philosophy [125].

[14]Charles Seife is a journalist with *Science* magazine and has also written for *New Scientist, Scientific American, The Economist, Science, Wired UK, The Sciences,* and numerous other publications.

[15]Tegmark has also formulated the "Ultimate ensemble theory of everything," whose only postulate is that "all structures that exist mathematically exist also physically." This simple theory, with no free parameters at all, suggests that in those structures complex enough to contain self-aware substructures (SASs) these SASs will subjectively perceive themselves as existing in a physically "real" world.

[16]In quantum mechanics, quantum decoherence is the general term for systems that typically evolve from quantum mechanical quantum entanglement to classical behavior. Decoherence occurs when a system interacts with its environment and thereby becomes an open system.

feeling, ultimately paranoid computer, in his book *2001, A Space Odyssey,* during which year real AI researchers were teaching small robots to find their way around rooms. As Penrose himself says, this is "no indication of any sort of intelligence, let alone consciousness," but then Penrose also disagrees with the majority view on how to decide whether a computer is conscious. Even so, Penrose's theories may not be so radical when used as a basis for understanding the "consciousnesses" of the hybrid sociotechnical machine that is the Web. Quantum concepts have helped explain many of the apparent inconsistencies in the most complex system known to man and in particular work well with the very nature of the Universe itself. They do this by specifically addressing the complex interactions of microscopic physical phenomena. Just as with mechanisms aimed at investigating the holistic characteristics of the Web, quantum physics has been devised to explain interactions best described in nondeterministic ways. It, too, addresses concepts that can only be characterized using the mathematics of aggregation and statistical probability, rather than the pinpoint accuracy of the deterministic macroscopic world. It turns out that there is much legitimacy to the theoretical physics of information and computing.

Like Alice following the white rabbit down a hole into a bizarre, peculiar wonderland, where "nothing is as it seems," studies of the quantum world can invoke a feeling of bewilderment in many of those who tread its seemingly ambiguous path [72]. But why should the quantum world be so like the Web world, even down to the use of familiar concepts such as entanglement? Perhaps this is purely a matter of scale and observability. As organisms, we are like meat in the middle of a sandwich of immeasurable complexity: below us are the complexities of the microscopic and subatomic worlds, too small for our clumsy measuring instruments to penetrate, while above us are the vast complexities of the cosmos, too grand for even our biggest implements to dent properly. It is in this latter type of domain that the Web is most likely to sit, too big for us to study in any context that directly relates to our own limited viewpoint. But there is some linearity across all layers. All are complex, perhaps differently complex, but complex all the same, so perhaps quantum theories are applicable to the workings of the Web. If so, they provide a pathway for Penrose's opinions on artificial consciousness to flow through. For small-scale computer systems, those employing, hundreds, thousands, or even tens of thousands, of nodes say, Penrose is undoubtedly correct and AI is indeed illusory. But ramp up the stakes somewhat and create a Web of literally millions of simple computational and informational nodes and there is strong evidence that new rules and behaviours emerge. Unpredictable beauty abounds, splitting unexpected symmetries as a result of strange and wonderful entangled loopiness. Could this be the consciousness that Penrose seeks, or is it just nature's failed attempt at fishing, having snarled its line in one immense entangled sea of connectivity?

CHAPTER 9

The Physics of Information and Computing

From a classical point of view we are machines, and in machines there is no room for conscious experience. It doesn't matter if the machine dies; you can kill the machine, throw it in the dumpster . . . it doesn't matter. If that is the way that the world is, then people will behave in that way. But there's another other way of thinking about the world which is pointed to by quantum mechanics, which suggests that the world is not this clockwork thing, but more like an organism. It's a highly interconnected orgasmic thing . . . which extends through space and time.

—*Dean Radin*

THE ATTRACTION OF "WHY" AND THE UBIQUITY OF COMPLEXITY AS A METAPROPERTY

Murray Gell-Mann, the Nobel Prize-winning physicist, once said the following about his beloved profession: "I think of the subject as a study of simplicity and complexity." "The simple laws of the Universe and its probabilistic character seem to me to underlie the whole subject—that and the nature of information and quantum physics." But then Gell-Mann would say that. A strong believer in symmetry and total reductionism, he was once even quoted as saying that the science of complexity is all about "the fundamental particles of which it was composed"—meaning subatomic quarks. He implied that metacomplex systems like social organizations or the Web are merely made up of lots and lots of quarks and you could follow the quarks through to various levels of aggregation. But the tide of opinion was against him, with many of his contemporaries believing that emergent, complex systems represented something new—that the fundamental concepts needed to understand that their macroscopic behaviors go well beyond the fundamental laws of force and linearity. And yes, the old schools of scientific thought were being challenged. Finally we were beginning to recover from Newton [67].

Murray Gell-Mann was clearly one of the major scientific figures of twentieth-century science. When he arrived on the scene as a young Ph.D. graduate in the 1950s, the subatomic world seemed an endless mess—a mess of π particles, σ particles, ρ particles, and so on, through the endless list of Greek alphabetical names assigned at random. But two decades later, largely due to the concepts that Gell-

Mann had pioneered, physicists were drawing up Grand Unified Theories of all particles as various combinations of "quarks"—simple subatomic building blocks that Gell-Man named after a made-up word in James Joyce's *Finnegan's Wake.*

The physics fraternity may well have been starting to unify their visions, at least around fundamentals at microscopic levels, but the notion of complexity was always there, nagging away to be recognized, pushing to be understood, breaking conventional thinking.

Physicists and mathematicians love all things fundamental and have an innate fondness for investigations centered on "why," the sharpest blade in their investigative toolbox. This is not a matter born out of preference, but is simply a result of their necessity to face off against some of the hardest, purest science there is [67]. They will happily strip away the surface layers of a given problem until they reach the bare bones of the answers they are seeking. This is their forte, like infants engrossed in the pleasure of a new toy, they strive to understand what is "provably real" and why it should be so. Needless to say, such fields have made unprecedented advances over the past few centuries, allowing us to at least be able to debate the entire spectrum of actuality in our Universe. For decades, fields like Theoretical Physics have been wrestling with the workings of our Universe at every level of detail. From the unimaginably small to the incomprehensibly huge, they have striven to match up their hypotheses with the precise observations of controlled experimentation, all in search of undeniable evidence at the heart of nature's magic. The ultimate aim of this is the discovery of one underlying theme—a grand Theory of Everything (TOE)[1]—of the way that quite literally everything interrelates. Such a theory would yield all the Universes secrets, merging the entire spectrum of physical systems into one family, a family where the subatomic and astronomic would sit at the same table. But nature is clever with its tricks, so far only taunting science with apparently irreconcilable differences in its household. At present the microscopic can still not be explained in terms of the macroscopic, despite all our best efforts. Dinner is not yet served, it appears, but this does not mean to say that our understanding is uncongenial in every respect. If we were to pull away from the data associated with raw observable fact and look instead at the inherent properties of the data itself—its metadata as it were—at least one commonality can be found: In the main, everything is complex, paradoxically a simple but honest truth.

Thus we have methods for quantifying and qualifying complexity in everything from the workings of galaxies right down to the inconceivably microscopic function of quantum interaction. Such methods have fortunately also focused on situations where both the real (observable macro phenomena) and the "unreal" (indirect-

---

[1]A theory of everything (TOE) is a theory of theoretical physics and mathematics that fully explains and links together all known physical phenomena. Initially, the term was used with an ironic connotation to refer to various overgeneralized theories.

There have been numerous theories of everything proposed by theoretical physicists over the last century, but none has been able to stand up to experimental scrutiny or there is tremendous difficulty in getting the theories to produce even experimentally testable results. The primary problem in producing a TOE is that quantum mechanics and general relativity have radically different descriptions of the universe, and the obvious ways of combining the two lead quickly to the renormalization problem in which the theory does not give finite results for experimentally testable quantities [126].

ly observable micro phenomena) naturally intertwine. This is an area of investigation sometimes summarized under the heading of "decoherence," a concept that appears exceptionally insightful when looking for analogies between real-world systems and the virtual workings of Web Life. Through such lines of research, points of overlap have been found containing rich veins of reputable thinking. These have nonetheless hitherto remained relatively untapped by the computing and information sciences communities, an interesting conundrum given that the physical Universe is itself the biggest computational device that could ever exist. In their original concepts, such understandings may well have been formulated to fathom potentially conflicting phenomena and relate to apparently sparsely interconnected fields, but this does not necessarily invalidate their use in helping to describe any of the various aspects of complexity itself, nor does it necessarily stop them from being applied in connection with complexity as seen in complex abstract systems like the Web.

SPIN GLASS

One really good analogy with the complexity on the Web comes from the field of material physics and in particular the study of a series of obscure magnetic materials known as spin glasses. These are highly disordered magnetic systems with competing ferromagnetic and anti-ferromagnetic interactions as found in some alloys, like copper/magnesium.

When a typically ferromagnetic material, like iron, is magnetized by an external magnetic field, electron spins are aligned with the direction of that field. When a spin glass is magnetized, the internal forces appear quite random—a state physicists call "glassy" [67]. This glassy quality is not really random at all, but is merely complex to the point where easily recognizable patterns are obscured. So, in much the same way as the Web, spin glasses are a maelstrom of interactions that accumulate into many higher orders of observable complexity.

The atomic scale disorder in spin glasses means that such materials are a complex mixture of positive and negative feedbacks as atoms try to align their spins in parallel with some neighbors but opposite to others.

Interestingly, it is time dependence which really distinguishes spin glasses from other magnetic systems. In particular, if one heats spin glass to above its transition temperature (T_c)—where it exhibits more typical magnetic behavior—and an external magnetic field is applied, the resultant plot of magnetization against temperature follows the typical curve found with more normal magnetic substances. This states that magnetization is inversely proportional to temperature until T_c is reached, at which point the magnetization becomes virtually constant—a property referred to as "field-cooled magnetization." When the external field is removed, the spin glass has a rapid decrease of magnetization to a value referred to as its remnant magnetization. This is followed by a slow decay as the magnetization approaches zero or some small fraction of the original value—a complex phenomenon that is particular to spin glass. If a similar procedure were followed for a standard ferromagnetic substance, when the external field is removed, there would be a rapid change to a remnant value, but this value is a constant in time. For a material like a paramagnet,[2] when the external field is removed, the magnetization rapidly goes to zero. In each case, the change is very rapid; if carefully examined, it is exponential decay with a very small time constant.

If instead, the spin glass is cooled below T_c in the absence of an external field, and then a field is applied, there is a rapid increase to a value called the zero-field-cooled magnetization, which is less than the field-cooled magnetization, followed by a slow upward drift toward the field-cooled value.

Interestingly, a great deal of early theoretical work on spin glasses has been used in a form of "mean field theory," a particular branch of science aimed at describing many-body or multi-agent systems involving complex interactions. The goal of mean field theory is therefore to resolve combinatorial problems in such systems.

The main idea of mean field theory is to replace all the interactions with any given entity in a system with an average of effective interaction. This effectively reduces multi-body issues into a single-entity problem. The ease of solving complex problems using mean field theory means that some insight into the behavior of complex systems can be achieved at a relatively low cost.

An influential exactly solvable model of a spin glass has been produced which has led to considerable theoretical extensions of mean field theory to model (a) the slow dynamics of the magnetization and (b) complex nonergodic[3] equilibrium state systems. The same variant of mean field theory has also been applied in the study of neural networks, where it has enabled calculations of properties such as the storage capacity of simple neural network architectures without requiring implementation of a training algorithm. Such practices have also now been directly applied to the Web and have proved useful in the producing new methods for extracting information [74] and predicting such properties as growth dynamics, connectivity distribution, and the scaling exponents [73].

QUANTUM COMPARISONS

In many respects, the complexity of the both life and the Web provides an accurate comparison to the strange subatomic worlds of quantum physics whose constitution has undergone significant scientific scrutiny in modern times. Quantum systems encode the probabilities of their measurable properties, or "observables," in much the same way that the holistic characteristic of complex macro-systems can only be fairly described in approximated ways. So, even though quantum physics, and in particular quantum mechanics, may appear to represent the ultimate approach to reduction-based analysis, by trying to establish that everything in the Universe is a consequence of a few types of subatomic particle, in fact, there are close comparisons to more holistic scientific disciplines, at least as far as complexity is concerned.

---

[2]Paramagnetism is the tendency of the atomic magnetic dipoles to align with an external magnetic field.
[3]Positive recurrent aperiodic state of apparently random systems; tending in probability to a limiting form that is independent of the initial conditions.

Although the particles that quantum physicists choose to study are much, much smaller and simpler than the proteins involved in DNA or the various communities strung together on the Web, for example, when one looks at those simple particles interacting in massive numbers to make up molecules and all other forms of higher level matter, all the same phenomena found in larger-scale complex systems can be seen. Tiny initial differences produce enormously different effects, simple dynamics producing astonishingly complex behaviors, with a handful of pieces falling into a near infinity of possible patterns [67]. Somehow, the underlying principles of all science are the same.

The practice of studying phenomena at such microscopic levels differs from most mainstream science. Generally, quantum-level investigations do not assign definite values to observables. Instead, they make predictions about their probability distributions—that is, the probability of obtaining each of the possible outcomes from measuring an observable. Naturally, these probabilities depend on the quantum state at the instant of the measurement, in exactly the same way as contexts in large-scale dynamic systems. There are, however, certain states that are associated with a definite value of a particular observable. These are known as "eigenstates" of the observable—"eigen" meaning "own" in German—and this notion bears a striking resemblance to the exact definitions now metered out through extensions to the mainstream Web, such as the Semantic Web. So just like the Web, in quantum mechanics, it is acceptable to both have exacting and heuristic description of the same problem space.

Quantum ideas also fall in line with the concept of symmetry in systems. Several hundred years ago, Gottfried Wilhelm Leibniz[4] came remarkably close to formulating an early version of Quantum Theory, without the benefit of any of the empirical evidence that aids us today. His Principle of the Identity of "Indiscernibles" states that no two different objects can have the same description. If two objects are indiscernible, with all their properties in common, then there is really only one object after all [66]. This principle has the ring of common sense and is self-evident to many philosophers, perfectly describing the notion of symmetry outlined in earlier chapters. Furthermore, if taken literally, it leads directly to a version of Quantum Theory, complete with all its strangeness. Leibniz only got partway there, but he got much further than hardly anyone gives him credit for.

According to some, quantum mechanics in particular is more strongly ordered than its classical macro equivalent, because while classical mechanics can produce chaotic systems, quantum mechanics cannot—an interesting comparison with the highly structured/randomly structured debate currently centered on the Web. For instance, the classical problem of three bodies under a force like gravity is not open to mathematical integration, while the quantum mechanical three-body problem is tractable and amenable in this way. That is, a quantum mechanical problem can always be solved to a given accuracy with a computer of predetermined precision, while the classical problem may require arbitrarily high precision, depending on the details of the motion. This does not mean that quantum mechanics is more deterministic, unless one already considers the wave function to be the true reality. Nev-

---

[4]Gottfried Wilhelm von Leibniz was a German philosopher and mathematician [127].

ertheless, it does highlight yet another link between the characteristics of the Web and other areas interested in highly complex systems behaviors.

But comparisons between quantum theory and the innards of the Web should come as no real shock. Quantum mechanics evolved as a new branch of theoretical physics during the first few decades of the twentieth century in an endeavor to understand the fundamental properties of matter. "It tells us that an understanding of our world can only be had by developing a theory of all possible worlds [66]" or "universal contexts." Our world can be said to have structure and order only if it is embedded in a larger ensemble of possible contexts, just as regions of the Web can only be truly understood when considered in relation to all other regions. This type of ensemble is referred to as the "wave function" of the Universe, and it is not definable under the traditional interpretation of quantum theory pioneered by Niels Bohr. Bohr did not believe in a wave function for the entire universe. He believed that an old-style classical, nonquantum object, such as an observer, was needed to "collapse" the possibilities down from many possible worlds to the one that actually exists. Even so, quantum theory is undoubtedly all about the interaction of "things" within a given set of contexts and is certainly self-reflexive in ways just like the Web. In the Web world the things might be meme-like ideas rather than "tangible" objects or particles, but nevertheless both the Web and quantum studies are fundamentally concerned with the nature of interaction.

Quantum theory began with the study of the interactions of matter and radiation. This was because certain radiation effects could not be explained satisfactorily by either classical mechanics or the theory of electromagnetism. In particular, physicists were puzzled by the nature of light. Peculiar lines in the spectrum of sunlight had been discovered earlier by the German physicist Joseph von Fraunhofer. These spectral lines were then systematically catalogued for various substances, yet nobody could explain why the spectral lines are there and why they would differ for each substance. It took around 100 years, until a plausible explanation was supplied by quantum theory.

In contrast to Einstein's Relativity, which is about the largest things in the Universe, quantum theory deals with the tiniest things we know, the particles that atoms are made of, which are called "subatomic" particles. As was the case with relativity, quantum theory was not the work of one individual, but the collaborative effort of some of the most brilliant physicists of the twentieth century, among them Niels Bohr, Erwin Schrödinger, Wolfgang Pauli, and Max Born. Two other names clearly stand out: Max Planck and Werner Heisenberg. Planck is recognized as the originator of the quantum theory, while Heisenberg formulated one of the most eminent laws of quantum theory, the "uncertainty principle," which is occasionally also referred to as the "principle of indeterminacy."

MORE ABOUT DIMENSIONS

At low levels of magnification the overwhelming complexity of the Web may well make it appear fuzzy and intangible. For some this may also only make it suitable for accurate classification using the uncertainty built into quantum-like formulae. But increase this magnification somewhat and distinguishable form soon comes into focus. In such ways the Web can be legitimately compared with both the macroscopic workings of the cosmos and the microscopic mechanisms of the subatomic. It quite literally presents a genuine juxtaposition of precise and estimated qualities. Both the Web and the cosmos, for example, are clearly vast and extremely complex in a number of ways and at a number of levels. Furthermore, by such tokens, neither can be "prestated across many of their individual dimensions and general themes [52]." In the natural world these dimensions are tied together into the space–time continuum, a region which, in the theories of special relativity and general relativity at least, is thought of as time and three-dimensional space treated together as a single four-dimensional object. But nothing prevents one from having more than four dimensions, per se. Space–time continua are the arenas in which all physical events take place—for instance, the motion of planets around the Sun—and may be described in a particular type of space–time. So it is the way with the Web for it too is its own "space," a valid universe of its own if you will, "a universe of discourse."[5]

Human minds have a hard time visualizing higher dimensions because we can only move in three spatial dimensions. And even then, we only see in 2 + 1 dimensions; vision in 3 dimensions allows us to see all sides of an object from appropriate viewing angles. One way of dealing with this limitation is not to try to visualize higher dimensions at all but to just think of them as extra numbers in the equations that describe the way that worlds work. This opens up the question of whether these "extra numbers" can be investigated directly via experimentation. If so, then such experiments must be able to show, ultimately, different results in 1, 2, or 2 + 1 dimensions to a human scientist. This, in turn, raises the question whether models that rely on such abstract modeling can be considered "scientific." But this conundrum has to be put to one side, at least for now, when dealing with multidimensional systems like the Web.

There are no exact equivalences between the Web dimensions of hyperspace and the real space–time of our physical actuality. As mentioned in Chapter 1, the Web does not necessarily conform to the Euclidian space–time[6] restrictions of our existence, nor is it necessarily mathematically imaginary[7] or complex as often portrayed in such concepts as Hilbert Spaces[8] or Riemann Surfaces[9] often used in physics. Instead its world extends beyond four dimensions, being capable of ontological representation through an almost limitless collection of semantic aspects and subsets that are, for all intents and purposes, topologically[10] irrelevant. Even so, the graphs that

---

[5]A class containing all the entities referred to in a discourse or argument. Also called a "universe."

[6]In mathematics, Euclidean space is a generalization of the two- and three-dimensional spaces comparable with height, depth, and breath [128].

[7]Corresponding to numbers involving the mathematical constant $i = \sqrt{-1}$.

[8]In mathematics, a Hilbert space is a generalization of Euclidean space that is not restricted to finite dimensions [129].

[9]In mathematics, particularly in complex analysis, a Riemann surface, named after Bernhard Riemann, is a one-dimensional complex manifold. Riemann surfaces can be thought of as "deformed versions" of the complex plane: Locally near every point they look like patches of the complex plane, but the global topology can be quite different. For example, they can look like a sphere or a torus or a couple of sheets glued together [130].

[10]A topology is an arrangement where the location of elements is spatially relevant.

can be extracted from the Web's various ontologies can be construed as comprising a kind of vector space, an eigenvector[11] space in fact, and thus can be studied mathematically. This makes the Web a truly multidimensional entity of materially irrelevant proportions, an n-dimensional "thing" eminently suited to description by advanced fields of mathematics and physics like phase analysis. Such fields model multifaceted abstract problems using the concept of n-dimensional "manifolds"[12] or "surfaces"[13]; shape spaces or algebraic topologies that allow the formalization of concepts such as convergence, connectedness and continuity. These can map a group of dimensions derived from a problem that need not have any direct physical relevance. In short, manifolds map out all the various occurrences of a given aspect across the dimensions chosen for representation. They, therefore, produce multidimensional "surfaces" that give such analytical techniques their name.

The hyperlinked associations that make up the Web can be modeled using graphs, which are a form of topology in much the same way as the surfaces and manifolds highlighted here. In fact, one is merely an extension of the other with surfaces able to express more dimensional data than graphs. Thus, in some respects, the makeup of the Web can be likened to that of a multidimensional ordnance survey map in which every referencable resource has its own unique set of coordinates and all hyperlinks act to lay out the contours of the intervening terrain. These have no correlation with their counterparts on normal maps of the real world, but they can help us understand the nature of the Web via far richer conceptualizations than usual.

Traveling across such surfaces can, in some cases, also be viewed as a process phase change between start and destination coordinates. Rather like inching from land to sea across a smooth beach in the real world, the dominant characteristics of the Web too can transition via minor incremental movements. Furthermore, change can also be extremely violent, just as if the flat beach were replaced with a steep cliff in our analogy. In fact, one can literally think of aggregated phase change as a landscape in this way.

STRANGE LOOPS, SPIN NETWORKS, AND PROBLEMS WITH THE WEB'S CONSTITUTION

Although the Web can be described using techniques such as surfaces and phase analysis, there are other issues. To start with, the Web is inherently loopy and intertwined, whereas many of the phenomena described by surface mathematics generally are not. Even so, on such "loopy" surfaces it makes no difference how "close" one loop might be to another. The only things that have significance are the ontological and topological "linking," "splitting," and "knotting," or "inter-

---

[11]Eigenvectors are a special set of vectors associated with a linear system of equations (i.e., a matrix equation) that are sometimes also known as characteristic vectors, proper vectors, or latent vectors [131].
[12]A manifold is a mathematical, abstract space that can be thought of as "curved" in various ways, but where locally (i.e., in a small enough neighborhood of any of its points) it looks like a section of ordinary Euclidian space [61], in which associations can effectively be modeled using straight lines.
[13]To be precise, a surface is a two-dimensional manifold. Examples arise in three-dimensional space as the boundaries of three-dimensional solid objects.

secting," regions amongst loops and the discrete level of "spin" associated with them [61].

This phenomenon is similar to the picture presented by quantum gravity, which is associated with a field of mathematics specifically concerned with the topology of knots and links. This a surprisingly sophisticated subject, considering the nature of its ingredients—basically untangling bits of string [60]. On the Web, hyperlink chains are without a doubt analogous to such "string"; they frequently loop back, intertwining and entangling with other such chains of links on their way. In such a manner the Web can be immensely self-reflexive at heart, incorporating many strange loops and frequently violating classical topologies like localized hierarchies or clusters. Furthermore, the very nature of a sequential path across the Web can be theoretically considered as being helical and "loopy" as outlined in Chapter 4, Figure 4.15a–c. But again this is not at odds with ideas relating to the notion of paths in the quantum arena. There, massless particles, such as photons, can "spin" about the direction of their motion, a characteristic often referred to as "helicity."

Helicity on its own it still not enough, however, to provide any overall characterization of complex connected problem spaces like the Web, spaces in which loops can intermingle and intersect. This leads to the idea of graphs that can use "intersecting loop lines," rather than straight point-to-point linkages. Such diagrams are commonly known as spin networks, a concept first described by Roger Penrose over half a century ago. These are graphs whose lines intrinsically contain spin and whose overall descriptive capability is often associated with irreducible representation of compact, complex or real manifolds. In layman's terms they are diagrams that can show the overall landscape of complex "loopy" problems.

Spin networks were designed to describe physics in terms of discrete combinatorial quantities, because part of a core belief that systems based in space–time should be strongly founded on the concept of discrete, rather than continuous, interactions. Since Penrose's work in this area the various fashions of the physics fraternity may have come and gone, but the absolute discreteness on which computational systems are founded has predominantly[14] not. So to that end, spin networks are eminently applicable to the description of complex digital schemes, being founded on the idea that everything can be expressed in terms of the relation between objects and not between an object and some background space [60]. For such reasons they are ideally suited to condensing representations of highly connected complex systems like the Web.

Spin networks (Figure 9.1) also lead to the mathematical idea that the structural entirety of a system can be summarized as a single value relating to its total spin. Also, given that each element in the structure can be uniquely characterized via a Gödel number it may also be plausible to suggest that an even more descriptive metric could come from some form of Gödelian spin product.

Thus comparisons between quantum gravity and the Web are not in the least farfetched. Given that the Web is a scale-free network, there is an inbuilt propensity for any new node to link to one which is already well-connected. In fact, this is

---

[14]Work on quantum computers does allow for "bits" of information to be both in "on" and "off" states at the same time.

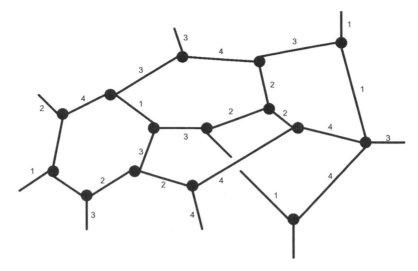

Figure 9.1. An example of a spin network, as originally envisaged by Penrose [60].

common across all scale-free networks such as social gatherings and protein–protein interactions. Hence, the greater the popularity of any one thing in such a network, the greater the likelihood that it will connect with more things in the future. They are attractors in a mathematical sense—as outlined in Chapter 2—almost as if they possess their own gravitational field or magnetism, their own form of energy sucking in elements from the environment.

In many ways the Web relies on this "energy" to maintain its scale-free characteristic. "For instance, Web pages that already have a high number of hyperlinks become well known and the natural choice for Web designers who want a pointer from their new page to a source of further information. In short, fame breeds fame in the guise of increasing returns [80]."

It would be nice to think that there is some underlying metric principle at work here—that is, that Web pages receive lots of links simply because they are "good." It would be surprising if that were not so. But goodness is an unfortunately subjective measure and popularity brings increasing returns to both good and bad. All that is a close to certain is that popular information and services will create a "pull" on other information and services. What makes them popular, and hence provides the energy for this attraction is much less clear.

COMPUTATIONAL DUALITY

Whenever anyone takes their first class in computing, there is a high chance that they will be presented with a diagram showing the simplest representation of computing there is. This is shown in Figure 9.2a and illustrates that computing is all about taking some kind of input, doing something with it to effect a change and then

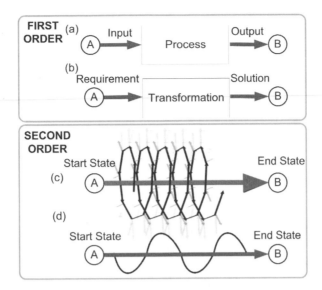

Figure 9.2. (a–d) Equivalent representations of the basic computational process.

serving up the result of that change as some form of output. To get philosophical for one second, at a high level, this simply boils down to nothing more than a first-order interpretation of that change, no matter how much second order detail is involved.[15] Make this diagram a little more informative, and then the ideas of "input," "output," and "process" become interchangeable with terms like "requirement," "transformation," and "solution."

But this is not the end of the all the equivalences available. Most of Chapter 4 was devoted to explaining the idea that broken symmetry in both sequential information and functionality can be seen to generate graph patterns that are conceptually helical in nature. When computing, regardless of whether the actual processing takes place as one long sequence of actions or as a collection of sequences acting in parallel, the underlying model is still conceptually the same—a series of steps that change input into output. So, when oversimplification is the order of the day, a high-level, second-order conceptual model of computation can be seen to be analogous to an ordered "coil" of changes between any given input and its corresponding output, as shown in Figure 9.2c.

[15]In philosophical attempts to understand general principles, the notions of first and second order are used to separate statements from the detailed meaning of those statements. Some examples:

First Order: "A transforms into B"
Second Order: "What does it mean to say that A transforms into B?"
First Order: "The universe does not exist."
Second Order: "What is cosmological language, and how may cosmological assertions be verified?"

So second-order language or logic clarifies first-order assertions.

Take any such "coil" and flatten it into two dimensions and it will transform into the curves of a wave formation; a wave "function" to be more precise, as can be seen in Figure 9.2d. This is common practice in many areas of science and mathematics when the number of variables in a problem needs to be narrowed down for investigation purposes. Thinking of computation and information in terms of wave functions introduces an interesting paradox. Convention tends to treat a transformation or change between any two points or states—"A" and "B" in both Figures 9.2 and 9.3 in this case—in a first-order manner; as a straight line or vector in most common nomenclatures. This is fine from the perspective of relatively simple or direct statements of understandings, but when deeper clarification is needed, a further, second-order representation is needed. For this reason, conceptualization using wave functions may also be used, thereby differentiating every step change involved in a first-order concept. And the more numerous and regular the steps involved, the smoother the wave produced. In this way both computation and the data it acts upon can be thought of as being capable of representation using both vector and wave notation. In other words, there is a duality present in much the same way that in physics light can be considered as being both a collection of particles and wave functions—the two different models actually turn out to be equivalent.

THE WEB'S SUPERPOSITION

The Web is unquestionably an eclectic place, being a melting pot of diverse opinion, need, and belief. In fact just about every conceivable viewpoint can be found on the Web these days. Go to any significant search engine like Google, type in a subject of your choice, and the chances are that hundreds, if not thousands, of links will be returned in response, all containing different interpretations of the subject matter in which you are interested. In such respects the Web is both explicitly noncommittal and implicitly knowledgeable on just about every aspect of human en-

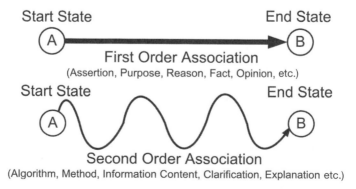

Figure 9.3. Vector wave duality in computation.

deavor. Not only does it possess many specific and individual pieces of information on most subjects, but these can also intertwine to produce a truly complex and rounded appreciation. Some might even interpret this as "knowledge" in the classical sense, being thought of as the information of which someone or something is aware.[16] But think instead of this "knowledge" being constructed from a collection of information in the form of wave functions or vectors as outlined above and a further possible interpretation is possible—that of superposition.

Superposition (Figure 9.4) is a concept often referred to in quantum mechanics involving the addition of the amplitudes of waves from interference. It is the amplitudes of wave functions, or state vectors, that add. It occurs when an object simultaneously "possesses" two or more values for an observable quantity. Usually quoted physical examples include the position or energy of a particular subatomic particle, but the various opinions manifest on a particular subject on the Web provide an equally valid illustration. Thus the cumulative sum of all the Web's capability and content, each piece superimposed upon another, can be seen as its superposition on any particular topic or purpose.

COULD PENROSE BE RIGHT AFTER ALL?

In the last chapter the opinions of Roger Penrose were highlighted as an example of significant objection to Artificial Intelligence. Nevertheless, the complete case for his point of view was deliberately not presented at that point. This is because Penrose is a physicist of some merit and much of the evidence in support of his argument rests on concepts that have only just been covered in this chapter. In particular, Penrose proposes that consciousness comes about when the superposition of neurons within the brain reaches a certain threshold and then spontaneously collapses due to quantum gravity effects (this is similar to the collapse of the wave function due to observation), bringing a vast array of possibilities down to a localized point value. According to Penrose, what he calls "objective reductions" are intrinsic to the way consciousness operates. "Objective reductions convert multiple possibilities at the preconscious, unconscious, or subconscious level to define perceptions or choices at the conscious level, rather like considering pizza, hamburgers, and noodles, all in superposition, and then selecting just one for your choice of dinner" [60].

But there are too many similarities with the Web to be ignored here. Accept the ideas of wave functions and superposition on the Web and think again of using Google to enquire on a particular subject. The way that normal hyperlinks work means that when you browse Google's results, you can only select one of them at a time—the enquiry process literally affects your perception of the information available in a nondeterministic, but statistically predictable, way. Surely this is equivalent to the collapse of superposition due to observation. Selection of a particular search result in effect reduces the entire collective knowledge of the Web

---

[16]The term *knowledge* is also used to mean the confident understanding of a subject, potentially with the ability to use it for a specific purpose.

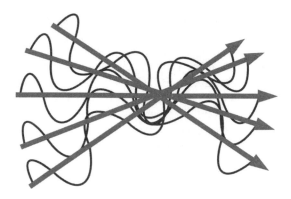

Figure 9.4. The Web's superposition.

down to one URL at one time, a single and unique reference point on the Web, an isolated perspective, an individual statement. In reality, you might as well be canvassing the opinion of the Web's consciousness in accordance with Penrose's theory.

Objective reduction need not only be considered as the collapse of two dimensional wave functions due to observation. It is just as valid to think of it as the collapse of superposition composed from multiple helixes or spins of raw information or computation. Therefore it also represents the deflation of many contributions, an ultimate consensus as seen from a specific vantage point. It is quite literally the ultimate metamodel of the Web and a model also not unlike the concept of a Quantum Brain.

QUANTUM BRAINS

In his book *The Quantum Brain: The Search for Freedom and the Next Generation of Man,* Jeffrey Satinover has constructed a rigorous mathematical argument demonstrating the workings of the human nervous system and the particular way that it implements quantum effects—very distinct, specific ways, not general, not fuzzy, not imprecise. "He absolutely does create a pathway for the possibility of free will while still not violating modern scientific standpoints" [80].

This is based on the idea that objective reduction takes place in tiny microtubes present in the brain. These are the hollow, straw-like structures found within every cell including the brain's neurons. Once thought of as merely the cytoskeleton or scaffolding of the cell, microtubes can be found to display extraordinary self-organizing ability. They serve as the cell's nervous and circulatory system, and they transport materials and organize the cell's shape and motion. They interact with their neighbors to process and communicate information and organize neighboring cells into a unified coherent whole [87].

The structural changes, information processing, and communication amongst microtubes within the neurons of the brain are directly influential one physical level up, on the organization of neurons into neuronets. But the microtubes themselves are affected from deep within their own structure by quantum phenomena: The proteins from which they are constructed respond to signals from what appears to be an internal quantum computer consisting of single electrons. As Stuart Hameroff from the University of Arizona explains: "These quantum mechanical forces in the pockets inside proteins control the conformational shape of the protein. That, in turn, controls the actions of the neurons and the muscles, and ultimately our behaviour. So, proteins changing their shape are the amplification point between the quantum world and our affecting the classical world in everything that mankind does, good or bad."

Hameroff also says that it is the spontaneous collapse though the objective reduction of microtubes, roughly 40 times a second, that provides a "moment of consciousness." Our consciousness is therefore not continuous, but instead a discrete sequence of "ah-ha moments." He says, "consciousness kind of ratchets through space time, and that consciousness is a sequence of now moments: now, now, now . . . [87].

"At the macro level all events, from orbits of planets to the movement of molecules, are mechanical and determined by precise mathematical laws. Thus, it is only if the randomness of the quantum level could be relevant on the macro level that choice and free will might be possible" [87].

"At the level of the brain," says Satinover, the neural networks "produce a global intelligence that's associated with the brain as a whole. But then when you look at individual neurons, the interior of the neurons is a different physical implementation of the same principle. And, in fact, at every scale as you go down, like Chinese boxes nested one in another, each individual processing element at one scale can be shown to be composed of innumerable smaller processing elements within it" [60]. In truth, the underlying physical architecture is fractal in nature.

Starting at the "lowest" level, or smallest scale that can be freely observed, the process whereby proteins fold—the process Stuart Hameroff described as operating within the microtubule—"obeys essentially the same mathematical self-organising dynamic as how a neural network processes information. So, the folding of a protein is mathematically identical to the generation of a thought, or the solving of a problem. And that's really where the notion of the quantum brain comes in. Not that the brain as a whole entity is a quantum entity, but rather that quantum effects at the lowest level are not only capable of, but of necessity are amplified upward because of the fractal arrangement of the nervous system. . . . It is through a very particular kind of neighbour-to-neighbour interaction amongst the neurons that global intelligence, at the level of the brain as a whole, emerges" [87].

According to this theory, the brain has in fact been designed to magnify these quantum effects and project them "upward" to larger and larger processing elements, until they reach the level of the brain [87].

In short, concludes Satinover, "Quantum mechanics allows for the intangible phenomenon of freedom to be woven into human nature. . . . The entire operation of the human brain is underpinned by quantum uncertainty." This is because "at every scale, from the cortex down to the individual proteins," the brain "functions as a parallel processor. . . . These processes form a nested hierarchy, an entire parallel computer at one scale being a processing element in the next larger one" [80].

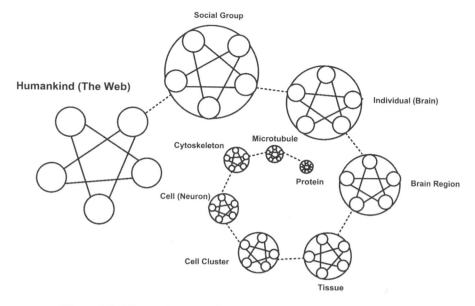

Figure 9.5. The continuation of computational integration across scales.

Sound familiar? Of course it does. This model is almost perfectly analogous to the Web, right down to the fact that the cylindrical structure of microtubes might as well be thought of as the helical configurations produced by sequential pathways across the Web. There is literally a continuation of computational integration and likeness across scales (Figure 9.5). To researchers like Satinover the link is obvious, so obvious in fact that he even refers to the brain as "the Wet Net" and to life as "a universal computer." He maintains that the basic model of quantum computing at microscopic scales, and thus quantum interdeterminacies, continues to scale up from individual brains to groups through complete societies and on to world-wide concepts such as the Web itself. This scaling needs not take into account any metaphysical effects to produce coherence at the level of all humanity. To Satinover, the Web and the brain are as if one—simply actualizations of the same mechanisms, just at different physical scales.

ONE BIG SPINY STRING THING

Of all the ideas presented so far, the notion of the Web as one big entangled assemblage of splitting and reforming sequences, or pathways, is clearly central. Sequences may of course be viewed simply as being lists or "strings" of ordered elements or concepts. For the computer scientists, in this context, such strings do not literally relate to any underlying data type, but rather to the concept of ordered "things" that are important to the existence of other "things" in a collective sense. In this way, numbers, sentences, functions, Web pages, and hyperlink chains can all be thought of as strings. When they split and converge, sets of concurrent activity or data are created and closed, thus realizing all the parts needed for a computational machine to be created.

Without wanting to mislead, for many the very name "World Wide Web" invokes a false image, implying a regular configuration akin to the cobwebbed constructions of the planet's arachnids—an amusing comparison when one considers that most species of spider use spiral patterns to construct their gossamer dwellings! Unfortunately the Web is not like that. Although highly structured, it really is something much messier, but no less beautiful. It is just "one big string thing" that writhes, coils, and knots about itself in a self-similar, self-organizing, and apparently emergent manner. But here again there are obvious and uncanny parallels with many advanced fields of physics.

String Theory is a model of fundamental physics that has attracted much attention in recent years. Its building blocks are one-dimensional extended objects—referred to as "strings"—rather than the zero-dimensional points, or particles, which are the basis of the Standard Model of Particle Physics. String theories are therefore attractive because that are able to avoid problems associated with the presence of point-like particles in a physical theory. Studies involving strings have, however, revealed that they are most useful when used with other objects, variously including points, membranes, and higher-dimensional objects in much the same way that hyperlinks on there own are relatively useless in a Web context.

Although it is a very loose comparison, String Theory, like all systems theories, relies heavily on the notion of symmetry in systems, having a specific need to describe problem spaces with more than four dimensions. It was originally invented to explain peculiarities of particular types of subatomic particular behavior. For instance, in particle accelerator[17] experiments, physicists observed that the angular momentum[18] of such particles was proportional to the square of their energy. No simple model, such as picturing this behavior as a set of smaller particles held together by spring-like forces, was able to explain these relationships. So, in order to account for these "Regge trajectories," physicists turned to a model where each specific particle, or "hadron," was in fact a rotating string, moving in accordance with Einstein's Special Theory of Relativity. This led to the development of Bosonic String Theory, which is still the version taught to many students.

Interestingly, String Theory is driven largely by the hope that it will prove to be a theory of everything, so perhaps it is not so crazy that similarities can be found between it and the workings of the Web. It provides a possible solution to the quantum gravity problem and can naturally describe interactions similar to electromagnetism and the other forces of nature. Work on string theory has led to advances in mathematics, mainly in algebraic geometry, and has also led to insight into supersymmetric gauge theories—a class of physical theories based on the idea that symmetry transformations can be performed locally as well as globally—again similar to the

---

[17]A particle accelerator is a device that uses electric and/or magnetic fields to propel electrically charged particles to high speeds.

[18]In physics the angular momentum of an object with respect to a reference point is a measure for the extent to which, and the direction in which, the object rotates about the reference point.

concept of manifolds built from collections of base interactions and pathways across multidimensional problem spaces like the Web.

QUANTUM DARWINISM

It may be all well and good that the Web is a complex multidimensional space capable of being investigated by existing physical theories, but what has this got to do with life? Although many influential physicists have found their way though an inbuilt curiosity in biology, fields like quantum mechanics don't contain any close correlations to the higher level notions like life, right? Wrong, or not at least according to the findings of respected physicists like Wojciech Zurek at Los Alamos National Laboratory in New Mexico.

If, as quantum mechanics says, observing the world tends to change it, how is it that we can agree on anything at all? Why doesn't each person leave a slightly different version of the world for the next person to find? Because, says Zurek and his colleagues, certain special states of a system are promoted above others by a quantum form of natural selection which they call Quantum Darwinism. Information about these states proliferates and gets imprinted on the environment. So observers tend to see the same "preferred" states of the world. In fact, if it wasn't for Quantum Darwinism the world would be a very unpredictable place: Different people might literally see very different versions of it and life itself would then be hard to conduct because we would not be able to obtain reliable information about our surroundings. It would just conflict with what everyone else was experiencing [75].

Quantum Darwinism sheds new light on the workings of environment-induced superselection or einselection—a process proposed a quarter of a century ago to explain the behavior of quantum systems that are open—that is, that continue to interact, however, weakly, with their surroundings. In Quantum Darwinism "survival of the fittest" is key, just as in normal life processes. The theory was first presented in 2002 to explain how the objective essences of our everyday reality emerge from the quantum substrate of our Universe. Now, the results obtained by Zurek and his coworkers support this initial hypothesis, but before diving into the significance of the findings, however, there is a need to outline the theory [72].

Simply put, instead of the classical world most believe they are casually experiencing, we are actually observing multiple imprints of only the "fittest" quantum states that are made by any quantum system on the state of its environment. These are often called pointer states and they emerge from the quantum "mush" to become good candidates for "classical reality"—the common day surroundings we know and trust. Such states can persist for a long time without being affected by the environment, and their stability is the reason for the success in making multiple imprints on the environment. They are, in effect, multiple copies of themselves that we then detect. "In simple terms, pointer states can take a beating and make a dent in the environment . . . over, and over and over again," says Zurek [72]. Or to put it another way, they have prominent characteristics that drown out the noise of less capable properties, a common occurrence in other life-like systems such as the Web. Here, gross generalization of information is often essential just to convey underlying intent. What is presented overall is not actually what is perceived by the audience, just as the title of a book might be remembered over its overall content and be enough sell many thousands of copies.

Because of the abundance of information about these pointer states and the indirect nature of our observations that involve only a small part of the environment, these states do not get "messed up." Rather, they continue to persist and propagate, surviving multiple observations [72]. In such ways, Zurek claims that Quantum Darwinism is a natural extension of decoherence, a theory that explains how open quantum systems interacting with their environments differ from closed, isolated systems [72].

"The old way of thinking of the forefathers of quantum mechanics assumed that all systems are isolated, and that measurement involves a direct interaction—that one must 'bump into the system' to observe it. But scientists at the time did not recognize that the environment was bumping into the system as well," states Zurek [72]. Decoherence describes what happens as a result of such measurements carried out by fragments of the environment. In effect, it shows that an open quantum system ceases to respect the quantum principle of superposition, which is the key to its quantumness [72]. Quantum collapse has to take place for the actualities we experience to be actual at all.

The theory of decoherence developed by Zurek and others over the past quarter century is now especially relevant in quantum engineering. For instance, to build a quantum computer one must make sure to limit the impact of the environment to eliminate unwanted decoherence effects. But Quantum Darwinism shows that decoherence is not the whole story. Zurek explains, "Recently, we realized that there was an extra twist. We never directly bump into a system to measure its state. We actually use the environment that has already bumped into the system to find out about it." [72] For example, when you are looking at the words on this page, you are not interacting with the page directly. Rather, your eyes are intercepting photons of light that have already interacted with the text. According to Zurek, this is how we actually observe, how we get information [72]. Essentially we never deal with it directly and, for all intents and purposes, it is wholly ethereal!

"In Quantum Darwinism the environment becomes the middle man, the communication channel through which the information is propagated from the systems to the observer," he said [72]. And so it is the same with the Web also. In reality we never actually interact directly with any Web resource, rather the Web itself becomes the middleman, being the resource's own immediate environment. So when we interact with information on the Web, it is like we are cutting through the many skins of an onion, physical first, Web next, and so on.

Another piece of the puzzle that eventually led to Quantum Darwinism is the fact that one never observes the entirety of the environment, just like it is impossible to take in all the Web in one go. Instead, individuals observe merely a fraction of it, but still can see the same systems in the same states—all the observers get the same big picture. This means that many copies of the same information must have proliferated throughout the environment [72].

How does this "advertising" happen? Why is the information about some states readily proliferated while data about competing alternatives—their quantum superpositions, which according to the quantum superposition principle are "equally good" when a quantum system is closed—are, in effect extinct? [72]

Zurek and his team have demonstrated that the already familiar pointer states, which are distinguished by their ability to survive decoherence, are the same states that advertise best—states that are easiest to find by intercepting small fragments of the environment. This makes sense: Pointer states live on. Survival is the precondition to reproduction, be that proliferation of the species or of information, be it in the domain of quantum mechanics, on the plains of the Serengeti, or over the complex surfaces of the Web. And only pointer states can continue to be measured by the environment without suffering any ill effects of such inquisition. So, as time passes, they tend to leave a redundant, prolific, and, thus, noticeable imprint on the environment [72].

As Zurek says, results prove that "quantum Darwinism works." "In our quantum Universe the environment is promoted from a passive role of a reservoir selectively destroying quantum coherence to an active role of amplifier selectively proliferating information about the system." Does it sound more like philosophy than science? Well, Zurek is able to prove the identity of pointer states and claims that they are easiest to find using small fractions of the environment through a complex, yet rigorous, sequence of equations [72].

For those who are intrigued by the unique wisdom behind Quantum Darwinism but are still unclear as to its real-world implications, the whole idea can sound a bit intangible in much the same way as the concept of Web Life can appear surreal. However, of late, such seemingly abstract ideas are becoming increasingly valuable for tangible applications [72]. For instance, "smaller is better" is the mantra of nanotechnology, computer hardware, and other high-tech areas. And, things begin to be more susceptible to "quantum weirdness" as they get smaller. For instance, if the size of the smallest parts of computer chips continues to shrink at the present rate of development, halving every 16 months or so, then withinin a decade researchers will have to deal with individual atoms and, hence, individual quanta. According to Zurek, that is where quantum Darwinism enters the picture [72]. "Understanding what happens on the quantum-classical interface helps us prepare the necessary documents for this inevitable border crossing" [72].

CHAPTER 10

Counter Arguments

> If at first the idea is not absurd, then there is no hope for it.
>
> *—Albert Einstein*

ALL THOSE AGAINST

It is one thing to present a case in favor of Web Life, but including a certain amount of skepticism along side is surely healthy. Even though the ideas presented so far have been taken from mainstream, and hopefully "safe," thinking wherever possible, it would still be quite incorrect to consider them to be indisputable truths.

One of the great things about science is its assumption that what it thinks it knows today will probably be proved wrong tomorrow. In all fields of science the real lesson to be learned is that truth is merely a transient property, retaining its respect only until the moment that a better truth comes along. And even when truth appears absolutely unquestionable, there are always subtleties of definition, interpretation, and application to take into account. So it is with both the idea of life and computation. Although there are definitions available that cover the broadest of cases, there are also other understandings that deliberately challenge the limits of what we might consider normal. This is only right and proper, because any one of these could, some day, prove a stepping stone in our next leap in understanding. What follows is therefore a brief summary of some of these alternatives, all counter arguments facing up against some of the most fundamental propositions on which the concept of Web Life is based.

COMPUTING THE INCOMPUTABLE

For those who choose to study conventional computer science, the Universe might seem a safe and dependable place. For them, their comprehensions are based on fundamentally discrete simplicities. George Boole and Alan Turing showed us a set of realities that were that way when they laid down their thoughts on algebraic rules and computability, and thus pointed the way forward for the modern digital revolution. Ordinarily such understandings are sound and practical, but it would be a miscalculation to cling to them in the hope that all computation can be neatly pigeonholed. In many cases the black and white depictions of Boole and Turing's discrete mathematics simply cannot come to the rescue of computation, and the work of modern-day computer scientists has spilled over to pay testament to this fact:

"In everyday life, it is common to talk about doing "computation." For example, we can speak informally about balancing a chequebook, working out the miles per gallon of gasoline obtained by our automobile, or converting U.S. dollars into pounds sterling. Each of these operations involves the processing of numbers in a particular way to obtain the desired result and the procedure by which we process the numbers is an example of what's more formally termed an algorithm. The problem faced by theoreticians is how to convert this very common, but informal, notion of carrying out a computation into a precise, formal mathematical structure within which we can actually prove things about the properties of algorithms" [84].

Such a formally mathematical system is technically a model of the computational process [84], with the Turing machine being the most common variant in use today. Turing's model is powerful and dictates exactly what is and is not computable in any discrete system—that is, any system where broken symmetry plays a fundamental part, making all the facets of computation easily discernable from one and other. But there are other possible models for computation, quite different in form from that of the Turing-machine model. These alternatives, in turn, determine their own sets of computable quantities. So what is really at issue is whether any of these models are more encompassing than Turing's, and by being so, can they provide a "better" general description of computation? Or to rephrase this specifically within the context of Web Life, can computation readily take place without reliance on asymmetry between its parts? "At present, no one really knows, but it is worth considering what some of these other models look like" [84].

Without symmetry-breaking we are led toward an indistinct world of continuity and sometimes confusion, a world where nothing really begins and nothing really ends. How can that be so one might think? How and where can such notions exist and be of value? In fact, in mathematics such ideas are relatively commonplace. Take any real number like π, for example. For most uses it can be rounded to several decimal places, but being a real number it is actually a number without end, the digits on the right-hand side of its decimal point stretching out toward infinity. In simple terms it cannot be expressed fully, ever, and this causes a real headache for computer scientists.

A few years ago Stephen Smale, a mathematician from the University of California at Berkeley, began to take an interest in this problem. As part of his effort to understand the theoretical basis of computation over nondiscrete things like real numbers, Smale started cornering colleagues, asking them the question, What do you mean by an algorithm? One reply was a Fortran[1] program. So, together with fellow mathematician Michael Shub and computer scientist Lenore Blum, Smale developed this notion of a Fortran program as an algorithm into a new model of computation, one that easily accommodates computation that operates on either whole numbers or

---

[1]Fortran (also FORTRAN) is a general-purpose, procedural, imperative programming language that is especially suited to numeric computation and scientific computing [132].

real numbers. This model is sometimes called a flowchart machine, Continuous Turing Machine (CTM), or, more simply, a BBS machine after the initials of its creators [84], and it differs quite substantially from Turing's original model.

Turing's typical model of an abstract machine has a fixed number of "states," represented on an infinitely long tape containing discrete "cells" where any one of a finite set of "marks" may be placed. The machine "looks at" a particular cell and, depending on the contents of that cell and the current state of the machine, executes a specific action—possibly replacing the mark in the cell with some other mark and changing its own "state"—and then 'moves its attention' to some other cell at a specified relative position on the tape [85].

Suppose, instead, we define a machine whose "state" at any time t is a real number $s(t)$, and the "tape" is magnetized with intensity $m(x)$ at location x, where x is the real-valued distance from the starting position on the tape. The machine is initially set to the state $s(0) = 0$ and placed at location $x = 0$ on the tape, which has been 'programmed' with some initial profile of magnetic intensities over a finite range of the tape [85].

As time passes, the machine determines its real-valued acceleration $a(t)$ as a preestablished function of the current state $s(t)$ and the magnetic intensity $m(t)$ at the current location $x(t)$. The machine can also modify the intensity of the field at location $x(t) - d$, where d is a fixed constant, by setting it to any desired value, or it can leave the intensity at location $x(t) - d$ unchanged [85].

Notice that an ordinary audio tape recorder is an approximate model of a CTM, although its program is computationally trivial. With some fairly minor modifications it should be possible to turn a tape recorder into a more general computing machine [85].

Continuous models of computation like this raise several interesting questions, however. For example:

Is an ideal CTM well-defined in the traditional computational sense?

What sort of "computation" could a CTM perform? For instance, is it meaningful to say that a CTM has "computed" a real number if it terminates, leaving the exact value of the number undetermined?

Is it at all meaningful to compare the computational power of a CTM with a discrete Turing machine, and so is it relevant to any discussions on computation in living systems?

CTMs seek to unify the fields of theoretical computer science and numerical analysis. Practical numerical algorithms involve the computation of real numbers, while the classical Turing machines manipulate discrete sets. Given that the CTM model for computation operates iteratively, it thus encompasses the 0–1 world of Turing machines and the real-complex number setting required for numerical analysis.

Other nontraditional computational models also exist, and these too have blurred their reliance on the discreteness of strongly broken symmetry. Quantum computers, for example, take advantage of the ability of a quantum system, say an atom or a single photon, to be in more than one quantum state at the same time. So, for instance, the spin of a photon can be in both the up and down states simultaneously. If we represent these two states by 0 and 1, respectively, then calculations on the superposition act on both values at once. Therefore, a quantum computer containing n photons or atoms in superposed states could do a calculation on 2 to the power n

numbers simultaneously—a degree of parallelism that is inconceivable for everyday, classical computers. Even so, as explained in the previous chapter, comparisons can still be found with this type of model and grander computational scales as found on the Web, scales at which the vast quantities of content present start to blur the boundaries created by lower levels of discreteness. In particular challenges to strongly discrete models of computation, such as the Solovay–Strassen algorithm,[2] insert an element of uncertainty into computation that is not all at odds with many realities confronted regularly on the Web. Sometimes it is not always possible to find a "perfect" answer to a given problem, but that's one of the Web's most fascinating paradoxes—it absorbs uncertainty and turn it to its advantage, transforming it into discrete outcomes as a consequence of its compensating sociotechnical makeup. It decoheres as part for its inherent computational capability.

OBSERVATION AND PRACTICALITY IN COMPUTATION

But why should the models presented here be important to the concept of Web Life? It's simple; the entire premise of this book, the idea that the World Wide Web might be thought of in the same vein as living systems, is based on the acceptance of one fundamental concept—that discreteness, or asymmetry, can be seen as a ubiquitous property across both naturally living and technologically abstract systems. This is a concept on which large parts of the classical Universe work and one on which the whole framework of digital representation is based. It is at the heart of Turing's model of computation and is fundamental to notions of absolute definition and understanding.

Turing himself drew the distinction between discrete and continuous machinery in 1948, likening the latter to the telephones of his day. In fact he made light of the difficulty of reducing continuous problems to the discrete model of the Turing machine and, though citing "the brain" as a continuous machine, stated that it could probably be treated as if discrete. He gave no indication that physical continuity threatened the paramount role of computability. Furthermore, the thrust in his work of 1947 was to promote the digital computer as more powerful than analogue machines such as the differential analyzer.[3] When he discussed this comparison he gave the following informal version of the Church–Turing thesis: "One of my conclusions was that the idea of a 'rule of thumb' process and a 'machine process' were synonymous. The expression 'machine process' of course means one which could be carried out by the type of machine I was considering"—that is, Turing machines. Turing gave no hint that the discreteness of the Turing machine constituted a real limitation, or that the nondiscrete processes of analogue machines might be of any

[2]The Solovay–Strassen primality test, developed by Robert M. Solovay and Volker Strassen, is a probabilistic test to determine if a number is composite or probably prime.
[3]The differential analyzer was a mechanical analogue computer designed to solve differential equations by integration, using wheel-and-disc mechanisms to perform the integration. It was one of the first advanced computing devices to be used operationally.

The analyzer was invented in 1876 by James Thomson, brother of Lord Kelvin. A practical version was first constructed by H. W. Nieman and Vannevar Bush starting in 1927 [133].

deep significance. Nevertheless, this is really just skimming an important issue. Turing may have talked about the use of approximation to tame continuous quantities, but we should really try and understand why such an approach is satisfactory.

SPACESHIPS CAN COME IN HANDY

Let's approach Turing's "rule of thumb" idea by way of an analogy: If you stood on the moon and looked down at the Earth, our world would look pretty spherical, a perfectly continuous thing, flawless in the contours of its surface.

If we travel much closer to the Earth, then the discrete boundaries of land and sea would soon become clear. Come in closer still and any number of individual types of terrain would be noticed. Yet closer and individual cities, animals, plants, molecules, and atoms would start to materialize. And even that's not the end of the story, because further magnification would move you past subatomic particles like protons, quarks, and who knows what else.

Admittedly, this illustration is deliberately contrived for particular purpose, but there are a number of points to be highlighted here. Although the actual process of observation may indeed be smooth and continuous—zooming in on the Earth in this example—what may appear continuous and symmetrical at one level might just be masking finer collections of discreteness below. Hence it is plausible to think of the distinction between the discrete and the continuous as merely a matter of the level at which an observation is taken—its "abstraction" to be technically precise. Overarching themes may represent a perfect continuum, but the things from which these themes are constructed may, often, be open to interpretation in discrete ways. In fact the Web is exactly like that. From one perspective its structure is indeed continuous by the very fact that it has fractal properties. Continually similar logical pattern within similar logical pattern is a common theme on the Web, and it is often irrelevant to even contemplate where one pattern ends and another starts. It is therefore an abstractionless continuance in that respect. But there are also breakpoints present; letters differ from words, words from Web pages, Web pages from Web sites, and so on. Thus the Web is both discrete yet continuous. What really matters, however, is the fact the enough precision can be achieved via its discrete parts to be able to interpret, appreciate, and understand its continuity. This is Turing's "rule of thumb." If it's "good enough," then it's good enough. And given the vast scales of the Web and the great detail in which modern digital technology can process it, Turing's discreet model of computation appears more than up to task of representing the Web at every level.

WHEN IS A CURVE NOT A CURVE, WHEN IS A BRAIN NOT A BRAIN?

This proposition of a harmony between discreteness and continuity goes still further, as Turing himself pointed out. Large sections of this book have again been devoted to promoting the idea (a) that the very building blocks from which the Web is built are curved to the extent of being helical and (b) sequences of information, hyperlinked pathways, and processes conceptually curve by the plain nature of their fundamental logical geometries. Yet here again the same paradox between discreteness and continuity can be found, given that mathematically curves are continuous and smooth, not disjointed and lumpy.

But does this really matter when the practicalities of abstraction are introduced into the picture? In practical terms probably not, as once more the same concept of "rule of thumb" comes to the rescue. DNA is also famously helical, for example, in fact so much so that it has made the helix iconic. Yet still there is discreteness present, not least at in the breakpoints between its macromolecular and molecular components. Furthermore, the information that DNA carries is also certainly discreet, but still, overall, there are aspects of DNA that can quite properly be seen as continuous. There is no pragmatic conflict really.

Moving up several abstractions in comparison, it would also be wrong to consider biological brains to be either characteristically discrete or continuous. The mechanisms by which natural brains work are not strictly digital. Neurons do not "switch" per se, they "fire" when a certain threshold of stimulus is reached, and it is indeed appropriate to measure such stimulus on a continuous scale. Nevertheless, here too it's all just a matter of observation, because the same type of scheme can also be seen to be applicable to the millions of transistors embedded in today's modern computer chips. All that is different is the rate at which the respective devices switch. The brain's neurons function in approximately one-thousandth of a second, whereas switching frequencies of 500 GHz are not unheard of in solid-state devices these days.

Information storage in natural brains is also somewhat less than digital. We do not hold our memories in the form of bits and bytes, like mainstream computers. Instead many more subtle schemes exist based on cumulative biological structures, and these are again open to continuous interpretation. Nevertheless, the very act of a neuron's firing can be generalized as a discrete event and thus makes the brain amenable to explanations based on discreteness. Simulate such a brain using enough discrete parts and at some point the simulation will become so rich that its discrete foundations will become fuzzy and appear subtly smooth in character. Thus it is the way with the Web. As a whole, its various high-level aspects might as well be considered as continuous, even to the extent where if it does become susceptible to processes of overall transition, this will be as smooth as the lead up to those changes seen in any natural and continuous phenomenon. Such happenings will simply be a consequence of continual being and not some contrived and instantaneous switching brought about by deliberate engineering.

A MATTER OF WHAT, NOT HOW

A further theme running through this book has involved an exploration of the importance that organization plays in complex systems such as life. But if this were inspected in detail, it could be argued that scant attention has been paid to the nature of just exactly what is being organized and the environments in which such organization is taking place—the very things from which organization is formed. Surely this is important. After all, in natural life systems physical matter is an absolute prerequisite for life to exist, isn't it?

So does matter matter when it comes to basic life definitions? Some would appear to think not. Ideas such as Chris Langton's A-Life and Richard's Dawkins memes do not dwell on such needs, being quite happy to discuss wider ethereal notions of life. Nonetheless, A-Life has been severely criticized for focusing on the mechanics of organization while ignoring the role of what is being organized. This is because, from the perspective of the A-Life believer, the what does not matter. Those who share more rational opinions, however, feel this to be unreasonable, protesting that if life were not tangible, how could it be observed and proven to be real? Both of these perspectives have merit in their own right, so the real question must be, can they be reconciled?

If one were to forget for a moment about the need or not for life to be a material thing, other definitions can be discussed without the need for so much controversy. In particular there is no real need to philosophize deeply about life being a sort of "system," a very special type of system maybe, but a system nonetheless. If one agrees on that at least, then a number of truths come to light. Not least of these is the fact that mathematical equations are also systems. They take in concepts such as numbers and transform them using distinguishable operations in ways that are hopefully meaningful. In this way they have purpose in much the same manner as we would hope life to be purposeful too. In mathematics, numbers merely provide one possible vehicle for equations to be able to "equate," "compute their outcome," "do their business," or "reach their destiny." Take your pick of the expression you prefer, but numbers fulfil much the same purpose in mathematics as physical matter in natural life processes, quite literally providing a way in which mathematical results can "materialize."

Besides, numbers are not actual, they are just abstract concepts used to convey notions of quantity and distinction. You cannot see, touch, hear, smell, or feel them, for example, or the mathematical equations in which they take part for that matter. But surely is that not also the case with life? We may be able to interact with the very materials from which we are made, but are we actually experiencing life itself or just the effects of particular molecules caught up in its process of completion—its computation by any other name? This brings us back to the philosophical issue of what is real and what is not. Are mathematical equations any less real than any of us? Are they any less alive? Think about it, mathematics is all about rigorous proof, precision, and determination. A mathematical equation can be proven beyond all reasonable doubt, but could we ever prove that we, as individuals, are truly alive? Maybe not, or at least not in a truly mathematical way that would do justice.

CHAPTER 11

Objective Opinions

To hate is to study, to study is to understand, to understand is to appreciate, to appreciate is to love. So maybe I'll end up loving your theory.

—*John A. Wheeler*

OPINIONS OF THE UBER-GEEKS

Sir Tim Berners-Lee quite rightly once stated the understandable fear that "one day the big brother of the Semantic Web will become a programming language, and library cards will start composing music, and cheques will be made payable to a person whose name can be calculated only by using two hundred years of computer time" [4]. Nevertheless, he later went on to address his fear admirably. The "answer" he advocates, "is that within many applications we should (control capability), but in the Web as a whole we should not." Why? "Because when you look at the complexity of the world that the Semantic Web must be able to describe, you realise that it must be possible to use any amount of power as needed. The success of the (current) Web is that hypertext is so flexible a medium that the Web does not constrain the knowledge it tries to represent. The same must be true of the Web of meaning. In fact, the Web of everything we know and use from day to day is complex; we need a strong language to represent it" [4].

He adds that, "the art of designing applications in the future will be to fit them into the new Web in all its complexity, yet make them individually simple enough to work reliably every time. However, the total Web of the data from each of the applications of semantic technologies will make a very complex world, in which it will be possible to ask unanswerable questions. That is the how the world is. The existence of such questions will not stop the world from turning, or cause weird things to happen at traffic lights. But it will open the door to some very interesting new applications that do roam over the whole intractable, incalculable Web and, while not promising anything, deliver a lot" [4].

This leads to the conclusion that if the Web is truly evolving in a natural sense, it will become self-organizing in the very near future, if it has not done so already. In doing so, its combined computational power will increase dramatically in a very short space of time. Furthermore, if the Web's evolution is also being driven in a truly dynamic and complex manner, this change will be irreversible in a spectacular way according to the law of entropy [5].

The Web's Awake. By Philip Tetlow

There is a warning here as the analogy of a global brain is tempting, because the Web and brain both involve huge numbers of elements—neurons and Web resources—and a mixture of structure and apparent randomness. However, a brain has an intelligence that emerges on quite a different level from anything that a neuron could be aware of. Indeed, many famous writers, like Arthur C. Clark, have contemplated an "emergent property" arising from the mass of humanity and computers. But remember that such a phenomenon would have its own agenda. We would not as individuals be aware of it, let alone be capable of controlling it, any more than a neuron controls the brain [4].

No sensible person would ever pretend that the growth of the Web to date has been without social difficulties. Nevertheless, to try and restrict the capabilities of a self-organizing "Web Machine" must surely be short-sighted. The child that was once the Web is now starting to grow up. The question now is whether it is destined to mature into an independent adult like us, mankind, its natural parents. Through self-organization it is more than possible that the Web could help solve problems until now thought impossible—an old ambition, but one which still holds as much promise as when the first electronic computers emerged more than half a century ago [5].

ARE WE RIGHT TO TALK ABOUT A GLOBAL "BRAIN"?

Some critics freely compare the Web to a "global brain" uniting all the world's disparate pools of information, while other visionaries, such as Bill Joy[1] and Ray Kurzweil,[2] believe that the computational powers of digital technology are accelerating at such a rate that large networks of computers may actually become self-aware sometime later this century. Did Arthur C. Clarke and The Matrix have it right all along? Is the Web itself becoming a giant brain? Many still think no, but consider that it is still worth asking why not.

Begin by jettisoning two habitual ways of thinking about what a brain is. First forget about the gray matter and the synapses. Here any reference to a giant brain relates to a more fundamental device for processing and storing information. Second, accept the premise that brains can be a collective enterprise. Being individual organisms ourselves, we are inclined to think of brains as isolated things, possessed by individual organisms. But both categories turn out to be little more than useful fictions. As already seen, bees and ants do their "learning" collectively. The swarm mind is the sum of thousands upon thousands of simple decisions executed by individual members.

Replace bees or ants with neurons and pheromones with neurotransmitters and one might as well be talking about the human brain. So if neurons can swarm their way into sentient brains, is it so inconceivable that the process might ratchet itself up one more level? Couldn't individual brains connect with one another, this time via the digital language of the Web, and form something greater than the sum of

---

[1]The co-founder of SUN Microsystems.
[2]Raymond Kurzweil is a pioneer in the fields of optical character recognition (OCR), text-to-speech synthesis, speech recognition technology, and electronic musical keyboards.

their parts—what the fashionable philosopher and priest Teilhard de Chardin[3] called the *noosphere*.[4]

In fact, one can go further. As Douglas R. Hofstadter has so eloquently stated in the twentieth anniversary edition of his Pulitzer Prize winning book, Gödel, Escher, Bach: An Eternal Golden Braid , "the brain that nestles safely inside one's own cranium is purely a physical object made up of completely sterile and inanimate components, all of which obey exactly the same laws as those that govern all the rest of the Universe, such as pieces of text, or CD-ROMS or computers. Only if we keep on bashing up against this disturbing fact can we slowly begin to develop a feel for the way out of the mystery of consciousness: that the key is not the stuff out of which brains are made, but the patterns that can come to exist inside the stuff of the brain" [39]. This is a liberating shift, because it allows us to move to a different level of considering what brains are: as media that support complex patterns that mirror, albeit far from perfectly, the world, of which, needless to say, those brains are themselves inhabitants—and it is in the inevitable self-mirroring that arises, however impartial or imperfect it may be, that the strange loops of consciousness start to swirl [39].

It is this change of focus from material components to abstract pattern that allows the quasi-magical leap from inanimate to animate, from the meaningless to the meaningful, to take place [39], whether in our heads, on the Web, or wherever. But how does this happen? After all, not all jumps from matter to pattern give rise to consciousness or any greater notions of "self," quite obviously. In a word, not all patterns are conscious. But the strange and complex self-referencing patterns prevalent on the Web fit the bill perfectly and certainly appear to signpost potential routes to higher levels of being.

Today the problem is not establishing whether the Web contains these strange yet special swirly, twirly, vortex-like patterns [39], which has long been established fact. Rather the real issue concerns whether it is possible to draw a practical line between the emerging Web and any resultant entity that we might normally choose to describe as living. This is not for lack of rigor in our understandings however, because for one thing we have a good grip of the underlying mathematics involved. We appreciate, for instance, that the Gödelian strange loops that arise in formal systems in mathematics allow such systems to "perceive themselves," to talk about themselves, and to become "self-aware," and in a sense it would not be going too far to say that by virtue of having such a loop, a formal systems acquires a form of "self" [39]. No, the real problem is one of complexity and volume. The Web is now such a copious thing that it breaks down human understandable models involving reduction and classification. To label it as a whole would be just as meaningless as to try and dissect it for the purposes of anatomical analysis. But then that is both the beauty and the dilemma at the heart of complexity.

---

[3]Reverend Pierre Teilhard de Chardin, a Jesuit priest trained as a palaeontologist and a philosopher [134].
[4]The noosphere can be seen as the "sphere of human thought" being derived from the Greek νους ("nous") meaning "mind" in the style of "atmosphere" and "biosphere." Just as the biosphere is composed of all the organisms on Earth and their interactions, the noosphere is composed of all the interacting minds on Earth. The word is also sometimes used to refer to a transhuman consciousness emerging from these interactions.

So, today's talk of a giant global brain is cheap. But there's a difference. These days, most people who talk this way are speaking loosely. Tim Berners-Lee has noted parallels between the Web and the structure of the brain, but he insists that the concept of a "global brain" is a mere metaphor. Teilhard de Chardin, in contrast, seems to have been speaking literally: Humankind was coming to constitute an actual brain—like the one in your head, except bigger. Certainly there are more people today than in Teilhard's day who take the idea of a global brain literally. Are they crazy? Again philosophy quickly gets in the way of a clinical answer, but there is mounting evidence to suggest that they are not as crazy as one might at first think.

There are those who point to evidence that *Homo sapiens'* brains already have a long history of forming higher intelligence. Individual human minds have coalesced into "group brains" many times in modern history, most powerfully in the communal gatherings of cities. The city functions as a kind of smaller-scale trial run for the Web's world-wide conjoined extravaganza, like an Andrew Lloyd Webber musical that irons its problems out in the provinces before opening on Broadway. As in the urban explosion of the Middle Ages, a city is not just an accidental offshoot of growing population density, it is a kind of technological breakthrough in its own right. Sustainable city life ranks high on the list of modern inventions, as world-transforming as the alphabet or the Web, that latter of which may well be its undoing. It is no coincidence that the great majority of the last millennium's inventions blossomed in urban settings. Like the folders and file directories of some oversized hard drive, the group brain of city life impregnated information with far more structure and durability than it had previously possessed. So it appears a natural progression to conclude that the Web looks to be the digital heir to that proud tradition, uniting the world's intellects in a way that would have astonished the early social networks of Florence or Amsterdam. Macrointelligence emerged out of the bottom-up organization of communal life, and it will do the same further on the Web [45].

There are others who are sympathetic to this view but believe that it still needs further clarification. Emergence, they argue, is not just some mystical force that comes into being when agents collaborate; there are environments that facilitate higher-level intelligence, as well as environments that suppress it. To the extent that the Web has connected more sentient beings together than any technology before it, you can see why one might sensibly consider it as a kind of global brain. But both brains and societies do more than just connect, because intelligence requires both connectedness and organization. Plenty of decentralized systems in the real world spontaneously generate structure as they increase in size: Cities organize into neighborhoods or satellites; the neural connections of our brains develop extraordinarily specialized regions. Has the Web followed a comparable path of development over the past few years? Is the Web becoming more organized as it grows? The apparent and overwhelming answer is "yes."

The Web is in some ways like a brain, but in important ways not. The brain does not just let information ricochet around the skull. It is organized to do something, to move the muscles in ways that allow the whole body to attain the goals set by the emotions. The anatomy of the brain reflects the fact that it is not a uniform web or net per se, but has a specific organization in which emotional circuits interconnect with the frontal lobes, which receive information from the perceptual system and send commands to the motor system. This goal-directed organization comes from an important property of organisms in that their cells are in the same reproductive boat, and thus have no "incentive" to act against the interests of the whole body. But the Web, not being a cohesive replicating system, has no such organization.

Again, the point here is that intelligent systems depend on structure and organization as much as they do on pure connectedness, and another point is that intelligent systems are guided toward particular types of structure by the laws of natural selection. A latter-day Maxwell's demon,[5] who somehow manages to superglue a billion neurons to each other, wouldn't build anything like the human brain, because the brain relies on specific clusters to make sense of the world and those clusters only emerge out of a complex interplay among neurons, the external world, and our genes, not to mention many other factors. Some systems such as the Web are geniuses at making connections and are overloaded with structure, but are they an outcome of natural selection? Again a moot point, but as a social machine the Web has certainly developed out of a dynamically natural consensus of human contribution, so perhaps such consensus could be construed as resembling a "natural" form of selection, a meme-like vote of confidence.

Yet in the midst of the entire Web's networked complexity, a few observers have begun to detect macro-patterns in its development, patterns that are invisible to most observers and thus remain largely unnoticed. The distribution of websites and their audiences appears to follow power laws for instance: The top 10 most popular sites are 10 times larger than the next hundred more popular, which are themselves 10 times more popular than the next thousand sites. Other online cartographers have detected "hub and spoke" patterns in traffic flows, similar to the bow-tie configurations highlighted in Chapter 5. But none of these macro-shapes, even if they do exist, actually makes the Web immediately more navigable or informative. These patterns may be self-organizing, but they are not adaptive in any direct way. Even so, regardless of the endless conjecture available, brain or no brain, one thing is certain; the Web is a fascinating and phenomenal creation that has to be admired if only for its rapid rise and unquestionable impact on us.

OVER THE HORIZON

Future gazing may be fascinating and have popular appeal, but from the perspective of good science it can often be dangerous. Nevertheless, the idea of Web Life is an enticing concept and if there are a number of objective comparisons available from other scientific fields to point to its existence, perhaps these might also provide some grounded predictions on just how the Web might develop in the longer term.

If Web Life is an emergent property, we have been studying many systems with similar types of emergence for some time with varying degrees of success. Weather

---

[5]Maxwell's demon is a character in an 1867 thought experiment by the Scottish physicist James Clerk Maxwell, meant to raise questions about the second law of thermodynamics. This law forbids (among other things) two bodies of equal temperature, brought in contact with each other and isolated from the rest of the Universe, from evolving to a state in which one of the two has a significantly higher temperature than the other. The second law is also expressed as the assertion that entropy never decreases [135].

is an emergent property, for example: Take water vapor out over the Gulf of Mexico and let it interact with sunlight and wind, and it can organize itself into an emergent structure known as a hurricane or typhoon. The mind also is an emergent property, the product of several billion neurons obeying the finer biological laws of the living cell. In fact, as Brian Anderson Pointed out in a 1972 paper, one can also think of the Universe as forming a kind of hierarchy: "At each level of complexity entirely new properties appear. At each stage, entirely new laws, concepts and generalisations are necessary, requiring inspiration and creativity to just as great a degree as in the previous one" [67]. In such a way, psychology is not applied biology, nor is biology applied chemistry.

So can we formulate a kind of weather forecasting method, or psychology for the Web? The answer is probably not, or at least until we can describe the entire Web in far more formal ways; not until we can calculate and model with it in other words. Such capabilities may not be that far off, but for now we can only really speculate from a distance.

However, studies of other highly complex systems, such as spin glasses, indicate that the future of the Web may be open to rigorous theoretical investigation. Just as ideas like mean field theory have been applied in material science, it is not unreasonable to assume that other theories will be applicable to the complexity of the Web. Even so, paradoxically they may need the power of modern computers to help them. Possible candidates for such application include Curie's Law, which relates the magnetization of a material to an applied magnetic field and temperature. But how could laws such as Curie's be analogous to the Web? In this case replace the external magnetic field with some strong ongoing movement in society and heat with society's desire to align with or repulse such an influence, and there is a strong likelihood that large sections of the Web could be seen to coalesce in a "magnetic" sense.

So what does this mean for mankind? The answer is almost sublimely simple: In times of great trouble, success or joy, society will both polarize and join together as it always has, only this time it will use the Web as a primary conduit for its communication. We have seen this happen many times already on the Web, but mostly on small scales. The various clusters of suppliers who have embraced the e-commence revolution provide a good case in point, for instance. Furthermore, within such clusters there are bound to be other smaller clusters, all fighting for and against each other as should be the case in any truly complex system. Their edges will also most certainly be blurred and dynamic in the same way that weather fronts wash over the planet or thoughts rush through the mind.

A FINAL SPRINKLE OF PHILOSOPHY

Conjecture and coincidence may be one thing but as for the Web as a true living organism, we as individuals may never truly be capable of encountering it in a manner that we would usually perceive as "life." But this does not necessarily mean to say that the Web is not, or ever could be, truly alive. The disparity arises simply as a consequence of our inability to experience existence on the same scale needed to support the Web as a living whole.

It has long been an established scientific theory that life on our planet grew from some form of complex primordial soup containing the right basic hydrocarbon ingredients. Consequently, could the current-day Web be considered as such a soup in a virtual sense? Certainly there is strong evidence to support this thinking and the right abstract ingredients and structures appear more than abundant. Furthermore, it is clear that the Web is capable of spontaneous expansion in much the same way that evolution has advanced on our planet for billions of years. Indeed, as Joseph Ford, an eminent founder in the field of nonlinear science, once said, "evolution is chaos with feedback." The Universe is random and dissipated, yes, but randomness with direction can produce surprising and mystical complexity. Maybe the lesson to be learned is that evolution hasn't stopped. It's still going on, both in a classical and universal sense, exhibiting the same phenomena it has always done in biological history. Except now we are seeing it take place in the sociotechnical plane, with a lot of the same kinds of extinctions and upheaval, but this time at a much higher and more abstract level. We no longer see technologies like "Gopher"[6] prevalent on the early Web, for instance, but the rise of the wiki is everywhere. New replaces old and evolution fills the gaps created by the extinction of the unfit. It's the age-old story.

All the same is this enough to truly speculate whether the Web is "alive," or should we engage in further philosophical debate of a metaphysical nature? Was the Web "born"? Will it eventually "die"? Can, and will, it reproduce? Does it have to occupy a place in space and time to truly exist? And does it embody such concepts as "thought," "self," and "conscience"? Some would side with the Web on such issues, while others would, quite correctly, firmly hold opposing views. That is our prerogative as a society capable of constructive debate. Even so, pattern born amid formlessness is indisputably nature's basic beauty and its basic mystery. Life sucks order from a sea of disorder, and this is precisely the same everyday purpose of the Web in its current form. As Erwin Schrödinger, a quantum pioneer and one of several physicists who made a nonspecialist foray into biological speculation, put it so concisely nearly half a century ago, a living organism has the "astonishing gift of concentrating a 'stream of order' on itself, thus escaping the decay into atomic chaos" [10]. For Schrödinger, as a physicist, it was plain that the structure of living things differed from that of the kind of material he and his colleagues studied.

Schrödinger's view was, and probably still is, unusual. That life was both orderly and complex is a truism, but to see nonlinearity as the source of its special qualities verged on being unthinkable. In Schrödinger's day, neither mathematics nor any other field of human endeavor could provide genuine support for such ideas. There were no tools for analyzing irregularity as a building block of life. Now these tools exist.

So, let's try and reach a rounded conclusion. Are we now capable of definitively demonstrating that the Web is alive? In the short term the answer is most probably not, but over the past few decades mankind has certainly made some significant

---

[6]Gopher is a distributed document search and retrieval network protocol designed for the Internet. It was released in late spring of 1991 by Mark McCahill, Farhad Anklesaria, Paul Lindner, Dan Torrey, and Bob Alberti of the University of Minnesota.

progress in addressing deep questions similar to this. When we ask questions like how life emerges and why living systems are the way that they are—the kind of questions that are really fundamental to understanding what we are and what makes us different from inanimate matter—the more we know about these things, the closer we're getting to fundamental questions like "What is the purpose of life?" Currently, in science we can't attempt to make a formal assault on such quandaries, but by addressing different questions like "Why is there an inexorable growth in complexity?", we may be able to learn something very basic about life that suggests its purpose, in the same way that Einstein shed light on what space and time are by trying to understand gravity. A suitable analogy might be to think of averted vision in astronomy: If you want to see a faint star, you should look a little to the side because then the eye is more sensitive to faint light, and as soon as you look straight at the star it disappears [67].

We can speculate all we like about life, but many more solid proofs from a number of fields will have to be established and unified before we even get close to a good definition—a unified connectionist theorem if you like. Nevertheless, the case for such a line study has been laid out by many serious and respected experts on a number of occasions and the road ahead will indisputably be interesting. We can, however, safely state a few things that the Web is not. It is not, for example, an artificially intelligent or neural system as understood by everyday computer scientists. It is much more than that. Such systems attempt to store and reproduce the workings of already developed brains for a specific purpose [11]. The Web may certainly embody such technologies, but its overall scale, complexity, and richness swamp even the largest of attempts at imposing overall direction. For now it is unquestionably floating free, dependent on its human creators. It is not self-sufficient or independent in the same sense as any truly autonomous life form. It still most definitely relies on social interaction for its advancement through ongoing human stimulation. For now it is merely a self-consistent, mutually supportive network of interactions in human and, more recently, machine societies [67]. Even so, technologies are being developed to make the Web more mature in this respect, and the technical advances needed to achieve the next stage of development appear remarkably small [5].

So, whether correct answers are available or not, some rather deep questions now need to be asked openly and honestly. Artificial life, and in particular Web Life, is more that just a challenge; it is facing up against the most fundamental social, moral, philosophical, and religious beliefs of the modern world. Like the Copernican model of the solar system, it will force mankind to reexamine its very place in the Universe and its role in nature [67].

Finally let's attend to unfinished business and return to the very beginning of this story. Was our friend the technician being treated unfairly? At the end of the day, who knows and does it really matter? Let's ask Google!

An Outline of the Semantic Web and Its Potential for Software Engineering

We are getting into semantics again. If we use words, there is a very grave danger they will be misinterpreted.

—*H. R. Haldeman*

BLUE CHIPS

So, the stage has been set. The arguments have been laid out to present the case for the Web as a living being. But how are these arguments grounded? Other more pragmatic questions remain. For example, what shape is the Web in today and what new, yet real, technologies do we have before us that could make a tangible difference to the Web's future development?

Many take it for granted that the Web is advancing at a pace, but shear momentum is not enough to make real progress. Change for change's sake is not normally associated with the onward march of technology, so if there are any blue chips, who's holding them and, if we wanted to gamble, what are the safest bets in the short-term Web game?

SEMANTIC WEB TECHNOLOGIES MAKE THE WEB'S MEANING MUCH MORE SPECIFIC

The Web may indeed currently possess sophistication well beyond that of the computer systems with which mankind has previously collectively engaged, but it is still undoubtedly weak in a number of areas. Notwithstanding, work is ongoing to improve large sections of its core architecture with the ultimate aims of improving automation and content accuracy. Like the characteristics of any living organism, the Web now has fledgling capabilities that can make its 'metabolisms' extremely specific and unambiguous in certain situations. No more the realm of our collective, clumsy musings, the Web has started to accurately classify itself as part of a deliberate movement.

When Sir Tim Berners-Lee first started his work on what would become the World Wide Web, his immediate goals, although revolutionary, were somewhat limited by the circumstances of his employment. His original intention was merely to create a system that would link together a disparate collection of electronic documents primarily for his colleagues to assimilate information more easily for research purposes. In so doing his driving force was "communication through shared knowledge" [4]. This he accomplished with the use of text-based hyperlinks, an invention first envisioned by Ted Nelson in 1965 in a system which he called Xanadu [48]. These replaced traditional referencing techniques with direct linkages between points in individual electronic documents.

Berners-Lee's work was undoubtedly an act of genius but, nevertheless, the Web's early architecture relied on a core failing, using literal text to form the linkages between resources. Misinterpretation of hypertext was, and certainly still often is, commonplace, but could be easily compensated for by the Web's originally intended audience: intelligent individuals like us. Move mankind further down the food chain, however, and ask "dumb" computers to interact directly with the Web instead and the problem of misinterpretation becomes almost insurmountable with the technologies present on the original Web. This failing was soon realized and by the late 1990s, work had begun on improving the mechanisms used to convey absolute meaning of Web-content—its semantics in other words—and the Semantic Web initiative was born.

In a perfectly engineered world, Web pages will be written in more sophisticated markup languages with a universally accepted metadata description format. XML and Semantic Web languages like the Resource Description Framework (RDF[1]) have made great strides in that direction, especially in specific areas like e-commerce. "Nevertheless it is almost certain that the Web will always remain adventurous enough that it's most interesting and timely content can never be shoehorned into such rigid frameworks" [82]. Having said that, the Semantic Web represents a significant leap forward in Web architecture and its cumulative capabilities should not be underestimated.

Semantic Web languages, such as the RDF, the Ontology Web language (OWL[2]), and the Semantic Web Rules Language (SWRL), have been developed specifically to prevent the Web from relying on our literal interpretation as the pri-

---

[1]Resource Description Framework (RDF) is a family of specifications for a metadata model that is often implemented as an application of XML. The RDF family of specifications is maintained by the World Wide Web Consortium (W3C).

The RDF metadata model is based upon the idea of making statements about resources in the form of a subject–predicate–object expression, called a triple in RDF terminology. The subject is the resource, the "thing" being described. The predicate is a trait or aspect about that resource, and often expresses a relationship between the subject and the object. The object is the object of the relationship or value of that trait [136].

[2]OWL is a markup language for publishing and sharing data using ontologies on the Web. OWL is a vocabulary extension of RDF (the Resource Description Framework) and is derived from the DAML+OIL Web Ontology Language. Together with RDF and other components, these tools make up the Semantic Web project.

mary vehicle to associate resources. Instead, abstract terms can be introduced that can be sourced and qualified from their particular problem space's individual lexicons (QNames[3] and Namespaces)—dictionaries for all intents and purposes. Such terms are typically combined to make statements about resources in the form of subject–predicate–object expressions (in RDF terms, called a triple). This may sound overblown, but in reality it is quite easy to understand. The subject in such statements is essentially the resource, the "thing" being described, the predicate is a trait or aspect of that subject, and the object is a possible value of that trait. For example, in the sentence "London is a city" the subject, "London" in this case, is linked to the object "city" by using "is a" as a predicate. It really can be as simple as that!

Where humans have a natural talent for literacy and hate the application of abstract concepts, computers just eat them up for breakfast, so with the advent of the Semantic Web a whole new set of computational possibilities has opened up to provide an exciting "basis for the Web's evolution" [4].

AUTONOMIC SYSTEMS AND SOFTWARE ENGINEERING

There are two contributing factors that are vital to the success of semantic interpretation on the Web. First, through the use of core Web languages like XML,[4] just about anything that needs representation can get it. With hardly any exception, XML, or one of its many derivatives, can now be used to describe problem spaces and their constituent parts regardless of the level of detail or scale required. Second, with the advent of the Semantic Web, the accuracy with which meaning can be conveyed has increased dramatically. The consequence of these two statements is quite profound, because levels of formal semantics are now being reached on the Web that mean that computer systems themselves can automatically use the raw descriptions society chooses to put in front of them, inferring their own contexts and making their own deductions. Just stop for one moment and think about this properly. What is actually being discussed here is the capability of computational systems to "understand" just about anything we can asscribe to them. This is not like traditional tailored programming for a specific problem, and it is more encompassing than most realms of mainstream AI technology. With a few layers of interpretation software, it is already proving practical to use XML-based derivatives, such as Web Services Description Language (WSDL), to create skeletons for complex Web Services, and this is only the start.

---

[3]A QName is a qualified name, as specified by XML Schema Part 2. It is a name made up of a namespace Universal Resource Indicator (URI), a local part, and a prefix. The prefix is not really a part of the QName and remains only to provide lexical information.
[4]The Extensible Markup Language (XML) is a W3C-recommended general-purpose markup language for creating special-purpose markup languages. It is a simplified subset of SGML, capable of describing many different kinds of data. Its primary purpose is to facilitate the sharing of data across different systems, particularly systems connected via the Web. Languages based on XML (for example, RDF, RSS, MathML, XHTML, SVG, and cXML) are defined in a formal way, allowing programs to modify and validate documents in these languages without prior knowledge of their form.

But there is more to the use of Semantic Web technologies than just clearer descriptions of data on the Web. Computer systems' engineering, and in particular Software Engineering, are fundamentally interested in the same problem that XML was designed to address—namely, describing things in a useful manner. In the case of Software Engineering the aim is predominantly to describe a particular problem to determine the best method to implement a software solution, whereas XML is intended to cover a much broader spectrum.

Many methods exist within the Software Engineering community that rely on the development of reduced descriptions in a language-based form. Some of these languages are admittedly graphical in nature, but most, if not all, can still be represented in a textural format such as XML. The Unified Modeling Language (UML) is a highly popular example of such a set of methods, for instance, which is central to the concept of Model Driven Architecture (MDA)—a proven engineering technique in the area of professional software development. To manage quality across the Software Lifecycle, UML and MDA have been further incorporated into higher-level frameworks like the Rational Unified Process (RUP), a toolset intended to assist with software engineering issues beyond software design, through construction and test and finally into real-world deployment.

RUP is usually adopted on significant software development projects, being used by experienced staff to architect large and complex systems. It has provided unquestionable benefit in real-world software development for a number of years by facilitating the systematic description and communication of relatively involved problems and their solutions. Yet it still relies on the personal experience, interpretation, and skill of those applying it to produce the "most appropriate" end products.

Such reliance fundamentally flaws the development process because there will always be gaps of experience and knowledge of any project team, no matter how capable or professional those involved might be. Therefore, it is common sense that under normal circumstances the probability of engineering the "perfect" solution to anything other than a trivial problem is low. This is an inescapable fact of life in most professional endeavors and not a criticism of the professional capability of the Information Technology industry.

THE FUTURE OF SOFTWARE ENGINEERING LIES WITH DISCOVERY

There is no escaping from it, serious software is currently unavoidably difficult to construct. Admittedly, techniques like software prototyping try valiantly to address this problem, allowing multiple iterations of design and development to get the solution right. Furthermore, the discipline of software patterns[5] undoubtedly helps, providing professionally assured solutions to particular types of problems. But still both approaches ultimately depend upon personal interpretation of the descriptions involved at every stage. As such, in most cases, a compromise is actually reached,

---

[5]In software engineering, a design pattern is a general repeatable solution to a commonly occurring problem in software design.

an agreement between designers and users of a system. The designers declare that they have done their very best to satisfy the particular users needs, while the users grudgingly accept that better versions of the software will eventually appear in time once the remaining areas of weakness are better understood.

A better answer may well be to attack gaps in understanding head-on, and it seems that by doing this the Semantic Web might be able to help.

It is reasonable to expect that utilizing the skills, understanding, and output of 100 professionals would unearth a better solution to any given problem than if only 10 were used. So imagine the possibility if this number were increased to a potential resource pool numbering tens of millions and all the software components they had individually written. "Impossible," the managers amongst you will shout, "no system's budget could ever stand such a large resource." Well, actually no, with the correct use of the Web, this is a distinct possibility. The real problem is not the amount of resource available, but rather finding it and phrasing the right questions to ensure you get what you need. This is where Semantic Web technologies come into play and why they can add so much value to the Web. As Grady Booch has said recently, as part of his involvement in the Semantic Web, "the future of Software Engineering is no longer in the construction of suitable components, but rather their discovery."

With such a prophecy in mind, it is easy to think of scenarios where the Semantic Web might help with software construction. This is because the thing that does not scale when the complexity and size of a man-made problem grows is intuition; the ability to solve problems without a well-defined logical method [55]. A team's inherent intuitive capability to transcend the limitations of any particular method is therefore restricted when its members fail to ask questions of those who have the right answers. This may be because communication breaks down within the team or because those with the right answers are not team members. But, it is important to remember that there are no rules that say that the right questions cannot be asked, or that the individuals with the right answers cannot be found with the right assistance.

Imagine that a number of software gurus have been working hard on designing a software-based system but are still not happy with one or two aspects of the models they have created. They broadly understand the issues at hand but are not absolutely confident that they have completely solved some of the important specifics. Still, they know the problems facing them and are capable of describing them via a list of meaningful attributes that are internationally recognized within their particular field. Rather like using International Standards Organisation (ISO) units of measure, the gurus could describe their remaining issues as having a certain set of features; size in cubic meters, mass in kilograms, and color in levels of red, green, and blue are all analogies that spring to mind from other less abstract disciplines.

Given that their original designs are capable of being described in an XML, this new list of semantic attributes could then be used to "mark out" and annotate the remaining problem areas, rather like running a highlighter pen over a diagram to make issues stand out.

With these additions, their designs could theoretically be submitted to a Semantic Web search engine, like TAP [49] or Swoogle, and used to search the Web for as many suggestions or "candidate solutions" to the highlighted problem areas as is applicable. This would be rather like using a traditional search engine to help answer any problem, but in this case the search string would be much more specific in conveying its requirements.

If this Web search were formally semantic, then results returned would be almost guaranteed to be applicable. They may not necessarily be relevant or useful, but they would accurately correspond to the search criteria entered. Determining relevance and usefulness would be a task returned back to the architects involved, but at least they would be in a stronger position than before, having asked the collective opinion of their global architect communities.

In performing such a semantic search, anyone interested in information about a resource should be able to easily aggregate data about that resource from different providers [49], and it is clear that the more semantically specific the attributes matched, the greater the probability, applicability, and opportunity for relevance and usefulness. In essence, the more a problem description (the XML-based search criteria) matches a solution description (the XML-based search result), the greater the likelihood that the located resources are suitable. In this way, using semantic properties as "mutually comprehensible references" [49] provides a powerful method for coalescing content from disperse, yet semantically related, Web-based materials. It is a technique currently causing great debate within the Semantic Web community, having been lovingly given the term "Smushing" or Semantic "Mash up" by those in the know.

SMUSHING

The Semantic Web is all about connecting and aggregating resources, and this requires support for taking collections of semantic information and joining them, thus merging individual resources or "communities" of resources using extra information. Through such practices it is easy to reason that the Semantic Web is just one large global database. But most databases in daily use are relational databases, and, strictly, speaking the Semantic Web is not. In relational databases, stored columns of data connect to each other, such as temperature, barometric pressure and location entries in a weather database, for example. In such databases, the relationships between the columns provide the semantics—the meaning of the data [55]. On the Semantic Web it may be common for such types of data collation to take place, but it is certainly uncommon for collections of "column" types to identify compilations of either literal data or Web resources.

RDF was, nonetheless, designed for generic, cross-domain data merging. Imagine taking two arbitrary Structured Query Language[6] (SQL) databases and merging them so that the new database could answer questions that required knowledge of things only described partially in one of the two original data stores. That sort of operation is hard to do because SQL wasn't designed in a way that makes this easy. Neither was XML, but RDF was. In RDF, there are "off-the-shelf" software tools

---

[6]Structured Query Language (SQL) is the industry standard for retrieving data from relational database technologies.

that can take RDF documents, "parse" them into a set of simple three-part statements, or triples, which make claims about the world, and store those statements
alongside others in a merged RDF database. This can extend to a point where both
datasets use the exact same identifiers when mentioning the things they describe,
and a rather handy data-merge effect is produced [56]. Unfortunately, however, if
two different RDF files are talking about the same thing but don't use exactly the
same URIs when mentioning that thing, how are poor stupid computers suppose to
understand such a conflict? In the real world there is a need to write RDF documents about things that do not yet subscribe to any agreed naming scheme, and this
is one of the core problems the Semantic Web has recently had to address [50].

Smushing does not solve such problems directly, but it is an attempt to help
bring the Semantic Web closer to the relational database model. It relates to an ill-
defined term for merging semantic metadata based on knowledge, using uniquely
identifying properties [55], and as such is similar to a relational join[7] in the traditional database world. It relies on identifying properties—commonly referred to as
Inverse Function Property (IFP) in specialised cases—to establish links between
disparate data sinks or data graphs. Unlike traditional database thinking, however,
rather than matching on property type and value explicitly, in the simplest types of
smushing, RDF predicates provide the primary vehicle for joining, with degrees of
equivalence potentially being used on triple subjects to infer the level of correlation
found. For example, if two resources share an RDF triple predicate relating to "res-
idential address" as part of a composite join and also hold object values of "10a
Downing Street" and "10b Downing Street," respectively, this may be enough to
deduce that both relate to the same building and hence share sufficient common
properties for an equivalence bond to be established.

In creating such a bond, however, it is essential that the sources of all the information used are trusted and the context in which they are being used is fully understood, because without trust the whole model of the Semantic Web breaks down.
Consequently, smushing basically attempts to deal with the problem of merging
data about things that might not be consistently identified. An individual's photo
database might mention a close friend by reference to their homepage, their calen-
dar might associate the same friend with one of his or her mailboxes, and their personal contacts might mention both their friend's homepage and their mailboxes, but
not a lot else. Semantic Web tools need to smush all these data together, so they can
get a more complete picture of what's going on.

So, returning to the original example of a team designing a software system,
imagine if a semantic search was undertaken using the amalgamated search string,
<SE:pattern> plus <SE:solution>. This is often referred to as a "composite key" in
relational database circles and in this instance specifically relates to the need for a
solution as a software engineering pattern, the pattern being both a sub-string and
a Discriminant Description [49] within each occurrence of a name–value-pair
search string used. By repeatedly undertaking such a search and smushing togeth-

---

[7]A join combines data sets (records) from two or more tables in a relational database. In the Structured
Query Language (SQL), there are three types of joins: inner, outer, and cross. Outer joins are subdivided
further into left outer joins, right outer joins, and full outer joins.

er the resources returned, it would be realistic to expect a combined knowledge-base being collated that contains references to software patterns relating to the other semantic names—value pairs within the string. This is equivalent to those in the example asking the question "Has anybody solved a problem like this before using software patterns?" Even more exciting is the possibility of using a name–value pair like <SE:Web Service>, which is a software engineering Web service that could be led to the a semantic search string being interpreted as "Has anyone solved a problem like this before who is also willing to let us use their solution directly?", a scenario that could yield a suitable solution with zero additional effort and no further investment.

RUNTIME AUTONOMIC SEMANTIC APPLICATIONS

There is nothing stopping us from taking Semantic Web technologies one step further and using them to provide data for use by live applications. For instance, imagine a Web Service designed as an emergency broadcast mechanism for use when, say, a ship capsizes or an aeroplane gets into difficulty. In such circumstances the service would most probably be triggered automatically, but once activated there is a problem: How do we best forward a distress signal to the right people, and who should they be? The service could be engineered to make a finite sequence of specific decisions and alert the "appropriate" authorities deemed best at the point at which its internal program code was written. But the world of communications moves fast, so who is to say that the built-in routes of communication are the very best at the point in time of any emergency. Here again semantic data enhancing and its possible uses on the Web could come into play.

As well as utilizing its usual lines of communication, by incorporating the use of semantic attributes, the service could be programmed to search for, and call, other Web-based services capable of forwarding its signal in ways that it cannot by default. This would be equivalent to sending a "semantic" flare high into the Web sky to get as much attention as possible. Drastic maybe, but in such life-threatening circumstances surely an overload of additional help is better than none. Much of the resulting communication frenzy may well be worthless spam, but there is always the potential that an unexpected and quicker rescue route could be secured.

This example demonstrates some of the potential behind ideas like dynamic self-extension using Semantic Web technologies, but there are some important implications of using the Web in this way. As semantic metadata allow computers to read and interpret information more readily, we should not forget that from certain perspectives the Web itself can be considered as one huge computer system. Given that it has already been outlined how the Web might use semantic data to return computer readable advice in the form of link or knowledge bases, it does not involve a significant leap of faith to see how a point could be reached where a core set of Web technologies could begin to "understand their own use." Progress this idea still further and it is easy to see how Web applications could be designed to become independently self-organizing. This is not science fiction and need not come as much of a shock as it might first seem. Self-organization is a characteristic often found in highly complex natural systems such as social communities. For some time now, we as a society have been interacting with the Web in a self-organizing manner to perpetuate hybrid social machines [4], involving both mankind and machine. Here, "the theme is human beings doing the thinking and machines helping it work on a larger scale, but nothing replaces wisdom in the end" [4]. Moving this concept forward to give machines more control and capability is not such a big step. In fact, it may well be a forgone conclusion if one believes in evolution as a pervasive concept.

STUMBLEUPON

So are there any examples of self-organization on the Web today? Plenty actually, although most still need a liberally sprinkling of human involvement to achieve their aims. For instance, StumbleUpon (www.stumbleupon.com) is a Web discovery service that integrates peer-to-peer and social networking principles with one-click blogging.[8] The Web browser plug-in associated with this site hence automates the collection, distribution, and review of Web content within an intuitive social framework, providing users with a browsing experience which resembles "channel-surfing" the Web. In short, it recommends sites for a user to visit based on a set of personalised preferences that are updated over time.

StumbleUpon's recommendations are based on feedback from its own user base. It combines collaborative human opinions with machine learning leveraged against personal preference to create virtual communities of like-minded Web surfers. Rating websites updates a personal profile and generates peer networks of Web users linked by common interest. These social networks coordinate the distribution of Web content in a self-organising manner, such that users "stumble upon" pages explicitly recommended by friends and peers interested in the same things. This social content discovery approach automates the "word-of-mouth" referral of peer-approved websites and simplifies Web navigation. "Stumblers," as users of this community dub themselves, also have the ability to rate and review each others blogs as well as join interest groups, which are community blogs for specific topics. Users can also post comments much like a discussion board in these groups and add websites that apply to the specific topic.

This is not only a really great idea for the communally inclined Web user with an interest in learning more through like-minded common consensus, but it works really well and is simple to use. What's more, this is surely an excellent and obvious example of self-organization at work on the Web, and the fact that it is both simple and effective is both encouraging and worrying at the same time. It is fantastic that such facilities can open up great swathes of the Web by group recommenda-

---

[8]A weblog or blog (derived from web + log) is a web-based publication consisting primarily of periodic articles (normally, but not always, in reverse chronological order). Although most early blogs were manually updated, tools to automate the maintenance of such sites made them accessible to a much larger population, and the use of some sort of browser-based software is now a typical aspect of "blogging."

tion, but also hints at just how amenable the underlying ideas might be to full automation.

StumbleUpon is growing in popularity fast, spreading beyond its native geek community with apparent ease. By doing so, it will be interesting to see just how popular it eventually becomes, given that with popularity undoubtedly comes wider realization that technologies with more powerful and autonomous capabilities are possible. As the Open Source software movement has demonstrated so many times in the past, once realization of a new idea reaches a critical point, soon many new technologies and products start to appear to implement its potential.

Beyond the Semantic Web

> There is nothing in the programming field more despicable than an
> undocumented program.
>
> *—Ed Yourdan*

OVERLAPS

Until very recently, most have considered the Web to be a predominantly static place, a vessel simply to hold mankind's worldly knowledge and contemplations. But the Internet of computers on which it rests is capable of much more, presenting billions of spare CPU[1] cycles that could be put to work on hitherto unimaginable tasks. This leads to the idea of a much more "active" Web, a Web on which software and data will live in closer harmony. On this Web the discipline of serious Software Engineering must play a much greater role, even though Web and software communities have chosen to remain relatively far apart until now. This is strange, given that obvious overlaps between both are apparent. Nevertheless, the similarities have now been recognized, and merits in a hybrid approach to Web-based semantic software development are starting to become accepted. This would involve combining Semantic Web technologies and techniques with more established software development formalisms like the UML and Java.[2] This is not only for the betterment of software in general, but also for the future good of the Web, as systems and Web Services containing rich Semantic Web content start to come online [65].

But just how will this new "Web muscle" be formed and how will it gel with the information and knowledge already prevalent on the Web? Some have talked of such concepts [5,65], but Holger Knublauch, formally of Stanford and Manchester University, is amongst those leading the way with some groundbreaking work, demonstrating just how the Semantic Web and established fields of Software Engineering, like Object-Oriented Development, can be interrelated. To give a much deeper insight into such concepts the remainder of this appendix essentially pro-

---

[1]Central processing unit.
[2]Java is a programming language expressly designed for use in the distributed environment of the Internet.

vides a reprint of the W3C note designed to introduce object-oriented programmers to the advantages of the Semantic Web. It is specifically targeted at a technical readership and is not intended to be of great value to the general reader. The original text of this note can be found at http://www.w3.org.TR/sw-oosd-primer.[3] *Note:* This reformatted version my contain formatting or hypertextual errors.

A SEMANTIC WEB PRIMER FOR OBJECT-ORIENTED SOFTWARE PRACTITIONERS

Descriptions of problems and their software solutions play a central role all through the software development process, from requirements analysis to design, to implementation and beyond. Such forms of description are more correctly referred to as domain models and great progress has been made in their consistent use throughout this process. Modern software development tools with support for graphical modelling and code generation hence allow developers to synchronize and verify software with user requirements using such models.

Nevertheless, the reusability of domain models is often limited because they are, by definition, problem-specific and only take into consideration the viewpoints needed to engineer solutions within the confines of their own individual problem's areas. But the Web is broader than that and is capable of referencing an almost limitless set of both problem domains and their relevant models. While software becomes evermore embedded in the Web, conventional software development processes do not fully exploit the potential for model reuse over the Web yet. A new idea to help lessen this dilemma is to use Semantic Web languages such as RDF Schema and OWL in software development directly, because they can be used in tandem with mainstream object-oriented programming languages like Java. This combination can then usefully serve as a platform on which domain models can be created, shared, and reused over the Web [64].

Table B.1. Outline System's Requirements

Outline Requirements (No Particular Order)	Domain Knowledge (No Particular Order)
Online sale of good	Purchase orders associate a customer with a list of products
International sales capability	Customers have a home country
Automated order processing	Germany, France and Australia are countries
Product catalogue	Germany and France are part of the European Union
Management of customer details	The European Union is a free-trade zone
	Orders from customers who live in a country that has a free-trade agreement with the online shops' country are duty free

It is common for a piece of software to be centered on domain models that represent aspects of its specified requirement. Consequently, domain models can describe relevant concepts and data structures from both the point of view of that software and that of its eventual users. They can also be used to encode knowledge that is useful to drive its behavior. For example, imagine a need to develop software for an online shopping application. In doing so, the needs and knowledge associated with this system might, in part, be listed as in Table B.1.

After some analysis of these requirements, it might be possible to construct an object-oriented view of the system like the UML conceptual class shown in Figure B.1. This is helpful because it can be used for discussion purposes and, after a few passes, will most likely prove important to the software development tasks that follow. From such a starting point, it is therefore usually possible to begin the design and development of software artifacts like user interfaces for both online customers and shop personnel. If these prove successful, more components can obviously be built around them to access the product catalogue through the likes of a Web service, for instance. If this does happen, any new functionality would want to share the same data structures and domain knowledge previously used so that they can be incorporated properly. And even if the original design is not particularly successful, there still might be the wish to at least reuse sections of it. So, obviously it would be

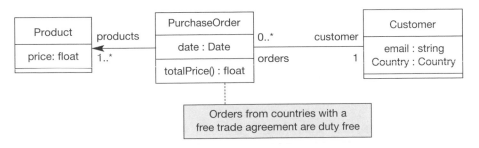

Figure B.1. A simple domain model in UML Syntax.

useful to have access to the underlying domain model in order to extract the relevant parts.

Since reuse is always a bonus in any engineering discipline, one of the most flexible approaches to software design is to use an approach commonly known as "Model-View-Control" architecture. This well-known software design pattern promotes the separation of domain models from more specific implementation considerations like user interface and control logic design, thereby making it potentially easier to reuse and share domain models between systems. Unfortunately, however, the promise of reusability in object-oriented models is often not fulfilled. In many such cases, domain models end up containing highly specific dependencies. This can be especially true once a domain model is translated in a particular programming language as a result of programming, where much of the knowledge that went into its initial design can be lost. To take the above example, the consideration of whether a *PurchaseOrder* is duty-free or not may end up being encoded by conditions lying deep inside the resultant software.

Another typical problem with such types of implementation is interoperability, the ability of one part of a software application to easily work with another. If some other system wanted to utilize data or services from our example, for instance, it would need to do so through a well-defined program interface, or API,[4] that is closely related.

By moving away from such levels of detail, underlying domain models offer the greatest engineering flexibility in most cases. Such models embrace detail at a much higher level and can be used to automatically produce lower-level application code in a number of ways. Even so, if two software components or entire applications have started with the same models, there is still no guarantee that they will share compatible implementations. For such reasons a large chunk of hand-crafted code may still be required to realize them. Certain types of domain model can also be notoriously ambiguous, easily prompting questions like, "In which format should customer data be stored and shared?" In one online store system, for example, reference data relating to countries may be stored using character strings, while others may choose to represent them as instances of a *Country* object class.[5] In either case it is unclear where and how the specific countries should be represented within any common domain model. What's more, unless software designers and developers choose to follow a consistent model-driven approach, domain models can often only be maintained as intermediate artifacts in the development process, used as the basis for programming but then tucked into drawers where they are frequently overlooked. It is a sobering fact of life that domain models are often hidden for a good reason, because they are no longer up to date with their intended software solution. This most often results in much wasted development effort through the unnecessary duplication of work and poor transfer of knowledge between those involved in design and development—an age-old problem common across many other fields of human endeavor. For such reasons, domain models need to be engi-

---

[4]An application programming interface (API) is a set of definitions of the ways one piece of computer software communicates with another. It is a method of achieving abstraction, usually (but not necessarily) between lower-level and higher-level software.

[5]"Class" in this context is a collection of both program code and associated data.

neered and maintained properly. In fact, such models should be the living language of any good software development activity, not just its archived doodlings.

In an ideal world, software developers would be able to discover shareable domain models and associated knowledge bases from a variety of interrelated sources and then use them in the development of object-oriented software—a practice slowly becoming known as "Ontology-Driven Architecture." All software sharing overlapping or similar domain models would therefore have a certain degree of interoperability built in. While this ideal world is still mostly a vision, some promising approaches are beginning to appear.

Rather unnoticed by mainstream Software Engineering communities, Semantic Web languages have started to mature and gain wide acceptance on the Web. These have the goal of making make Web content easier to understand by intelligent agents and software such as Web services. In fact, rather usefully as it turns out, Semantic Web languages and tools can also play a major part in software development in general.

The World Wide Web Consortium has produced a set of complementary Semantic Web technologies for developing, maintaining, using, and sharing models such as those found in Software Engineering. At their core are the languages OWL, RDF, RDF Schema, and now SWRL. So, domain models written in languages like OWL can hence obviously be uploaded onto the Web and shared. OWL also supports an unambiguous dialect of formal logic called Description Logics (DL)—a real advantage for models realized in software making them much clearer to interpret, both by humans and other software. This formal underpinning makes it possible to exploit intelligent reasoning services such as automatic classification and consistency checking tools. These can be used while software development is in progress to help the construction of reusable, well-tested program code amongst other software assets. Reasoning services can also be used when the finished software is actually in live operation. So, for example, automated inferencing makes it possible to define software dynamically, to reclassify examples of that software, and to perform complex logical queries across domain models during development. With their strong logic foundations, OWL and RDF Schema operate on syntaxes similar to object-oriented programming languages, making them ideal for integration with more traditional software artifacts.

In short, the key benefits using Semantic Web languages in parallel with object-oriented approaches in Software Engineering can be seen as follows:

- **Complementary Syntaxes.** RDF and OWL can be easily integrated with object-oriented programming languages like Java.
- **Formality and Accuracy of Information Conveyed.** RDF and OWL are built of mathematically formal, and hence provable, forms of description logic
- **Reuse and Interoperability.** RDF and OWL models can be shared among applications via the Web.
- **Flexibility.** RDF and OWL models can operate in an open environment in which object-oriented classes can be defined dynamically.
- **Consistency.** RDF and OWL allow quality checking across models.

- **Reasoning.** OWL has rich expressivity supported by automated reasoning tools.

Semantic Web technologies are therefore not just making the Web more specific in general, but they are starting to have deep and detailed relevance to its support mechanisms as well. Software Engineering may well be the first of these mechanisms to go mainstream, but this is simply because of its obvious and close association two of the Web's essential ingredients—obviously software and data. Other, more esoteric applications of this type of technology will surely follow, and in such ways the Web will slowly start to become more careful about it own upkeep. In essence, not only is the diversity of the Web's expanding at an alarming rate, but now there is potential to realize this diversity in far more understandable, accurate, and shareable ways.

References

1. Gregory Stock: *Metaman: The Merging of Human and Machines into a Global Superorganism,* Simon & Schuster, New York 1993.

2. How the Species Became, New Scientist, **180** (2416): 32, October 2003.

3. James Gleick, *Chaos—The Amazing Science of the Unpredictable,* Vintage, New York, 1987.

4. Tim Berners-Lee, *Weaving the Web,* Texere Publishing, Warsaw, Poland,1999.

5. Philip Tetlow, *SOA, Glial and the Autonomic Semantic Web Machine—Tools for Handling Complexity?* IBM, United Kingdom, 2004. http://www.alphaworks.ibm.com/g/g.nsf/img/semanticsdocs/$file/soa_semanticweb.pdf

6. Duncan J. Watts, *Six Degrees—The Science of a Connected Age,* W.W. Norton & Company, New York, 2003.

7. Albert-László Baarabasi, *Linked: How Everything Is Connected to Everything Else and What It Means,* Plume, New York, 2003.

8. J. Xu and Y. Chao, and R. Chen, *Fractal Geometry Study of DNA Binding Proteins.* Department of Protein Engineering, Institute of Biophysics Academia Sinica, Beijing, People's Republic of China. http://www.ncbi.nlm.nih.gov/entrez/query.fcgi?cmd=Retrieve&db=PubMed&list_uids=7869732&dopt=Abstract

9. Nestor N. Oiwa and James A. Glazier, *The Fractal Structure of the Mitochondrial Genomes,* Department of Physics, Center for the Interdisciplinary Study of Biocomplexity, College of Science, University of Notre Dame, South Bend, IN. http://biocomplexity.indiana.edu/jglazier/docs/papers/62_Fractal_Structure_Mitochondrial_Genomes.pdf

10. Erwin Schrödinger, Astonishing Gift of Concentrating in *What is Life?,* Cambridge University Press, Cambridge, UK, 1967.

11. Mel Thompson, *Teach Yourself Philosophy of Mind,* McGraw-Hill, New York, 2004.

12. Stephen Dill, Ravi Kumar, Kevin S. McCurley, Sridhar Rajagop Alan, D. Sivakumar, and Andrew Tomkins, *Self-Similarity In the Web,* IBM Almaden Research Center, San Jose, CA. http://www.almaden.ibm.com/cs/people/mccurley/pdfs/fractal.pdf

13. Mark Levene and Alexandra Poulvassilis (eds.), *Web Dynamics, Springer,* New York, 2004.

14. C. Martindale and A. K. Konopka, Oligonucleotide Frequencies in DNA Follow a Yule Distribution, *Computer Chemistry* **20**(1): 35–38, 1996.

15. M. Faloutsos, P. Faloutsos and C. Faloutsos, On Power Law Relationships of the Internet Topology, *Proceedings of the ACM SIGCOMM Conference,* pp. 251–262, 1999.

16. John Gribbin, *Deep Simplicity,* Penguin Books, New York, 2004.

17. Stuart Kauffman, *At Home in the Universe: The Search for the Laws of Self-Organisation and Complexity,* Oxford University Press, Oxford, UK, 1999.

18. Stuart Kauffman, *The Origins of Order,* Oxford University Press, Oxford, UK, 1993.

19. Evelyn Fox Keller, *Making Sense of Life: Explaining Biological Development with Models, Metaphors, and Machines,* Harvard University Press, Cambridge, MA, 2002.

20. David Fell, *Understanding the Control of Metabolism (Frontiers in Metabolism),* Ashgate Publishing, Aldershot, UK, 1996.

21. Kevin Kelly, *Out of Control—The New Biology of Machines, Social Systems, and the Economic World,* Basic Books, New York, 1995.

22. RNA, http://en.wikipedia.org/wiki/RNA

23. Richard Solé and Brian Goodwin, *Signs of Life—How Complexity Pervades Biology,* Basic Books, New York, 2000.

24. Gary William Flake, *The Computational Beauty of Nature,* The MIT Press, Cambridge, MA, 1998.

25. Fibonacci Numbers and Nature—Part 2 Why is the Golden Section the "Best" Arrangement? http://www.mcs.surrey.ac.uk/Personal/R.Knott/Fibonacci/fibnat2.html

26. Logarithmic Spirals, http://alumni.media.mit.edu/~brand/logspiral.html

27. Chaos Theory, http://en.wikipedia.org/wiki/Chaos_theory#History

28. Steven Potter, The Meaning of Life. http://www.ibiblio.org/jstrout/uploading/potter_life.html

29. Mark C. Taylor, *The Moment of Complexity—Emerging Network Culture,* University of Chicago Press, Chicago, 2003.

30. Mathworld, Continued Fractions. http://mathworld.wolfram.com/ContinuedFraction.html

31. Leonard Mlodinow, *Feynman's Rainbow, A Search for Beauty in Physics and In Life,* Warner Books, New York, 2004.

32. C. A. R. Hoare, *Communicating Sequential Processes,* Prentice-Hall Publishing, Upper Saddle River, NJ, 1985.

33. R. L. Martino, *The Dynamic Management of Information Systems,* 1968

34. Gerald Feinberg and Robert Shapiro, *Life Beyond Earth,* 1980.

35. Kevin Kelly, We are the Web, *Wired,* August 2005. http://www.wired.com/wired/archive/13.08/tech.html

36. Peter Johnson, Pornography Drives Technology: Why Not to Censor the Internet. http://www.law.indiana.edu/fclj/pubs/v49/no1/johnson.html

37. Gebreselassie G. Anenia, , The Challenges of Developing Localized Applications: Beyond the Standards. http://www.ethiopiaknowledge.org/Final%20Papers/Localised%20Applications,%20Gebreselassie.PDF

38. Genes, Macromolecules & Computers are Related by Strange Loops. http://www.ram.org/ramblings/dream/overview.html

39. Douglas Hofstadter, *Gödel, Escher, Bach: An Eternal Golden Braid,* Penguin Books, New York, 1979.

40. Introduction to the Post-Human Condition. http://www.post-human.net/

41. Matt Ridley, *Genome, The Autobiography of a Species,* 4th Estate (Harper Collins), New York, 2004.

42. Steven Johnson, *Emergence: The Connected Lives of Ants, Brains, Cities and Software,* Scriber, New York, 2001.

43. Roger Penrose, *The Emperor's New Mind,* Oxford University Press, Oxford, UK, 1989.

44. Charles Darwin, *The Origin of Species,* Gramercy Publishing, New York, 1859.

45. David Wells, *The Penguin Dictionary of Curious and Interesting Numbers,* Penguin Books, New York, 1998.

46. *The Best Short Works of Richard Feynman: Cargo Cult Science: The 1974 Caltech Commencement Address,* Basic Books, New York, 2001.

47. Seth Lloyd, *The Computational Universe,* originally published in *Edge,* Oct. 24, 2002, http://www.kurzweilai.net/meme/frame.html?main=memelist.html?m=3%23589

48. Chris Sherman and Gary Price, *The Invisible Web,* Information Today, Inc., Medford, NJ, 2001.

49. R. V. Guha, Object Co-identification on the Semantic Web, IBM Research. http://tap.stanford.edu/CoIdent.pdf

50. Dan Brickly, http://rdfweb.org/mt/foaflog/archives/000039.html.

51. Richard Dawkins, *The Blind Watchmaker,* Penguin Books, New York, 1990.

52. Stuart Kauffman, *Investigations,* Oxford University Press, Oxford, UK, 2000.

53. J. Kleinberg. The Small-World Phenomenon: An Algorithmic Perspective, *Proceedings of the 32nd ACM Symposium on Theory of Computing,* 2000. http://www.cs.cornell.edu/home/kleinber/swn.ps

54. J. Kleinberg. Bursty and Hierarchical Structure in Streams. *Proceedings of the 8th ACM SIGKDD International Conference on Knowledge Discovery and Data Mining,* 2002. http://www.cs.cornell.edu/home/kleinber/bhs.ps

55. Dan Brickly, http://rdfweb.org/topic/smushing,

56. Dan Brickly, http://rdfweb.org/mt/foaflog/archives/000039.html.

57. Grady Booch, *The Handbook of Software Architecture.* http://www.booch.com/architecture/index.jsp

58. Stuart Kauffman, Carsten Peterson, Björn Samuelsson, and Carl Troein, Genetic Networks with Canalyzing Boolean rules are Always Stable. http://www.pnas.org/cgi/content/full/101/49/17102

59. Richard Feynman, *Six Not So-Easy Pieces: Essentials of Physics Explained by Its Most Brilliant Teacher,* Perseus Books, New York, 1995.

60. Roger Penrose, *The Road to Reality—The Complete Guide to the Laws of the Universe,* Jonathan Cape Publishers, London, 2004.

61. Paul Benacerraf, What Numbers Could Not Be. http://hilton.org.uk/what_numbers_are_not.phtml

62. Population Division of the Department of Economic and Social Affairs of the United Nations. http://esa.un.org/unpp

63. James O. Coplien, Symmetry Breaking in Software Patterns. http://users.rcn.com/jcoplien/Patterns/Symmetry/Springer/SpringerSymmetry.html

64. Holger Knublauch, Daniel Oberle, Philip Tetlow (IBM), and, Evan Wallace, A Semantic Web Primer for Object-Oriented Software Developers. http://www.w3.org/2001/sw/BestPractices/SE/ODSD/

65. Philip Tetlow, Jeff Pan, Daniel Oberle, Evan Wallace, Michael Uschold, and Elisa

Kendall, Ontology Driven Architectures and Potential Uses of the Semantic Web in Systems and Software Engineering, Sandpiper Software. http://www.w3.org/2001/sw/BestPractices/SE/ODA/

66. Allan F. Randall, Quantum Superposition, Necessity and the Identity of Indiscernibles. http://home.ican.net/~arandall/Indiscernibles/

67. Mitchell Waldrop, *Complexity—The Emerging Science at the Edge of Order and Chaos,* Simon & Schuster, New York, 1992.

68. Howard. H. Patee, (ed.) *Hierarchy Theory—The Challenge of Complex Systems,* George Braziller, Inc., 1973.

69. Robert L. Flood, *Dealing with Complexity—An Introduction to the Theory and Application of Systems Science,* Kluwer, Amsterdam, 1998.

70. Bruce Anderson, *Towards an Architecture Handbook,* OOPSLA'92 Conference Poster Session Submission, 1992.

71. Brian Clegg, *A Brief History of Infinity—The Quest to Think the Unthinkable,* Brian Clegg, Constable & Robinson, London, 2003.

72. *Los Alamos Laboratory Newsletter,* July 2005, http://public.lanl.gov/whz/images/Newsletter.pdf

73. A. Barabási, R. Albert and H. Jeong, Mean-Field Theory for Scale-Free Random Networks, http://arxiv.org/PS_cache/cond-mat/pdf/9907/9907068.pdf

74. Monika Henzinger and Steve Lawrence, Extracting Knowledge from the World Wide Web. http://www.pnas.org/cgi/reprint/101/suppl_1/5186.pdf

75. Philip Ball, Natural Selection Acts on the Quantum World. http://www.nature.com/news/2004/041220/pf/041220-12_pf.html

76. Philip Ball, *Critical Mass—How One Thing Leads to Another,* Arrow Books, London, 2004.

77. W. Huitt, Motivation to Learn: An Overview, http://chiron.valdosta.edu/whuitt/col/motivation/motivate.html

78. Susan Blackmore, *The Meme Machine,* Oxford University Press, Oxford, UK, 1999.

79. Kenneth W. Ford, *The Quantum World—Quantum Physics for Everyone,* Harvard University Press, Cambridge, MA, 2004.

80. Jeffrey Satinover, *The Quantum Brain,* Wiley, Hoboken, NJ, 2001.

81. Nielson Lesmoir-Gordon, Will Rood, and Ralph Edney, *Introducing Fractal Geometry,* Totem Books, Blue Ridge Summit, PA, 2000.

82. Soumen Chakrabarti, *Mining the Web,* Morgan Kaufmann, San Francisco, 2003.

83. Ehud Shapiro and Yaakov Benenson , Bringing DNA Computers to Life, *Scientific American,* May 2006.

84. John Casti, Computing the Incomputable. http://www.heise.de/tp/r4/artikel/2/2414/1.html

85. Continuous Turing Machines.http://www.mathpages.com/home/kmath135.htm

86. Websites as Graphs, http://www.aharef.info/2006/05/websites_as_graphs.htm

87. William Arntz, Betsey Chasse, and Mark Vicente, *What the Bleep Do We Know,* HCI, Deerfield Beach, FL, 2005.

88. Gregory Chaitin, The Limits of Reason, *Scientific American,* March 2006.

89. Richard Dawkins, *The Selfish Gene,* Oxford University Press, Oxford, UK, 1990.

90. http://en.wikipedia.org/wiki/Vannevar_Bush

91. http://en.wikipedia.org/wiki/Theodor_Holm_Nelson
92. http://en.wikipedia.org/wiki/CERN
93. http://en.wikipedia.org/wiki/Norbert_Wiener
94. http://en.wikipedia.org/wiki/Determinism
95. http://en.wikipedia.org/wiki/Euclid
96. http://en.wikipedia.org/wiki/Ergodic_hypothesis
97. http://en.wikipedia.org/wiki/Higgs_boson
98. http://en.wikipedia.org/wiki/The_Manhattan_Project
99. http://en.wikipedia.org/wiki/Thomas_Stearns_Eliot
100. http://en.wikipedia.org/wiki/Werner_Karl_Heisenberg
101. http://en.wikipedia.org/wiki/Jules_Henri_Poincar%C3%A9
102. http://en.wikipedia.org/wiki/Edward_Norton_Lorenz
103. http://en.wikipedia.org/wiki/Wheel
104. http://en.wikipedia.org/wiki/Geoffrey_Ingram_Taylor
105. http://en.wikipedia.org/wiki/Hermann_Weyl
106. http://en.wikipedia.org/wiki/Cartesian_coordinate_system
107. http://en.wikipedia.org/wiki/Ren%C3%A9_Descartes
108. http://en.wikipedia.org/wiki/Jakob_Bernoulli
109. http://en.wikipedia.org/wiki/Johannes_Kepler
110. http://en.wikipedia.org/wiki/Gregor_Johann_Mendel
111. http://en.wikipedia.org/wiki/Titus_Livius
112. http://en.wikipedia.org/wiki/Quintus_Horatius_Flaccus
113. http://en.wikipedia.org/wiki/Publius_Ovidius_Naso
114. http://en.wikipedia.org/wiki/Principia_Mathematica
115. http://en.wikipedia.org/wiki/Bertrand_Arthur_William_Russell
116. http://en.wikipedia.org/wiki/Alfred_North_Whitehead
117. http://en.wikipedia.org/wiki/Douglas_Richard_Hofstadter
118. http://en.wikipedia.org/wiki/Ilya_Prigogine
119. http://en.wikipedia.org/wiki/Thomas_Alva_Edison
120. http://en.wikipedia.org/wiki/Christopher_Langton
121. http://en.wikipedia.org/wiki/John_Von_Neumann
122. http://en.wikipedia.org/wiki/Stanislaw_Marcin_Ulam
123. http://en.wikipedia.org/wiki/Craig_Reynolds_%28computer_graphics%29
124. http://en.wikipedia.org/wiki/Turing_test
125. http://en.wikipedia.org/wiki/Marvin_Lee_Minsky
126. http://en.wikipedia.org/wiki/Theory_of_everything
127. http://en.wikipedia.org/wiki/Gottfried_Wilhelm_von_Leibniz
128. http://en.wikipedia.org/wiki/Euclidean_space
129. http://en.wikipedia.org/wiki/Hilbert_space
130. http://en.wikipedia.org/wiki/Riemann_surface
131. http://en.wikipedia.org/wiki/Eigenvector
132. http://en.wikipedia.org/wiki/Fortran

133. http://en.wikipedia.org/wiki/Differential_analyser
134. http://en.wikipedia.org/wiki/Pierre_Teilhard_de_Chardin
135. http://en.wikipedia.org/wiki/Maxwell%27s_demon
136. http://www.w3.org/RDF/

Index

About the Author

Philip Tetlow is a Senior Certified IT Architect and member of the (UK and Ireland) Technical Consultancy Group in IBM's Global Business Services Practice. He is also a Chartered Engineer and an Open Group Master IT Architect. He has more than 20 years experience in the IT industry and has worked on a number of challenging client-facing projects. He specializes in the application of Web-based technologies, metadata and transformation techniques on large central government systems. He is member of the World Wide Web Consortium and coordinated their taskforce on the application of the Semantic Web in Software Engineering as part of the Semantic Web Best Practices and Deployment Working Group. He is acknowledged in the Object Management Group's Ontology Definition Metamodel (ODM) specification and has been a Software Engineering workshop committee member at the International Semantic Web Conference on two occasions.